THE CHANNELS OF
STUDENT ACTIVISM

The Channels of Student Activism

HOW THE LEFT AND RIGHT
ARE WINNING (AND LOSING)
IN CAMPUS POLITICS TODAY

Amy J. Binder &
Jeffrey L. Kidder

The University of Chicago Press
Chicago and London

The University of Chicago Press, Chicago 60637
The University of Chicago Press, Ltd., London
© 2022 by The University of Chicago

Published 2022
Printed in the United States of America

31 30 29 28 27 26 25 24 23 22   1 2 3 4 5

ISBN-13: 978-0-226-68427-7 (cloth)
ISBN-13: 978-0-226-81987-7 (paper)
ISBN-13: 978-0-226-81986-0 (e-book)
DOI: https://doi.org/10.7208/chicago/9780226819860.001.0001

Library of Congress Cataloging-in-Publication Data

Names: Binder, Amy J., 1964– author. | Kidder, Jeffrey L.
    (Jeffrey Lowell), 1977– author.
Title: The channels of student activism : how the left and right are
    winning (and losing) in campus politics today / Amy J. Binder &
    Jeffrey L. Kidder.
Other titles: How the left and right are winning (and losing) in
    campus politics today
Description: Chicago ; London : The University of Chicago Press, 2022. |
    Includes bibliographical references and index.
Identifiers: LCCN 2021054317 | ISBN 9780226684277 (cloth) |
    ISBN 9780226819877 (paperback) | ISBN 9780226819860 (ebook)
Subjects: LCSH: College students—Political activity—United States. |
    Education, Higher—Political aspects—United States. | Political
    activists—United States. | Right and left (Political science)—
    United States.
Classification: LCC LA229 .B525 2022 | DDC 378.1/980973—dc23/
    eng/20211106
LC record available at https://lccn.loc.gov/2021054317

♾ This paper meets the requirements of ANSI/NISO Z39.48-1992
(Permanence of Paper).

Contents

CHAPTER 1

The Channels of Student Activism

We met Georgia at the University of Colorado Boulder (CU) in 2018. Georgia goes by the gender-neutral pronouns they/them/their. On the day of our interview, Georgia had on a colorful kerchief tied into a front-facing bun. Everything else was black: black sneakers, a black high-waisted miniskirt, and a black crop-top worn off-the-shoulder. The ensemble had a '90s grunge rock vibe to it. As we talked, Georgia showed themself to be exuberant, self-aware, and very funny. Their major was a mind-bending mix of environmental studies, integrated physiology, and history. They discussed their plans to start a college radio show called "Woke in the Morning"—a show "directly tailored to calling out people on their bullshit and having some fun with it."[1]

We had contacted Georgia because they were a leader of CU's Black Student Association (BSA). During our conversation, we also learned that they were involved with UMAS y MEXA (a Latinx club on campus),[2] the Middle Eastern Student Association, and the Muslim Student Association. Their ties to these clubs arose out of friendships Georgia had formed through their activism on campus. As Georgia explained, "I'm for people having rights, and being appreciated, and having a civil society where we share funds and resources, instead of just being crazy capitalists making a profit off of people's bodies and labor." To this end, Georgia and the clubs they associated with had protested CU purchasing furniture made by prisoners because it is a form of "slave labor." These clubs also held actions at the school to raise awareness about minority students' sense of marginalization—like chalking the words "White silence is violence" across campus and chanting that slogan from the bleachers during a university basketball game.

Georgia had run into a few right-leaning clubs at their school, most notably Turning Point USA. Turning Point is a national organization, with chapters in hundreds of high schools and colleges, promoting a populist vision of conservatism. Its members tend to be unwavering Trump supporters. Walking through campus one day, Georgia told us they were lured in by some of the group's literature, without realizing who was distributing it—"because that's how they get you." Once Georgia figured out it was Turning Point, Georgia started to leave, but someone staffing the table tried to talk to them. Georgia's response was deadpan and rhetorical: "Well, is it going to be productive?" Georgia was certain the answer was "no," and so Georgia kept walking. When BSA, UMAS y MEXA, and several other clubs brought the former Black Panther Bobby Seale to CU, Georgia recounted, "There was a weird little counter-protest of losers from Turning Point USA." When asked what, exactly, the club was protesting about Seale, Georgia dismissed the question. "I don't know what their signs said, and I don't care." They then laughed about how "the anti-fascist people came to protect us. That was funny. They looked terrifying."[3] The Turning Point protesters, Georgia assured us, "just looked dorky."

Over 1,600 miles away, at the University of Virginia (UVA), we met the clean-cut, all-American Tony—decked out in a fleece pullover, fashionable jeans, and dress shoes. Throughout the interview, Tony was eager to tell us his opinions, often excitedly jumping from issue to issue but still managing to circle back around to thoughtfully address our questions in the end. While students like Georgia wanted to discuss the "trauma" inflicted on Black and Brown communities by "climate chaos," Tony wanted to talk about the US Constitution and free market policies. And Tony was deeply involved in Virginia's Republican Party politics. He explained to us that he was not initially a Donald Trump supporter, but eventually decided to back the 45th president. "I think, overall, he's been a little bit toward the net positive, and I think people just need to be objective."

Around the 2016 election—a period in which social unrest on many college campuses seemed to be reaching a boiling point—segments of UVA's student body began agitating for the removal of their school's memorial to Thomas Jefferson. According to those on the left, Jefferson's tolerance of slavery and his sexual relationship with Sally Hemings, which progressives consider inherently coercive (if not violent), does not warrant such commemoration. At one protest, the Jefferson statue was covered by a tarp, and a sign deriding the school's founder as a "racist rapist" was hung on it. Tony was at this event, standing to the side (aghast), livestreaming what was happening to his sizable social media following. The Jefferson demonstrations—which students like Georgia see as fighting for "people having rights and being appreciated"—were considered to be sheer lunacy by Tony. "These crazy disrupters, they don't want to be friends. They want to attack you." As Tony viewed it, they are part of a left-wing mindset that wants to prevent people from being able to "cherish and celebrate the good things" in our nation's history by only focusing on the "bad things."

After the statue's shrouding, which followed on the heels of the chaotic and deadly Unite the Right rally in Charlottesville,[4] Tony tried to organize what he called a nonpartisan "unity rally" at his school. "I was like, 'You know what guys? We're getting over the line. Tensions are high. Everybody, just come out waving an American flag, and, for a second, put behind our political tensions and just have a conversation and talk about something that's not politics.'" Tony told us he wanted to purchase flags to hand out to attendees, but the only organization he could find to help cover costs on short notice was the staunchly conservative American Legacy Center (ALC). Because of this sponsor, some left-leaning students and professors at UVA interpreted Tony's plan as nothing more than another provocation from the far right. For his part, Tony seemed genuinely dumbfounded by the hostile reaction to his efforts. "Somebody said, 'This looks like lots of White nationalist dog whistling.' I was like, 'What!?'" The basis of doing this rally, he insisted was, "Hey, we can be reasonable adults and stand next to each other, even if we don't agree politically or feel the same way. But, no, I got called a White nationalist."

ON THE FRONT LINES OF STUDENT ACTIVISM

Georgia and Tony were as far apart in terms of ideology as any two people we interviewed for this book. As student activists, though, they were remarkably similar. Both were seen by their peers as charismatic and impassioned leaders. Georgia helped direct the political focus of several progressive clubs at CU. Tony was not a formal member of any conservative club at UVA, but he knew all of their officers, and he provided counsel to many. Were Georgia and Tony enrolled at the same school, Tony would no doubt have lumped Georgia in with the "crazy disrupters" looking to "attack." And even though Tony might have perceived his own actions as encouraging bipartisan dialogue on his campus, Georgia would probably have dismissed any chance at conversation with him as inevitably "unproductive." Perhaps most importantly, neither saw social change at their university as the final goal post. Their ambitions were much grander, focused on change at the societal level. But the activism enabled through their schools' political clubs provided a means for them to move forward in asserting their vision of what American democracy should look like. This is to say, petitioning CU to stop buying products made by prisoners was just a small part of Georgia's critique of the carceral state. Likewise, standing up for the legacy of Jefferson at UVA was merely a starting point for how Tony wanted to protect a traditional version of national history.

In the course of their activism, both Georgia and Tony took part in events that drew the ire of the other side. BSA marching through the stadium (with their fists raised) as alumni, parents, and students watched a basketball game is an example of what right-leaning students at CU perceived as leftism run amok. And Turning Point members were clearly incensed by Bobby Seale's talk. The Black Panthers, after all, were champions of Maoism, and Seale was indicted (but never convicted) for the murder of a fellow revolutionary.[5] At UVA, attempting to squelch ongoing racial grievances with a banal celebration of patriotism set progressives on edge—especially after the Unite the Right rally (in which American flags were used as a preferred symbol by avowed racists) had taken place. Further, the fact that Tony eventually aligned himself with a pro-Trump organization moved his activism into unacceptable territory for those on the left. Even some of his compatriots on the right found this to be a step too far.

In different ways, Georgia's and Tony's activism also brought them into contact with school officials. CU administrators intermittently tap identity-based clubs like BSA and UMAS y MEXA to weigh in on pressing issues at the university. However, such efforts are often viewed cynically by club members. In Georgia's words, "They like having us as tokens." But "the second we try to do anything politically motivated, especially if we try to get athletes involved, that's when the administration is like, 'Oh no! This is a threat. This little game is over.'" Similarly, UVA's administration occasionally consults the College Republicans and Young Americans for Freedom, two conservative student-led groups Tony was connected with. Because students on the right assume, with good reason, that their schools are mainly staffed by liberals, the right-leaning activists we interviewed took great satisfaction in discovering conservatives in leadership positions.[6] As Tony gleefully told us, one of UVA's deans "calls himself a New England conservative." And, Tony explained, he "seemed like he'd had problems" with "fringe radical" students too.

If social change is going to take place on their campuses, activists like Georgia and Tony need administrative buy-in on some level. Political clubs—along with the student leaders behind them—are one of the primary means by which universities are forced to address student-based issues.[7] At times Georgia's and Tony's relations with school officials were congenial; on other occasions they were fraught or even hostile. As we will see throughout this book, progressive activists like Georgia were more embedded within their school's institutions, but they were also highly frustrated by the slow pace of change. By contrast, conservatives like Tony were skeptical about the liberal underpinnings of higher education from the start, but they were generally satisfied with their one-on-one experiences with faculty and administrators.

Beyond bringing them into contact with university leaders, Georgia's and Tony's political engagements also helped them link up with outside entities looking to harness the energy of college students. Leaders of these organizations know that social change in the educational field can percolate through society at large. In many ways, collegians can be the tip of the spear for generational alterations of American life.[8] In Georgia's case, they attended the annual MEXA conference, enjoying the opportunity to meet other activists and share strategies for more effective organizing on their campuses. At the same time, Georgia also explained that, as a national organization, MEXA provided very little guidance or resources to CU's chapter. As for BSA, members told us the group had no national organizations it could turn to for support. Whatever they did was cobbled together locally. Like Georgia, Tony had attended national conferences connected to his activism. But for him the cornerstone of this connection was the well-funded annual Conservative Political Action Conference (CPAC); through his networking at events like this, Tony was able to quickly hook up with ALC for his aborted unity rally.[9] Tony's ties to outside entities did not stop with ALC either. He had a variety of national, state, and local organizations to which he turned to help out UVA's conservative clubs.

A major difference, then, between Georgia and Tony's activism was the guidance and resources available from inside and outside their universities. There was a plethora of extramural funding to help student-led groups on the right to host guest speakers, distribute literature, travel to conferences, and secure internships in political campaigns or government offices. In short, while some of Tony's activism took place on UVA grounds, his political engagements were driven largely by organizations not associated with his school. By contrast, Georgia's activism pushed them into the university structure. For example, at CU there is the Center for Inclusion and Social Change, and Georgia was in regular contact with its head, the Vice Chancellor for Inclusion and Student Achievement. As Georgia half-jokingly explained, "She's in charge of us, basically. She's in charge of all the angry Brown students." Georgia was far from sanguine about how committed someone like the vice chancellor might be to social change, or how effective the Center would be at enacting it. Regardless, the Center provided a set of formal pathways through which student-led groups like BSA and UMAS y MEXA could work to air their grievances and demand action from administrators.[10] Tony's activism, on the other hand, fit less easily within the institutional environment of UVA. There was a "New England conservative" dean who griped about leftists, and a few identifiable professors who were known for their conservative views. But these individuals lacked the networks progressives had access to through multicultural centers and administrators on campus. Thus, Tony turned outward—to well-funded organizations that explicitly sought to encourage students to critique academia. These organizations have their own agendas and, through issuing harsh condemnations of universities as liberal indoctrination mills, are often committed to slashing the budgets of public institutions and weakening the influence of higher education in American civic life.[11]

THINKING ABOUT CAMPUS POLITICS FROM
THE OUTSIDE IN AND THE INSIDE OUT

Previous studies by a variety of scholars confirm the general assumption that American colleges and universities are home to more leftist and liberal faculty than to conservative professors. On top of this, academic disciplines (particularly in the social sciences and humanities) reinforce progressive worldviews.[12] And then there are the students themselves. Recent surveys of incoming freshman reveal that the number of collegians identifying as liberal or leftist is on the rise. Activism is also on their minds, with more students saying they are likely to take part in a protest compared to past cohorts. Finally, the formal policies of most colleges and universities, as laid out by administrators, promote the liberal goals of diversity and inclusion, even if the results of these efforts are disappointing to left-wing activists. From the inside out, then, progressive students—relative to conservatives—have staked out a position of greater power and comfort on their campuses.[13]

Yet, progressives' taken-for-granted status at most schools has created openings for challenge from the right. The leaders of conservative organizations have been adept at employing a civil rights framing that uses the values of liberalism to promote their own causes. Following the lead of these outside groups, right-leaning students and faculty often position themselves as merely promoting free expression of undervalued viewpoints, for which they claim they are marginalized and silenced on campus.[14] This strategy, first championed by the conservative icon William F. Buckley Jr. in the 1950s, is well-funded and highly organized and has successfully chipped away at the progressive vision of academia.[15] The result is that critiques of higher education as too liberal, too esoteric, and too expensive have become increasingly mainstream. Such critiques can be heard in congressional committee meetings and state offices. They fill hours upon hours of commentary on Fox News. They are then echoed through social media channels. Ultimately, such anti-progressive positions have not only created conditions for provocative forms of conservative student activism; they have also lowered the public's trust in the academy, particularly among Republican voters.[16]

In this book we draw upon a culturally informed organizational perspective[17] to understand the student activism that has rocked colleges

and universities in recent years—from demonstrations and building occupations to shouting down invited speakers and even riots.[18] In looking
at these issues, many social scientists rely solely on data gleaned from
large surveys to measure how students' political engagement is impacted by their demographic characteristics.[19] In contrast, we emphasize the importance of school institutions in shaping the experiences
and perspectives of matriculants, and we examine the role that outside
groups play in attempting to guide the content and direction of campus
politics. Past sociological research has mostly looked at progressive activism.[20] Fewer scholars have studied the conservative response to these
leftward social movements, whether through student-led mobilization
or concerted efforts to redefine the structures of higher education. Even
more crucially, little scholarship tries to make sense of the left and the
right at the same time, using a coherent framework to see the back-
and-forth of these ideological forces.[21] Ultimately, what we are able to
show is a contested political arena, with progressives and conservatives
building on their advantages (institutional embeddedness or outside insurgency) while also suffering from distinct deficits in relation to their
opponents. Outsiders lack institutional influence, but compensate for
their disadvantages by building up a powerful external ecosystem that
lends considerable support to student followers and future conservative leaders. Insiders have greater institutional support, but can become
disillusioned with existing arrangements, both within their universities
and toward outside organizations that lend too little support.

Our analytic approach follows what we call an outside-in/inside-out
strategy, which gives us the ability to grasp the ways students are steered
into particular types of activism. Despite the dizzying speed at which
current events are constantly unfolding, we do not see these dynamics
shifting anytime soon. Our research reveals how right-leaning activists
like Tony are encouraged by organizations external to their schools to
adopt a discourse hostile to the academic enterprise. This is a winning
tactic. Turning Point's "Professor Watchlist," used to intimidate and
harass progressive faculty, comes to mind here, as do PragerU videos
decrying the professoriate as a threat to Western civilization. We refer
to these various outside influences as the conservative channel for student activism. Further, we emphasize that today's political engagements
from the right are mainly (although not exclusively) oriented toward

targeting a liberal campus culture, which plays into a larger Republican game plan. Many outside organizations encourage students on the right to plan events specifically designed to incite outrage among their left-leaning peers.[22] Once outrage is successfully sparked, and progressive students demand that administrators do something in response, the front line of conservative politics shifts to protecting the speech rights of reactionaries and provocateurs. This tactic fractures collegians along a variety of ideological lines, opening the door to more sustained attacks on the value of academia. It also garners enormous airplay on conservative television networks and websites, where conflagrations in higher education frequently go viral. Ultimately, the conservative channel promises to funnel its young participants into pathways for future political careers by linking them to right-leaning politicians, think tanks, and media outlets.

Activists on the left, by contrast, are drawn inside their universities—even those on the far left who see themselves as dissidents battling the administration. That is, the progressive channel for student activism embeds individuals within their campuses' institutions through student affairs offices, multicultural centers, and even academic departments. For instance, Georgia not only was connected to CU's Center for Inclusion and Social Change; they also worked at CU's Environmental Center, and they were majoring in Environmental Studies, among other fields. The Environmental Center supports a bevy of progressive causes under the banner of "climate justice." The Center is also run by former activists, and the staff offer tacit support to the leftist campaigns initiated by students like Georgia. Robust as these bureaucratic ties are, however, they often chafe against progressives' desire to see school officials enact sweeping changes. So, while the demands of leftists have succeeded—to a degree—in restructuring higher education,[23] students invested in social justice causes can still come to have contempt for their administrative partners. What is more, the progressive channel offers a much murkier route into post-baccalaureate political work than we observe on the right. That is, the career benefits for left-leaning mobilizations are vague at best.

As we see it, the conservative and progressive channels for student activism create the contours of contemporary campus politics. These channels influence the identities and ideologies of the collegians operating within them. They also shape the debates and protests taking place in higher education, among students, faculty, and administrators. This is always a two-way process. Just as these channels produce campus politics, they also are a product of them. In particular, we focus on the relationship between political clubs operating at schools and the channels they are part of. It is student-led groups, after all, that enable collegians to mobilize effectively on their campuses. But the clubs can exist only because of the support they receive from the internal and external resources the activism channels provide. In other words, Tony could rely on organizations like ALC, but he found that little help was available from his connections within UVA. If anything, administrators, professors, and other students stymied some of his efforts. Conversely, Georgia's work in BSA depended almost entirely on resources funded through CU. That is, their activism was made possible formally through the Center for Inclusion and Social Change and informally through other campus connections (even if their activism was not always sanctioned by the university or appreciated by school officials).

In many respects, our argument can be positioned as a sociological rejoinder to the book *The Coddling of the American Mind*, written by Greg Lukianoff, the CEO and president of the Foundation for Individual Rights in Education (FIRE), and Jonathan Haidt, a psychologist at New York University.[24] The authors offer sweeping generalizations based on extreme examples to support a grand claim about the emotional fragility and stunted intellectualism of young people. While Lukianoff and Haidt make many worthwhile observations, we do not think it is all that useful to point fingers at the supposed shortcomings of Generation Z (that is, those born since the mid-1990s). Instead, we use our research to consider the social structures that make certain types of student activism more or less acceptable in different contexts. This involves thinking about the institutions and organizations behind political clubs, and the practices they encourage or discourage. In short, we argue that students are channeled, not coddled. At the same time, like Lukianoff and Haidt, we are troubled over some matters related to free expression on campus, and we support the general tenor of Haidt's efforts in encouraging transpartisan dialogue (via Heterodox Academy and BridgeUSA).[25] However, we also believe an adequate analysis of contemporary campus politics requires a serious engagement with the multitude of players operating in the field of higher education.

STUDYING CAMPUS POLITICS

In making our cultural-organizational argument from the outside in and the inside out, we primarily rely on a qualitative analysis of semi-structured interviews that we conducted with 77 politically engaged college students in the academic year 2017–2018. All student respondents were enrolled at, or recently graduated from, the University of Arizona (UA), the University of Colorado Boulder (CU), the University of North Carolina at Chapel Hill (UNC), and the University of Virginia (UVA). All four are the flagship schools in their university systems. We wanted to study public universities because they enroll a far larger share of the American student population than private colleges.[26]

We selected these four states because at the time we were designing our study, they were considered toss-ups in presidential elections.[27] In 2016, Colorado and Virginia voted for Hillary Clinton, while Arizona and North Carolina went for Trump. Four years later, and by the thinnest of margins, Arizona flipped for the Democratic nominee, Joe Biden, while North Carolina stayed with Trump. These four states were also seen as battlegrounds that could help determine Democratic control of the Senate in 2020, with Republicans eventually losing seats in Colorado and Arizona. The schools we chose, therefore, were campuses where the motivation for local activism and outside influence was (and will continue to be) high. We initially selected students based on their affiliations with political clubs at their schools—such as College Democrats, College Republicans, Black Students Association, Young Democratic Socialists of America, Young Americans for Freedom, and so on. Additional respondents were snowballed through referrals. Our goal was to speak to the individuals most involved in activism at these pivotal public institutions during an especially contentious time in American politics, and to see how local events—such as speakers invited to campus or attempts to shroud monuments—shaped their political lives.

Nearly all of the collegians we spoke with were between the ages of 19 and 23. Our two oldest student interviewees were 28; another two were 25.[28] Based on the family descriptions they provided, half of the collegians grew up in working- or lower-middle-class households. The other half came from professional elite backgrounds. We spoke with 42 progressives (13 leftists, 28 liberals, and 1 self-described moderate who leans Democratic) and 35 conservatives (7 libertarians, 26 self-identified conservatives, and 2 self-described moderates who lean Republican). Thirty-four of the collegians in our study were women, 41 were men, and 2 told us they preferred non-binary designations. The vast majority of our respondents self-identified as White (86 percent). Eight students were Latinx, 5 were Black, 2 were Asian, and 2 were biracial. Our progressive interviewees were somewhat more diverse in terms of class (55 percent were from non-elite backgrounds), gender (only 48 percent identified as men), and race (26 percent were non-White), compared to the conservatives in our sample (66 percent from the professional elite, 89 percent White, and 60 percent men). Based on our own firsthand observations of conservative college groups, reviews of the clubs' official social media posts, and survey data of college students, we assume women were overrepresented in our interviews with right-leaning students. Conversely, we have inevitably underrepresented non-White progressive activists in our sample.[29] Much of our racial over- and under-representation results from the predominance of Whites at our four field sites.[30] When referring to specific respondents, like Georgia and Tony, we use pseudonyms and obscure identifying information. However, we do report the names of their universities and the clubs with which they were affiliated, except in cases when doing so would compromise confidentiality.

In addition to our student interviews, we talked with twenty-one leaders of political organizations operating in higher education. Our organization leader interviews include eight representatives from conservative groups (including the American Enterprise Institute, Young Americans for Liberty, and PragerU), six representatives from progressive groups (including US PIRG and NextGen America), and seven representatives from trans-partisan dialogue groups (such as BridgeUSA and Sustained Dialogue). Two of these respondents were Asian, two were Black, and the rest were White. We use the real names of the organization leaders we interviewed, as they are all public figures. Our sample also includes sixteen faculty and staff: seven conservatives and nine progressives. These people were involved with activism at their schools in one way or another:

serving as advisors to political clubs, supporting student-led initiatives, and hosting controversial lecture series. All were White, save for one Asian respondent. Because faculty and staff often discussed sensitive topics related to their employment, we keep their identities confidential.

The real significance of our data, when compared with the surveys frequently relied on by other researchers of campus politics, comes from the open-ended nature of the questions we asked our interviewees. Students knew we were interested in their experiences at school and their participation in political activities. But we generally gave them (and our faculty and organizational leader interviewees) the opportunity to dictate the specifics of what we discussed—which allowed them to identify the issues they viewed as important in relation to higher education, democracy, local causes, and civic participation. Where survey data collapses distinctions through fixed choices, our respondents had free rein in providing their answers. We also were able to ask follow-up questions—a lot of follow-up questions. It is in their richly detailed depiction of the reasoning behind our respondents' initial answers that our more than two hundred hours' worth of transcripts offer new insights into campus politics.

We should add here that we do not necessarily take what students, organization leaders, faculty, or staff told us as objective facts. For instance, we assume respondents will avoid discussing some activities and opinions while embellishing others. This happens not so much because interviewees care to impress nosy sociologists like ourselves, but because this type of narrative selectivity is a way to construct idealized self-images. Every person does this to some extent; it is part of what makes us human. Further, depending on the situation, different aspects of a respondent's self will come to the foreground or recede from view. Our goal, therefore, was not to uncover some immutable truth about our interviewees, but to offer them a chance to put what they felt was their best foot forward so we could then try to understand why they considered a particular choice the right step to make while talking with us. The result, we believe, is a highly nuanced picture of what campus politics looks like today—predominantly from the perspectives of the young people directly engaged in the mobilizing efforts that will define our democracy in years to come.[31]

OVERVIEW OF THE BOOK

We begin the next chapter with the help of Ellen Stolzenberg of the Higher Education Research Institute (HERI) at the University of California Los Angeles. Stolzenberg uses national data from the CIRP Freshman Survey to describe a variety of long- and short-term trends in campus politics.[32] Although our qualitative data collection included mostly upper-level students and not first-years, over fifty years of annual survey data allows us to situate our findings within a wider context. After exploring the quantitative findings, we turn to the students we spoke with and describe their ideological orientations. We highlight how they thought about their experiences on campus vis-à-vis their interactions with peers, professors, and administrators. Among our other findings, we see significant divisions between leftists and liberals (the progressive wing of campus politics). Conversely, there is a general sense of social solidarity on campus, if not also stylistic tendencies, among libertarians and other students on the right (the conservative wing of politics).

In chapter 3, we turn to describing the actual process of mobilization. There are, of course, conflicts between progressive and conservative clubs, but there are also intra-ideological disagreements among activists on the same end of the political spectrum. This is, at least partially, the result of how student-led groups sort and shape the activism styles of their members. We show that progressive clubs (especially those on the far left) focus their efforts on targeting administrators to change school policies. In contrast, conservative clubs home in on trying to change the hearts and minds of their fellow students, whom they consider to be unthinkingly liberal. A subset of student-led groups on the right specializes in shocking their peers with events designed to unsettle progressive sensibilities.

In chapter 4, we look at the power of the conservative channel for student activism using three case studies: the American Enterprise Institute, Turning Point USA, and PragerU. These organizations differ in their goals, styles, and models of mobilizing students, but taken together they illustrate the bountiful extramural support available for right-leaning students. This outside sponsorship takes various forms, including financial resources for campus recruiting, opportunities to bring speakers to campus, templates for media blitzes, subsidized conference travel, for-credit internships and paid summer fellowships, leadership training seminars, and rubbing elbows with celebrity politicians, policymakers, and pundits on the right. Beyond just channeling activism, we show how these organizations create something of a career funnel—or at least the appearance of one—for the most committed participants, helping undergraduate students find occupational opportunities in the conservative political sector. Through this funnel, a cadre of young conservatives trusts that it will be salaried and groomed year after year for future advocacy and activism.

We look at the progressive channel in chapter 5. While those on the left do have access to outside organizational support, we find significant asymmetry with the right. Progressive students must navigate a more do-it-yourself environment where activism is largely a matter of finding one's own external resources and opportunities. Left-of-center organizations provide less funding for travel, speakers' events, and member-recruitment drives. Yet, while they are relatively under-resourced externally, leftist and liberal students benefit from being embedded within their universities. Progressives take courses that speak to their life experiences. They major in disciplines that amplify their ideological positions. They socialize at events hosted by multicultural centers that bolster their identities. And when they have concerns about issues on their campus, they often take their disputes straight to administrators, who frequently grant them an audience. Such meetings, of course, are not the same thing as enacting tangible changes to school policy. Yet, administrators' open-door policy gives progressives more attention than most activists on the right believe they receive. Overall, we show that the outside infrastructure for student activism is not nearly as built up on the left as the organizational ecosystem is on the right. This fact, plus the generally progressive tilt of the higher education sector, draws progressive students inward toward their universities while enrolled in college, and leaves them with fewer outside contacts to forge their political career pathways after graduation.

Perhaps no issue in higher education has captured the public's eye in recent years more than the battles over free expression and inclusion. What limits are there to "free speech," and where are the boundaries of "hate speech"? What compromises to individual rights should be made to protect collective interests? This is the matter we turn to in chapter 6.

We explore how students form their arguments about the First Amendment and diversity at their schools. On the right, we see the very apex of how outside organizations can successfully channel students' thinking, by producing an easily available script justifying constitutional protections for expressions that offend, and sometimes frighten, many collegians. On the far left, we see students seriously questioning the underpinnings of speech rights—often in ways that make centrists and liberals deeply uncomfortable. Nonpartisan First Amendment organizations like the American Civil Liberties Union (ACLU) or PEN America have been less successful than conservative groups in supplying a satisfying script for how to think about these matters. This has left progressive students—and really, all students—at a disadvantage for navigating these controversies, as the very mission of academia has come under attack, and colleges and universities seem to have been caught on the back foot as this long-brewing dispute boiled over following the election of Trump.

In the final chapter, we turn to the role that trans-partisan organizations play in creating opportunities for students to talk across political divisions. Although still in the minority, a growing number of students from the left, right, and center are abandoning tactics that lead to hostility in favor of talking with one another to build empathy. BridgeUSA and Sustained Dialogue are two examples of outside national organizations that work with schools to confront political polarization. Using norms that prize taking the perspective of others and practicing "epistemological humility" (that is, not trusting your own first impressions and judgments), these groups are committed to civilly hashing out topics that ordinarily lead to acrimony. We find much to admire when students choose to talk courageously across the political aisle about abortion, gun rights, and climate change without shouting at one another. However, we also find limitations in the model, particularly if groups stop at mere "dialogue" and refrain from concerted action.

Overall, we contend that an analysis of higher education without adequate attention to institutional and organizational influences—from both within academia and outside it—cannot fully explain students' political engagements. Looking across all four of the campuses we visited, we see that external organizations (particularly on the right) and internal campus institutions (mostly on the left) form significant social structures contouring how collegians make sense of the world and mobilize to change it. In the process, students are channeled into distinct types of activism. Conservatives are winning as an insurgent force, but they do so at the cost of alienating classmates and undermining the pedagogical mission of the university. Progressives have the ideological backing of the academy, but with this support comes frustration among the far left at bureaucratic inertia and weak career paths outside of academia. The end result, when grafted onto a polarized national landscape,[33] is heated battles between political factions—with each side playing to its strengths, even if doing so exacerbates its weaknesses. So, for example, we see universities adopting policies on social issues that can seem outlandish to "middle America," and far-left students demanding even further concessions to the progressive agenda. But we also see increased hostility toward higher education from mainstream conservatives, and right-leaning collegians inviting bombastic speakers to campus as a retort to the leftists and liberals they feel dominate their schools. Understanding the channeling of student activism is a necessary step in making sense of such campus politics and—ideally—developing strategies for more civility on the quad and beyond

CHAPTER 2

Generation Z and Campus Politics

with Ellen Stolzenberg

In this chapter, we study the ideological orientations of students belonging to Generation Z. We first look at national trends in collegians' political views. Using the CIRP Freshman Survey from UCLA's Higher Education Research Institute,[1] we can see that many stereotypes and assumptions about young people—that they are uniformly leftists or that hardly any hold beliefs to the right of center—are not true. Conservative pundits and politicians frequently deride colleges and universities as catchment areas for left-wing radicals. However, fifty-plus years of data on incoming freshmen demonstrate that the proportion who identify as far left is just slightly higher than those identifying as far right. For example, in 1969, just over two percent of students identified as far right, while just under three percent identified as far left. And in 2018 these figures were nearly the same (two percent as far right and less than four percent as far left). Furthermore, over the history of the Freshman Survey, the difference between these two outer poles of the political spectrum averages just over one percent, meaning that on a typical campus you are nearly as likely to find an extremely reactionary student as you are an extremely radical one.

After using the Freshman Survey to analyze incoming collegians' political identities, activism, and civic participation, we turn to our qualitative data to examine the worldviews of the students we interviewed. We focus on five main ideological orientations: leftists, liberals, libertarians, conservatives, and moderates. Leftists (to whom we also refer as the far left and the left wing), along with liberals, comprise the left side of the political spectrum—which we collectively denote as progressivism. Libertarians and conservatives (none of the students we met called themselves "far right") comprise the right side of the political spectrum—what we group together as conservatism.[2] Finally, we also look at the few students in our sample who call themselves moderates. Moderates represent a very small portion of our interviewees (despite the preponderance of "middle of the road" responses on the Freshman Survey), likely because they are less inclined to get involved in politically active clubs.

With the responses from our interviews, we explore how students stake out their positions along the political spectrum, trace the origins of these viewpoints, and describe whether they feel their beliefs have shifted through college. Students' ideological orientations (a term we use interchangeably with political identities and political ideologies) are the building blocks of civic participation; these individual-level identities are the necessary platform from which mobilization arises. In subsequent chapters, we will go beyond personal political affiliations to show how the clubs students join connect them with new ideas and styles of activism. And beyond that, we use our outside-inside approach to show how students are associated not only with a variety of institutions and practices rooted on campus—coursework, peer groups, multicultural centers, student affairs offices, and clubs—but also with external national organizations, all of which help to channel their beliefs and actions in particular directions.

THE POLITICS OF GENERATION Z—NATIONAL TRENDS

While the proportion of freshmen at the political extremes has remained relatively consistent for decades, the Freshman Survey shows that there has been greater fluctuation among those identifying as conservative, middle-of-the-road, and liberal. Of these three political ideologies, conservatives have varied the least, with a low of just over 14 percent during Nixon's presidency, and peaking in 2006 at nearly 24 percent during George W. Bush's second term in office. Figure 1 shows almost an inverse relationship between the trend lines for middle-of-the-road and liberal

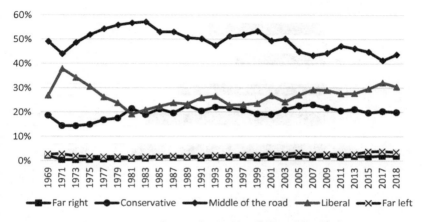

FIGURE 1   Trends in incoming college students' political views, 1969–2018

students, highlighting that much of the variation in the student population over the years has occurred between these two groups. For example,
the proportion of collegians identifying as middle-of-the-road hit its
highest point in the early 1980s, the same time that the proportion of
students identifying as liberal was at its lowest ebb. Focusing on the past
fifteen years, the general proportion of liberals has increased as those
identifying as middle-of-the-road has gone down. Along with middle-
of-the-road, there has also been a slight decrease in those identifying as
conservative.

Women make up more than half of the first-time, full-time students
who started college in 2018 (55.4%). Relative to their total numbers, however, women are overrepresented among those who identify as liberal
(70.1%) and far left (61.5%), as seen in figure 2. By contrast, though men
comprise less than 45 percent of incoming students, they represent
nearly 60 percent of those who identify as conservative and almost
65 percent of those who identify as far right. Put another way, first-year
college women are nearly twice as likely as men to be progressives.

The Freshman Survey also sheds light on the race and ethnicity of incoming students. Figure 3 shows that in 2018, slightly over 57 percent of
freshmen identify as White. A bit more than 10 percent identify as Black.
Asian and Latinx collegians comprise just under 10 percent each. Identifications with other races or ethnicities collectively represent less than

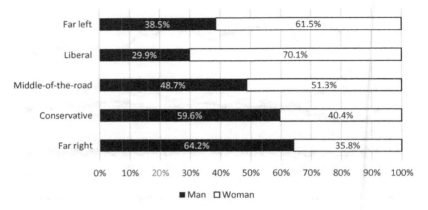

FIGURE 2   Gender and political view

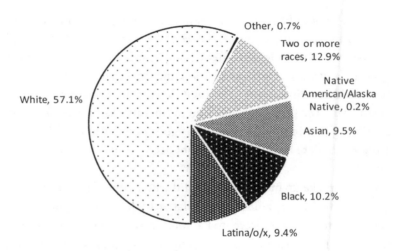

FIGURE 3   Race/ethnicity group for 2018 freshmen

1 percent of incoming students, while nearly 13 percent identify with two or more races or ethnicities.

As seen in table 1, when analyzed alongside political identity, White students are overrepresented among conservatives and those who identify as far right, and they are underrepresented among leftists and liberals. Latinx students, on the other hand, are underrepresented on the right side of the political spectrum, represented proportionately in the middle of the road, and overrepresented among progressives. Interest-

TABLE 2 Leftists

Respondent	School	Primary club	Political party	Gender	Race	Class background	Parents' ideology
Alejandro	CU	UMAS y MEXA	Unknown	Man	Latinx	Working class	2 conservative
Georgia	CU	BSA	Unknown	Non-binary	Black	Middle class	2 liberal
Levi	CU	Fossil Free CU	Socialist	Non-binary	White	Professional elite	1 liberal / 1 libertarian
Molly	CU	Unaffiliated	Democrat	Woman	White	Middle class	1 liberal / 1 conservative
Vanessa	CU	BSA	None	Woman	Black	Middle class	1 liberal / 1 conservative
Alexa	UA	Planned Parenthood	None	Woman	Latinx	Middle class	2 liberal
Ash	UA	YDSA	Socialist	Man	White	Middle class	Missing
Dean	UA	Unaffiliated	Socialist	Man	Biracial	Working class	2 conservative
Donovan	UA	YDSA	Socialist	Man	White	Middle class	2 liberal
Iona	UA	YDSA	Socialist	Woman	Latinx	Professional elite	1 conservative / 1 liberal
Lydia	UA	MSUA	None	Woman	Latinx	Working class	1 liberal / 1 conservative
Pierce	UNC	YDSA	Socialist	Man	White	Professional elite	1 missing / 1 liberal
Isaac	UVA	Students United	Socialist	Man	White	Professional elite	1 liberal / 1 moderate

in capitalism," and an immigrant mother who "grew up pretty rich" and voted for Trump. Before she arrived at UA, Iona had considered a future working in the federal government—perhaps even for the CIA. But, through her classes in American history and political science, she told us that her eyes had been opened to a new reality. In fact, her leftism was deeply informed by the college courses she had taken. Describing this evolution, Iona explained:

> I took this Latin American politics class, and I started really seeing a little bit more about American foreign policy, how it affected Latin America. [. . .] That affected me strongly because I'm a Mexican citizen and an American citizen. So, I can see what the Americans have done in the name of [. . .] peacekeeping and safety. Really, it's about controlling drugs and oil. And just like being a capitalist for America at the expense of [other] people. [. . .] I was just like, "Oh my god!"

We heard similar stories about the influence of college courses from other leftists as well. Isaac, for example, told us, "I've definitely always had marginally similar views" even before coming to UVA, "but I never had the right words for it. I never had the right kind of political education to understand what I was thinking." He added, "I don't think I have radicalized since I came to college, but I've developed more, and become more critical of, the system around me. That has allowed me to put a word on it and understand what I'm really thinking when I'm saying something that is a critique of capitalism."

Iona and Isaac also attributed their enhanced leftism to fellow students. For Iona this was—perhaps uncharacteristically—precipitated by her time in Model UN as a freshman. A friend she met in the club became a mentor. "We talked about [politics a lot], and it just moved me to the left a little bit." This exposure to more progressive ideas helped motivate Iona to start a Young Democratic Socialists of America (YDSA) chapter at her school with a handful of other students. She left Model UN because she eventually came to see it as overly careerist and not in line with her developing views. For Isaac, social ties led him to become involved with the far-left group Students United. Reflecting back on his early days at UVA, he said, "A couple friends told me, 'We're going to this organizing meeting. Come with us.' Then it just kind of snowballed from there. I was politically active in high school, but I was never going out to rallies and helping organize protests." But at UVA, it "just became a really central part of my life."

All leftists in our sample emphasized an anti-capitalist position, but their political concerns were about much more than economics. As Lydia told us, "I am anti-capitalist, anti-racism, you know, like, [a] general leftist." Or as Levi stated, they are "anti-capitalist, intersectional, feminist" and "for social justice." Levi summed this up by saying that they felt themself to be "pretty far left," adding that they strive "to be anti-oppressive in a whole slew of ways, whether that's in terms of ableism, sexism, or transphobia, or all sorts of racism."[6] Alexa said she was "actively against" the oppressions of "White supremacy and patriarchy." To this end, top-of-mind issues for Alexa included "unequal pay" for women and "changing laws to reflect better rules for people to not be victims of gender-based violence, providing more social support for people who are victims of abuse, [and] creating comprehensive types of education [to] diminish rape culture." Donovan said, "I'm very, very pro, like, sexual liberation," describing this as being about "queer liberation."

In service of these views, some on the far left said that they may be willing to vote for establishment Democrats, but leftists all disparaged liberalism as an ideology with known failures, and they critiqued the DNC for pandering to the interests of the elite at the expense of ordinary people. Or, to take historian Mark Lilla's perspective, the far left—especially as it is manifested on college campuses—has little tolerance for the horse-trading and compromise required in democratic governance.[7] As Lydia explained, "Yeah, I don't identify as a Democrat, because, you know, I just don't really agree with liberalism. I don't think it really solves anything. [. . .] I see liberals as wanting to work within capitalism, wanting to work within our system. I'm like, 'No, you cannot use our system to help things, but also profit off of that at the same time.'" Georgia stated quite simply, "Liberalism is on par with conservatism" because "a lot of times liberals are like, 'I'm socially liberal but fiscally conservative.' And those things can't go together." Pierce added that "Basically, I've moved to a point where I [. . .] do not discriminate between Republicans and Democrats. I do not differentiate between them."

In other words, the leftists we talked with wanted to fundamentally change existing social hierarchies. They understood valuable civic participation as primarily happening through mobilizations that occur outside of the established political system. From such a vantage point, liberals are not adequately invested in overturning intersectional injustice, and the Democratic Party is no less beholden than the Republican Party to what the sociologist Immanuel Wallerstein describes as the capitalist world-economy.[8] In essence, leftists were deeply critical of mainstream American politics and distrustful of the political figures operating within it. These misgivings about institutionalized power also colored their opinions of school officials.

LIBERTARIANS

The Freshman Survey does not allow students to select "libertarian" as their ideological orientation, but several of our right-leaning interviewees preferred this term to describe their beliefs. Like leftists, the students who called themselves libertarian do not come from families who share their worldview, which means that they, too, have done considerable work to develop their political identities. While they tended to think of themselves as being somewhere on the right, they (like some of the leftists we talked with) were prone to point out the problems of plotting political ideology along a unitary axis. Beyond an economic question of left and right (x-axis), there is a question of personal freedom (y-axis) running from authoritarian to libertarian.[9] The students we interviewed in this ideological segment considered themselves economically on the right. That is, they generally believed market forces are positive and state interventions are a negative. But they also supported expansive personal liberties on issues like drug legalization, the free movement of people across national borders, and LGBTQ+ rights. Thinking in these two dimensions means it can be hard for libertarians to know where they belong in a political system that collapses such distinctions. However, a few still called themselves Republicans. And even among the libertarians who avoided the Republican label, most felt strongly at odds with the Democratic Party.

   Hugh told us, "I used to be your standard bearer, middle-class, White, conservative kid." He "grew up in a normal household," and he had "slightly conservative social values, slightly conservative economic values." Things began to change once Hugh got to high school, when, he

TABLE 3 Libertarians

Respondent	School	Primary club	Political party	Gender	Race	Class background	Parents' ideology
Steve	CU	YAL	Independent	Man	White	Professional elite	1 moderate / 1 leftist
Jerry	UA	Strive	None	Man	White	Professional elite	1 liberal / 1 conservative
Arlo	UVA	CR	Republican	Man	White	Missing	2 moderate
Ernest	UVA	SIL	Libertarian	Man	White	Professional elite	1 liberal / 1 libertarian
Hugh	UVA	SIL	None	Man	White	Professional elite	2 conservative
Jack	UVA	SIL	Libertarian	Man	White	Professional elite	2 conservative
Sandra	UVA	CR	Republican	Woman	White	Professional elite	2 moderate

said, "I ended up making some friends that had very liberal lifestyles." From there "I started to realize that some of the stuff that I was told [. . .] was actually just kind of false." Hugh began to feel "it's a little bit less black and white than I thought." He went on to explain, "I have a lot of issues with your average conservative, Republican, evangelical revivalist." Too many conservatives, in Hugh's view, are "trying to promote religious interference in our country." Against this, he insisted, "It's perfectly fine if you don't do drugs or if you don't engage in unprotected, extra-marital sex, but you have no right to force that on someone else if they are not harming an un-consenting third party." All of this over time, according to Hugh, "made me leave the whole conservative-esque identity" behind. While embracing personal freedoms on what we have called the y-axis, Hugh's right-leaning politics on the x-axis did not draw him any closer to Democrats. According to Hugh, the DNC's "tax the rich" platform and "entitlement spending without any movement toward restraining it" is "detrimental to our economy." Further, Hugh felt the Democrats disingenuously take on a "holier-than-thou" attitude as they promote "social welfare."

Fed up with Republicans and Democrats, Hugh came to UVA wanting "to take a step back and just work on issues and philosophical discussions." It is this shift, he said, that led him to the group Students for

Individual Liberty (SIL), and "led me to more moderation of beliefs." As he described it a bit later in the interview, "In general, I want to err on the side of individual responsibility, personal freedom, economic freedom." As he saw it, "there are a lot of market failures and behavioral failures where we actually do need the government to either enforce or have some form of active policy, but taking a more neutral slant and not favoring one party over another" was his preferred route. All of which is to say, Hugh expressed an ideology with no worthwhile party home—not even the Libertarian Party, which most of those we interviewed (including Hugh) considered hopelessly disorganized and doomed at the ballot box.

Unlike Hugh, libertarian-identified Sandra had no problem calling herself a Republican. In fact, she was an active member of UVA's College Republicans, but in 2016 she could not stomach pulling the lever for Trump (none of the libertarians we interviewed said they had voted for the 45th president). Calling herself "socially liberal and fiscally conservative," Sandra explained that "I'm probably more libertarian" than most Republicans "since I believe in things like marijuana legalization. I believe in gay marriage. I believe in abortion rights." Her reasoning was that "I think the government has no role in regulating people's private lives." The fiscally conservative side of her balance sheet, though, pointed to concerns about making "individuals reliant on the government" because "government spending can only increase," and it "never decreases with time." What Sandra's comments underscored was a desire to reduce the influence of government in everyday life—which was also why Hugh reacted so negatively to the association of the religious right with Republicans.

While there are numerous issues that animate different libertarians—decriminalizing drugs, ending corporate subsidies, supporting gay rights, de-escalating military conflicts, reducing the carceral state—what we heard most uniformly in our interviews was a frustration with not fitting into the existing political system.[10] In effect, the libertarians we talked with had lots of complex and nuanced ideas that could not be easily pigeonholed, and, like those on the far left, many libertarians were highly dubious of the role played by American government. At the same time, even though they shared many overlapping concerns with progressives (like criminal justice reform and distrust of the military-industrial complex), they did not view left-leaning students as allies on campus. Further, their activism was not oriented around the boycotts, sit-ins, and protest marches favored by leftists. Instead, libertarians saw themselves as more squarely aligned with conservatives, despite their numerous disagreements with them.

LIBERALS

Along with leftists, liberals occupy the left side of the political spectrum. Together, the two groups comprise what we commonly refer to in this book as progressives. But, as we have already seen, there are divisions within the different political segments. Here, we highlight three important themes in our interviews with liberals. First, for all of the students in this ideological segment, being "liberal" was synonymous with being a Democrat. Indeed, our interviewees used the terms interchangeably. Second, most liberals we talked with were pragmatists. They wanted to work within the established party structure to create a better system, which they said contrasted with leftists, who they said agitated without any realistic endpoint in mind.[11] Finally, liberals talked about having undergone quite a bit of political change in college. Several reported becoming more progressive compared to their parents, while a handful of others said that their experiences in school opened their minds to perspectives further to the right.

When asked how she would describe her political views, Melissa answered, "I would say liberal, yeah, liberal Democrat. I always vote Democrat." Prompted to reflect on what else being a liberal meant to her, she responded, "It means voting Democrat, but also working together with other people who vote Democrat, because at the end of the day, Democrat is the party that I align with." Similarly, Kristen told us, "I would definitely say I'm pretty liberal. [. . .] I mean when you look at most of the pretty standard Democratic platforms, I'm going to agree with most of those. There might be a few small things that I would do a little bit differently, but for the most part I am pretty much, like, check the boxes of what you would expect the Democratic platform to be." Or as Anthony explained, "I would say I'm liberal. I wouldn't say I'm moderate left, but I wouldn't say I'm far left. I'm probably a pretty typical mainstream Dem."

Liberal students voiced many of the same concerns that occupied leftists. Edward, for example, talked about "equal opportunity, social

TABLE 4 Liberals

Respondent	School	Primary club	Political party	Gender	Race	Class background	Parents' ideology
Donato	CU	College Democrats	Democrat	Man	Latinx	Professional elite	2 liberal
Edward	CU	College Democrats	Democrat	Man	White	Middle class	1 liberal / 1 conservative
Jace	CU	College Democrats	Democrat	Man	White	Middle class	1 liberal / 1 moderate
Katherine	CU	College Democrats	Democrat	Woman	White	Middle class	2 moderate
Lulu	CU	PIRG	Democrat	Woman	White	Professional elite	2 liberal
Maddox	CU	College Democrats	Democrat	Man	White	Middle class	1 moderate / 1 conservative
Atlas	UA	Planned Parenthood	Democrat	Man	Latinx	Middle class	1 liberal
Liana	UA	Catalyst	Democrat	Woman	White	Professional elite	1 liberal
Madeleine	UA	Young Democrats	Democrat	Woman	White	Middle class	1 liberal / 1 moderate
Sheridan	UA	Planned Parenthood	Democrat	Woman	Asian	Working class	1 missing / 1 conservative
Abigail	UNC	Young Democrats	Democrat	Woman	White	Professional elite	2 liberal
Adele	UNC	Young Democrats	Democrat	Woman	White	Middle class	2 moderate
Anthony	UNC	Young Democrats	Democrat	Man	White	Middle class	2 conservative
August	UNC	BSM	Democrat	Man	Black	Working class	2 moderate

Blaire	UNC	BridgeUSA	Democrat	Woman	White	Professional elite	2 moderate
Dexter	UNC	Young Democrats	Democrat	Man	White	Professional elite	1 conservative / 1 moderate
Jerod	UNC	Young Democrats	Democrat	Man	White	Professional elite	1 liberal / 1 moderate
Jill	UNC	Young Democrats	Democrat	Woman	White	Professional elite	2 liberal
Kristen	UNC	PIRG	Democrat	Woman	White	Professional elite	2 conservative
Quinta	UNC	BSM	Democrat	Woman	Black	Middle class	Missing
Cody	UVA	University Democrats	Democrat	Man	White	Middle class	2 conservative
Jamison	UVA	University Democrats	Democrat	Man	White	Professional elite	1 moderate / 1 conservative
Mae	UVA	Sustained Dialogue	Democrat	Woman	White	Professional elite	2 moderate
Marco	UVA	Unaffiliated	Democrat	Man	White	Professional elite	2 liberal
Melissa	UVA	University Democrats	Democrat	Woman	White	Middle class	2 moderate
Piper	UVA	Sustained Dialogue	Democrat	Woman	White	Professional elite	2 liberal
Sasha	UVA	Queer Student Union	Democrat	Man	Asian	Middle class	2 moderate
Simon	UVA	University Democrats	Democrat	Man	White	Middle class	2 liberal

justice, and just human rights in general." Melissa stated that "Equality is the root value," which, for her, included fighting for the rights of animals, the LGBTQ+ community, and the working class. Adele echoed leftists when she told us she was especially interested in "gender equity" and "race equity." And she believed in "using government intervention, as opposed to relying on market structures," to get there. However, leftists and liberals diverged in what they thought was the best way to advance their causes. Most liberals argued that they were pragmatic institutionalists. They told us they wanted to work within existing foundations, as opposed to organizing disruptive protests. Liberals did not rule out street demonstrations in all situations—for example, many had participated in the 2017 Women's March (held the day after Trump's inauguration)—but they felt that tactics that went further than that could be divisive and were rarely necessary and at times even unhelpful. In discussing campus politics, in fact, liberals were inclined to bring up the actions of the far left as a reference point for the types of mobilization they were not interested in doing. For example, Madeleine huffed, "My problem with YDSA" is that "they're mad about everything." But, she went on, "The way to fix it is to elect people who can influence policy. [Just] being upset isn't going to get you anywhere." So, while the Freshman Survey reveals that leftist and liberal freshmen say they are about as likely to protest, our qualitative data show that the types of demonstrations they have in mind are quite different.

In some cases, liberals reported that their politics mellowed during their time at school. Abigail, for instance, said she "dabbled around in a few progressive clubs" on campus "like a feminist, left-wing magazine." But she was turned off by the ideological orientations of members. "The political views they were pushing were kind of anti-capitalist," she said, while "I've definitely kind of evolved to a pretty moderate-liberal viewpoint." Likewise, Jace told us that he considered himself to be "left of center," but added that he was "less hard to the left than I used to be." Jace explained that majoring in economics clued him in to the merit of some conservative ideas and opened his mind to other outlooks. "I think that markets are generally a good thing. I think that they need to be regulated, but, in general, they're the best way to get goods to consumers." After stating that the police and military were two sectors that should be public and regulated, he went on to say that he "can see the conservative argument" on keeping the minimum wage low, because "when you make labor more expensive, you're going to use less labor in your production mix." Jace also gave a nod to some of the underlying concepts of right-leaning arguments against gun control and abortion rights, even though he still supported both himself.

In contrast to students like Abigail and Jace, other liberals reported that college had shifted them leftward. As Jerod explained, "I would say my views have gone a little bit further left since coming to UNC." When asked if this was mostly due to coursework or interactions with peers, he gave credit to both, saying, "I've certainly gotten a better academic grounding and a better idea of how I talk about issues from my course-work. But I would say that things that are going on outside the class are equally valuable." Similarly, August told us, "I think being at UNC defi-nitely changed my views. It exposed me to different perspectives, differ-ent issues. It definitely made me a little more politically engaged. It put me in spaces to have conversations that I probably wouldn't have had." He then commented that these experiences "definitely shifted" his views "of what it means to be liberal." Liberals, then, may have altered their positions while in college, but they did not see themselves as straying too far left of the center of the political spectrum.

CONSERVATIVES

More so than liberals, conservatives are an ideologically diverse group, and these differences manifested in both the substance and the style of their activism.[12] However, much of this seeming diversity in com-parison to liberals is definitional. That is, whereas the progressives we interviewed were in general agreement about the divisions between the far left and liberals, there was considerably less clarity among self-identified conservative students on how to demarcate the ideological terrain belonging to the just-right-of-center and the truly far right—a problem made more difficult by the rise of Trumpism in the Republi-can Party. And many extremely conservative interviewees (if judged by progressives' sensibilities) eschewed the notion that they are "far right" at all, since they associated the term with overt racism and domestic ter-rorism. The leftists we talked with, by contrast, embraced the designa-tion of "far left."

In an effort to offer greater clarity, we divide our conservative respondents into three ideological strands: traditionalist, libertarian-leaning, and populist. Despite the distinctions between them, all three strands, as well as those in the libertarian segment we have already covered, generally felt bonded together by their right-leaning worldviews. This created a degree of cohesion among conservatives, irrespective of their political disagreements and tactical differences.[13] By contrast, we see less of a shared sense of community between the far left and liberals.

Andy explicitly proclaimed himself a "traditionalist" by pointing to his "political heroes, William F. Buckley and George Nash." These are two famed thinkers in the intellectual heritage of modern conservatism. Asked to say more about how this brand of conservatism resonated with him, Andy said, "Oh, a great respect for traditions and a distaste for reactionary politics." The latter, he said, includes both the far right and the far left: "Pretty much anyone who's shouting, I don't like." When asked to plot himself on a continuum from left to right, Andy marked himself alongside Ronald Reagan, who—though a product of a conservative shakeup in the 1970s[14]—is now considered a paragon of American traditional conservatism.

Traditionalists, like liberals on the progressive side, supported a pragmatic approach to politics. They were committed to supporting the Republican National Committee (commonly referred to as the GOP, or Grand Old Party) even when it meant backing politicians, like Trump, who they might have disliked. Jaiden was an especially ardent booster of the GOP. "When it comes to the [political] spectrum, I would say I consider myself a conservative Republican." But at the same time, Jaiden also assured us, "I think we need to reach across the aisle and work with Democrats as much as possible." Playing against being a dogmatic conservative, he added, "In the end, I think it's important to be able to work together on a lot of issues." In the next breath, though, Jaiden also explained that he campaigned for Trump in 2016, despite having favored the moderate Republican Jon Huntsman in 2012, because he was certain Trump would beat Hillary Clinton at the polls. In other words, for activists like Jaiden, pragmatism involved taking the electorate's pulse and making compromises that would capture the most votes.

Beyond the seven respondents we already discussed who declared their political ideology to be libertarian (over and above the label of con-

TABLE 5 Conservatives

Respondent	School	Primary club	Political party	Gender	Race	Class background	Parents' ideology
Traditionalists							
Chloe	UA	CR	Republican	Woman	White	Middle class	2 conservative
Denisse	UA	CUFI	Republican	Woman	Latinx	Working class	2 conservative
Jaiden	UA	TPUSA	Republican	Man	Latinx	Working class	1 conservative / 1 moderate
Miranda	UA	Unaffiliated	Republican	Woman	White	Professional elite	1 conservative / 1 liberal
Andy	UNC	CR	Republican	Man	White	Professional elite	2 conservative
Ava	UNC	CR	Republican	Woman	White	Professional elite	1 conservative / 1 liberal
McKenzie	UNC	CR	Republican	Woman	White	Middle class	2 conservative
Silas	UNC	CR	Republican	Man	White	Professional elite	2 conservative
Warren	UNC	CR	Republican	Man	White	Middle class	2 conservative
Billy	UVA	CR	Republican	Man	White	Middle class	2 conservative
Dante	UVA	CR	Republican	Man	White	Professional elite	1 moderate / 1 unknown
Jessica	UVA	Sustained Dialogue	Independent	Woman	White	Professional elite	2 conservative
Kalista	UVA	Unaffiliated	Independent	Woman	Black	Professional elite	2 conservative

continues

TABLE 5 (continued)

Respondent	School	Primary club	Political party	Gender	Race	Class background	Parents' ideology
Libertarian-leaning							
Chris	CU	AEI	Republican	Man	White	Middle class	1 liberal / 1 conservative
Sofia	UA	CR	Republican	Woman	White	Middle class	1 moderate / 1 libertarian
Audrey	UVA	CR	Republican	Woman	White	Professional elite	2 conservative
Tony	UVA	Young Republicans	Republican	Man	White	Middle class	2 moderate
Populists							
Ariel	CU	TPUSA	Republican	Woman	White	Professional elite	1 moderate / 1 conservative
Miles	CU	TPUSA	Republican	Man	White	Professional elite	2 conservative
Trevor	CU	TPUSA	Republican	Man	White	Professional elite	2 conservative
Josephine	UA	CR	Republican	Woman	White	Middle class	2 moderate
Charlotte	UNC	CR	Republican	Woman	White	Working class	2 conservative
George	UNC	TPUSA	Republican	Man	White	Middle class	2 moderate
Layla	UNC	CR	Republican	Woman	White	Professional elite	1 moderate / 1 conservative
Maxwell	UNC	BridgeUSA	Republican	Man	White	Professional elite	2 conservative
Joaquin	UVA	TPUSA	Republican	Man	Bi-racial	Working class	2 conservative

servative), several students on the right side of the political spectrum told us they were "libertarian-leaning." The main distinction was the degree to which they felt attached to the Republican Party. Whereas many libertarians eschewed the Republican Party (with the exception of Sandra, above), libertarian-leaning conservatives said they felt perfectly at home in the GOP, though they stressed their commitment to personal freedom. As Audrey explained, "I identify definitely as a Republican in terms of voting. However, I'm socially liberal." Audrey acknowledged her stance was probably the "typical" Republican description of Generation Z: "pro-choice, don't care about [banning] gay marriage, anything like that. So, [I have] more of a libertarian bent. As long as you're not hurting anyone else, I don't really care what you do." This theme of "do your own thing" differentiated conservative-identified libertarians from the traditionalists.

We should add here that some libertarian-leaning conservatives might have considered themselves to be straight-up libertarians except for social issues (a viewpoint that would confound the students we placed in the libertarian segment). Sofia summed up such views with the term "conservatarian," or "more conservative than libertarian and more libertarian than conservative." By which she meant, "I lean conservative on certain issues, and I disagree with libertarians generally on specific issues, like abortion. But then the same thing with conservatives: I don't agree with them on a lot of things." She concluded by telling us that if "someone else's decisions don't affect me, then I would just let them do what they want."

While traditionalists and libertarian-leaning conservatives had their differences, these often seemed like minor quibbles when contrasted with the positions of the students we categorize as populists (a designation probably most closely aligned with the Freshman Survey's "far right"). We find two themes animating these students—themes that put them at odds with other conservatives. First, Trump's brash, illiberal behavior energized these activists, and his deviations from conservative orthodoxy did not seem to bother them.[15] As Ariel explained, "I think he's good for the party because I think the party needed some shaking up. The party needed somebody to go in there and say, 'Hey, we're not going by X, Y, Z anymore. We're going to do it the way that we want and in a way that we see best fits.'" Second, populists, as the name implies, championed a new vision for the GOP. They told us Republicans should prioritize the economic needs of the working class over the interests of the highly educated and wealthy. Trevor broke it down by explaining that what was most important to him was "being more nationalistic, being more country-focused than being global-focused." Or, as George said, "I support more of a populist agenda than traditional corporate conservatives."

Speaking to her frustrations with politics as usual (that is, the sort of views supported by traditionalists and libertarian-leaning respondents), Ariel told us she believed that younger people "don't really like the term Republican anymore." Asked if she considers herself a party supporter, she responded, "There's a lot of politicians and people within the Republican Party who are in Congress that I don't want anything to do with," but "if I say I'm a conservative, I guess, people can understand me more." These complaints aside, Ariel told us she would cast her votes for virtually any Republican running against a Democrat (a level of support not necessarily reciprocated by leftists for the DNC).

As a final note on those who subscribe to the various strands within the conservative identity, it is worth remarking on how these students saw college as either strengthening or weakening their ideological positions. Some told us that they do not think college has specifically changed their views that much. All the same, Audrey told us, "I feel like I'm more empathetic and more understanding of other people's viewpoints." She described taking classes from professors who have been from the Middle East, which allowed her to see "how they respond to things like the Muslim ban" (a reference to the Trump administration's efforts to limit travel into the US from several primarily Muslim nations). And this exposure "had me go further to the left and be more empathetic on issues like that." Andy said that his experiences in college have made him a greater supporter of bipartisanship. Writing for the *Daily Tar Heel* (UNC's student paper), he said, "I've had to work alongside pretty much all liberal student journalists, and I don't really have a problem with that. It's easy to think of the other side sort of in the abstract when you don't have daily interaction with them." In other words, conservatives like Audrey and Andy highlight how just being in a diverse environment like college can lead to greater understanding of and compassion for others.[16]

Alternatively, Layla's sense of frustration with progressive classmates (especially their disrespect for Trump and their ad hominem attacks against his supporters) pulled her out of political apathy and into populist activism during the 2016 election. She recalled that other students would "diminish your character" for being pro-Trump, which "definitely made me more conservative." Coming from the traditionalist strand, Silas reported that until coming to UNC, he did not believe that students would be "as liberal as they are." He added, "Then I came here, and—surprised might not be the best word, but—I was *awakened* to the fact that, okay, there really are people that are this way." The result was to feel "pushed" further to the right. In short, proximity to others with different worldviews does not guarantee a move toward empathy. Indeed, it can lead to more confrontational styles, often with the goal of riling up the opposition.

MODERATES

A few words about the three moderates in our sample are in order. As the Freshman Survey indicates, over the past fifty-plus years, more incoming freshman have called themselves middle-of-the-road than have identified further to the left or right on the political spectrum. This remains true to this day, although their numbers have been falling as the political arena has become more polarized. Yet, as we have already discussed, it is difficult to know from surveys what "middle of the road" actually means to those who select it. Choosing to identify as middle-of-the-road may signal that respondents are centrist on the issues. But it also could mean that they are hesitant to state a political identity, are unsure of what their politic views are, cast their lot with no party and vote as independents, or that on some issues they are conservative and on others they are liberal. Although this population is significantly underrepresented in our sample, our qualitative data allow us to glean insights about what being a moderate means to those who are politically active in today's campus politics. One thing that is notable is that all three of our interviewees said they were particularly open to having less polarized discussions with other students at their schools, a point we will return to in chapter 7 when we explore trans-partisan dialogue groups.

TABLE 6 **Moderates**

Respondent	School	Primary club	Political party	Gender	Race	Class background	Parents' ideology
Gregory	CU	BridgeUSA	Democrat	Man	White	Professional elite	2 liberal
Amanda	UA	AEI	Republican	Woman	White	Professional elite	2 conservative
Bishop	UNC	BridgeUSA	Independent	Man	White	Middle class	1 conservative / 1 moderate

We talked with one moderate student from each university except UVA—a moderate Republican, a moderate Democrat, and a moderate independent. Demographically, all three moderates in our sample are White. Two are men and one is a woman. Two of them come from professional elite families and the third is middle-class. Also notable is that these three students do not generally come from moderate families. As table 6 shows, each felt they had moved toward the center from the left or the right, relative to their parents. This means that moderates, too, rather than being complacent, are taking on new political ideologies in college.

Amanda is a moderate Republican who at the time of our interview was a graduating senior at UA. Earlier in her college career, she had been a member of the College Republicans, had spent a lot of time campaigning for candidates in her party, and had traveled to the Conservative Political Action Conference (CPAC) more than once. While Amanda continued to identify as a Republican, she could no longer tolerate students, politicians, or campus clubs that use inflammatory tactics to ignite the passions of progressive classmates and faculty. A person who did not, and never would, vote for Trump, Amanda was turned off by the aspersions that conservative media, pundits, and politicians cast on higher education. For example, Amanda was appalled when a Republican candidate for state senator came to UA and promised that he would change the law so that "students don't have to go through diversity or inclusiveness training, or pronoun training, anything like that." She explained that as a student leader on campus, "I'd been through all those [trainings]. And I was just like, I didn't want to [support that candidate's negative] perspective about universities."

So, what does appeal to Amanda? "I really look for people who can work with both parties and are open and accepting to hear both sides." Asked if she would ever vote for a Democrat over a Republican, she readily said yes, and in fact she was supporting the Democrat candidate for a local congressional seat, which is something that in past years she "never would have thought" she would do. Now, though, for Amanda, moderation meant bipartisanship.

Both Bishop and Gregory were members of what we call transpartisan dialogue groups—organizations that seek to promote mutual understanding across the political spectrum. Bishop, a freshman at UNC, said that his core concerns ranged a great deal, from speech issues to free markets to climate change. "I believe climate change is happening," he said. "I really think it's an important issue that has to be dealt with." A student who would have supported John Kasich in 2016 had he been old enough to vote, Bishop said that these stances, in addition to "having been raised by a Catholic, mostly Republican mother and an atheist, mostly Democratic father," were the result of "both sides pulling on my brain my whole life." Throughout high school, he said, "I really struggled to figure out where I fit because I was just in this mindset of, 'Am I Republican or am I Democrat?' And then eventually I was just like, 'Well, who cares? I don't need to have a party.'" Bishop landed on just having "my individual beliefs." Being a moderate, in other words, meant not pledging himself to a political organization even while maintaining a keen interest in the major issues of the day.

CU's Gregory also found himself moving closer to the center than his parents, although from the other direction. Like Bishop, he was having serious second thoughts about affixing a party label to himself. The son of two liberal, reliably Democratic parents, Gregory said, "I definitely don't identify primarily as a Democrat. I'm still a registered Democrat, but I have my reservations about primarily identifying as that because I'm a lot more of a centrist. There are a lot of issues that I disagree with the mainstream Democrats on, and I think that the environment of our party politics today just does more harm than good." Asked to go into more detail, Gregory talked about distasteful identity politics. "I'm not far left-wing on anything." Explaining, he stated, "I would say I fall to the right on foreign policy, immigration to an extent," and "unfortunately—I think it should be a bipartisan issue—but free speech. I fall a lot more where the right is today." Reflecting on how he believed the left is shutting down intellectual inquiry on campuses, Gregory said his time at university has moved him further to the right than he had thought possible. For Gregory, being a moderate meant putting distance between himself and what he felt was the radical fringe.

As we can see, there is considerable variation among those who identify as middle-of-the-road. Because our sample of moderates is so small, and because we can make out in detail the political leanings of each interviewee, in subsequent chapters we group Amanda and Bishop in with conservatives and Gregory with progressives.

CONCLUSION

In this chapter, we started with the CIRP Freshman Survey to look at national trends among incoming college students. This gave us leverage for seeing how individuals, in the aggregate, refer to their political beliefs and activities. We then used our qualitative data to understand what these ideological labels mean to activists and how their worldviews have developed. Political beliefs are a complex affair. There is considerable variation not only across political affiliations (between, say, liberals and libertarians), but also within the same general ideological space (for example, between traditionalist and populist conservatives). Families, high school experiences, political parties, and especially campus interactions all deeply influenced the ideological orientations of these politically engaged students. Institutionally-minded education researchers such as Peter Kauffman, Kenneth Feldman, Ernest Pascarella, and Patrick Terenzini remind us that students—far from being atomized beings—interact with one another in a variety of college-level organizational structures and learn how to take on new ideas and identities,[17] often setting themselves apart from others, including their parents. Yet, the effects of college on political identity are not ideologically unidirectional—certainly not in the sense that all students become more liberal, or even that they stray from their family's political orientation at all. As the political sociologist Kyle Dodson argues, the degree to which college influences students' political beliefs is contingent on the particular academic and social groups with which they come into contact.[18] We saw this happening among our interviewees, as they took classes, joined political clubs, worked on student newspapers, and interacted with peers in dorms. Although a sample of 77 activists on four public university campuses cannot be generalized to all politically engaged students at flagship institutions (much less to all collegians in the US), our data go a long way to fleshing out the findings of national surveys—especially when considering that it is activists who often push the directions of the political conversation forward.[19]

In the next chapter, we go beyond individual-level perspectives to see how members of political clubs actually mobilize at their schools. As we move ahead in the book to discuss the channels of student activism, it is worth remembering how our interviewees said they came into their ideological orientations in the first place and how college has transformed them in large and small ways. Contentious campus politics arise through the interplay of collegians' identities with the institutions and organizations that promote particular forms of civic participation. By looking at how progressives are pushed from inside their universities and conservatives are pulled from the outside, we begin to grasp the complexities driving young people to act in these polarizing times. We will also see the deficiencies in how the left and right have built up their political infrastructures—shortchanging all students in the promise of learning better democratic values.

CHAPTER 3

Doing Campus Politics

We see that students' self-identifications are a first step in a larger process that leads them to join political clubs to mobilize for social change. But what does activism on campus really look like? In this chapter, we examine some of the campaigns, events, and protests that members of student-led groups engage in at our four universities. Our intention is not merely to list the many practices that club members take part in, such as distributing literature or conducting presentations on certain issues. Nor is it to simply lay out the ostensible goals of activism—such as Georgia's leftist clubs' efforts at CU to block the purchase of goods made in prisons, or Tony's conservative objective of protecting the legacy of President Jefferson at UVA (as we saw in chapter 1). Instead, we want to provide a "thick description" of what participating in political clubs achieves for student members, as they figure out what kind of activists they want to be.[1]

Political clubs are small interactional settings that function as sorting and shaping mechanisms for different styles of student activism, ranging from civil discussions with like-minded others to planning events that antagonize peers and faculty on campus. Beyond this, separating students into different groups that nurture (or stifle) particular repertoires of mobilizations affects collegians' perceptions of other political activists on campus. Classmates are transformed into opponents or potential collaborators. Finally, club differences influence the targets that members select for their activism. Left-leaning groups often try to spur administrators to change campus policies, while right-leaning groups tend to attempt to change the hearts and minds of their fellow students. In chapters 4 and 5, we will return to our outside-inside model to show how all of these campus-level club activities are encompassed in wider political and organizational contexts—or what we call conservative and progressive channels. But before we get to the influence of these larger structures, our campus-oriented exploration of club dynamics reveals new insights into what the sociologist Daisy Reyes calls "inhabiting" campus politics, or, in our terminology, how school-level organizational relationships mold student activism.[2]

Prior to our analysis, we need to clarify that a "political club," as we are using the term, refers to a student-led group brought together to conduct activism and campaign work or take part in civic dialogue. There are several important caveats that follow from this. First, the vast majority of university-affiliated clubs are not political. There are clubs for playing video games and learning horticulture. There are clubs for engineering majors and Francophiles. We are only interested in the small subset of clubs with political motivations. Second, while most of the student-led groups we looked at were officially recognized by their schools, some were not. There are usually perks that come with university affiliation, like funding from student government and office space. But there are also hurdles, like filling out forms and finding faculty advisors. Whether a student-led group is formally acknowledged by the administration is not our concern. What matters to us is whether the students are collectively organized for a political purpose. Third, we are defining "politics" quite broadly. In this category we naturally include clubs focused on campaigning for politicians—namely, College Democrats and College Republicans. But there are also issue-based clubs—groups advocating for drug legalization, fossil fuel divestment, gun rights, and so on. And there are identity-based clubs, like Black student associations and LGBTQ+ groups. These latter types of clubs might not prioritize activism or campaigning in their mission statements, instead aiming to foster a sense of community among members. We include them as political clubs because—as Georgia's actions illustrate—such groups often end up being the leading voices for progressive mobilizing on campus.[3]

SORTING MEMBERS: CLUBS AS SIEVES

The metaphors of the sieve and the incubator, as laid out by the educational sociologists Mitchell Stevens, Elizabeth Armstrong, and Richard Arum, are useful for understanding what happens to students when they join political clubs.[4] As sieves, clubs filter through potential recruits based on membership criteria. For example, if students want to be active in Democratic politics or learn more about libertarianism, they can join clubs, and can potentially take on leadership positions as they gain experience. Once the students are sorted into groups, the clubs incubate particular styles of activism among their participants. In nurturing the types of practices politically engaged students take part in, clubs function as miniature institutions—pressing adherents into their mold of idealized activism. Because these campus-based clubs are unlike conventional educational sieves (such as admissions and retention policies), and because they have low barriers to entry and exit at most schools, members can come and go as they please. But those who stay, almost by definition, come to share a sense of fit within the group.

To explain this process, we begin by noting that clubs initially attract students through ideological affinities and a desire to find like-minded peers. One common refrain in our interviews was a general frustration with the political apathy of the student body as a whole. As Jace explained, "A lot of the kids" at CU are "there for the wrong reasons—drinking away [their] parents' tuition, not going to class, and just bullshitting [their] way through college with a C average." Jace told us such hedonistic decisions were "okay" because "it's college." However, he was bothered because he felt many of his peers did not "want to advance themselves, and that offends me." During his sophomore year, having become disappointed with many of his classmates, Jace found a cohort of politically engaged liberals in his school's College Democrats, and that "made things easier." A related theme is that students looked to political clubs (much like any other student group) to form friendships and find support. For example, Dexter described the impact of social connections among his fellow Young Democrats. "It is cool to get a nice group of friends when you first enter college." To this he added, "I feel like most people, once they get connected to a group, it's in many ways just a friend group, more so even sometimes than a political group." And, speaking of UNC's Young Democrats specifically, "The people who come to the events each week" are "close friends" who comprise "the core of the club." Likewise, but from the other side of the political spectrum, Josephine explained, "I just enjoy the fact that I'm able to go somewhere and feel that I won't be ridiculed for my values." To this end, Josephine described the College Republicans and Turning Point USA as the clubs "where I can openly discuss my values."

Left-of-center collegians are drawn to progressive groups, while right-leaning students gravitate to conservative groups. That may seem like an obvious point, but between the far left and the far right, there is also a good deal of difference, and finding one's people requires trial and error. There are centrist Democrats, leftists who eschew party politics, traditional and populist Republicans, unaffiliated libertarians, and much more. And then, even within the same policy or party orientation, there is variation in how students envision advocating for social change. Students may join clubs because they want to meet elected officeholders and gain experience working on campaigns. Alternatively, students may seek opportunities to take part in reasoned debates where they can challenge others over differences in beliefs. All of which is to say, students sort themselves into clubs not just by ideology and party, but also by their interest in embracing particular political tactics. Potential members have to consider what kind of activists they want to be and learn which clubs will give them opportunities to engage with their preferred style of activism.

Melissa, a liberal member of UVA's University Democrats (UDems), for instance, kept her distance from left-wing groups at her school. She told a story about how leftist clubs disrupted a town hall meeting held on campus for a Republican congressman, Tom Garrett. In the wake of Donald Trump's 2016 election, many Republican representatives in swing districts across the nation were swarmed by angry progressives when they hosted forums with their constituents. Garrett drew even greater ire at UVA's town hall because a photograph had recently surfaced featuring him glad-handing Jason Kessler, the organizer of the Unite the Right rally.[5] "University Democrats were trying to host a more peaceful counter-protest" when the congressman visited, Melissa explained about her club. The leftist groups, however, staged "a counter-

DOING CAMPUS POLITICS   53

counter-protest," replete with banners condemning Garrett for being
cozy with White supremacists and including actions she deemed overly
confrontational. According to Melissa, "I remember going out with my
friends to get drinks after, and we were just reflecting on [how] that was
the problem with the left." The takeaway here is that Melissa was sympa-
thetic to leftists' anger at Garrett. She was protesting too. But she found
fault with how clubs like Students United went about trying to achieve
social change—in this case, by attempting to de-platform a seated poli-
tician. UDems, in other words, offered its members one set of practices
for supporting progressive causes (such as peaceful expressions of displeasure with Congressman Garrett), whereas Students United (a far-left
group) wanted to display more aggressively their opposition to social
injustices. From Melissa's vantage point, the UDems' civil approach was
more productive. Similarly at CU, Jace said he was receptive to at least
some socialist critiques of capitalism, and he concurred with his more
radical peers on needing to protect the dignity and safety of historically
underrepresented populations on campus. However, like other liberals
we interviewed, Jace was not interested in joining a far-left group, saying
that he shared the College Democrats' pragmatic goal of electing party
candidates.

Leftist groups, in turn, found plenty of flaws in the clubs wedded to
liberalism. Donovan underscored this difference, explaining that his
chapter of Young Democratic Socialists of America (YDSA) would never
partner with a mainstream Democrat club because "we have a lot of critiques of their party." And, in a move that would undoubtedly cause Jace
and Melissa to roll their eyes, Lydia—a member of the Marginalized Students of the University of Arizona (MSUA)—lumped the mainstream
political clubs together and dismissed both sets of members as uninterested in real social change. "Democrat, Republican [. . .] they're not
really involved in advocating for students." This is because "Their political life is like, 'Oh, I interned for John McCain.' On both sides: Democrats and Republicans." She concluded by stating, "I think it's just a club
for them or a résumé-builder." According to leftists like Donovan and
Lydia, the more moderate clubs (liberal or conservative) are insincere in
their activism, and their members are laughably careerist. In short, the
reform-minded approach of liberal clubs did not jibe with the dissident
identity adopted by leftists.[6]

We see equally deep divisions on the right. In particular, many College Republicans and libertarian groups were turned off by the antics of the populist-oriented Turning Point and the group's founder, Charlie Kirk. As Amanda, a moderate Republican, told us, "I would never join Turning Point." The organization's methods of recruitment at the Conservative Political Action Conference (CPAC) "wasn't a very positive environment." Specifically, Amanda told us, "They have an agenda on campus, and I'm like, 'That's just not something I want to take part in.'" Likewise, Dante said he was uninterested in joining Turning Point because they focus on "trolling type stuff." Or as Billy explained, his College Republican chapter would not want to bring former Breitbart News editor and provocateur Milo Yiannopoulos to UVA. He derided Turning Point, asserting that "They *want* to be the group that brought Milo." George would agree with Billy's assessment that Turning Point is brash, but for George that was the key reason to steer clear of the more straitlaced College Republicans. In fact, George helped create a Turning Point chapter at UNC because he was fed up with the existing conservative clubs. As he explained, "I don't see any leadership from the College Republicans" for doing confrontational activism on campus, and "I felt like there was a need for that." Which is to say, populists exude something akin to the dissidence of leftists, and this influences their tactical preferences.[7]

BUILDING COALITIONS OR AVOIDING EACH OTHER

Groups' power to attract activists on the basis of ideological and stylistic preferences has consequences for coordinated action down the line. In general, student groups that displayed the greatest distance from one another along the political spectrum were mostly unaware of what opposing clubs were doing on campus. Even the tradition of debate nights between Democrat clubs and College Republicans seems to have fallen out of favor in these divisive times. As Melissa told us about the UDems, "We try to get away from debates, just because we don't necessarily think it's incredibly productive." In her words, arguing with conservatives "just involves two student groups sharing their opinions, and, ultimately, there is no real work being done." Likewise, McKenzie, with UNC's College Republicans, explained, "We've explored debates in the past, but debates really don't work well for us." Overall, this decline in willingness to vigorously trade ideas across the aisle gives credence to the notion that young people are less interested in confronting differing viewpoints, and are instead creating their own echo chambers.[8]

Since there are not many links spanning the political continuum, that leaves most of the potential for collaboration to ideologically similar groups. On the right, Turning Point's relationship with other conservative clubs is instructive. In spite of the ill will directed at them by students like Amanda, Dante, and Billy—and their own distrust of College Republicans, as we saw in George's statement—Turning Point chapters remained connected to their fellow activists. For example, Christians United for Israel (CUFI) invited College Republicans and Turning Point to co-sponsor an event to bring Sebastian Gorka, the former deputy assistant to the president and strategist in the Trump White House, to UNC for a talk in 2017. Likewise, at CU, College Republicans and Turning Point collaborated to bring in Milo (as Yiannopoulos prefers to be called) as a speaker that same year. At UA, Jerry insisted that no one in the objectivist club[9] he belonged to admired Turning Point—neither the organization in principle, nor the activities of its members. "But we wanted to associate with them because they had the money to mobilize people—to get bodies in rooms, basically." For student-led groups on the right, in other words, a shared social identity can supersede tactical divisions and intellectual disagreements.[10]

Even more so, the coalition-building we see among conservatives is spurred by clubs' affiliation with national organizations. These outside entities often require student-led groups to find co-sponsors to help share the costs and public relations work for the event, as CUFI did to bring Gorka to UNC. Additionally, access to resources from organizations like Turning Point can be a major incentive to put differences aside. National organizations recruit and groom student leaders on campuses too. These leaders then establish connections between their organizations and other political clubs at their schools. In this sense, forming bridges to other conservative groups is part of the blueprint for student activism on the right. This has been a successful strategy for decades, historically led by CPAC and the Leadership Institute, and has helped keep clubs in relative alignment with each other, differences notwithstanding.[11]

Because the total number of conservatives involved in political clubs is fairly low (relative to progressives), the density of their social ties strengthens their connections on campus. As Josephine mentioned above, she came to rely on her political clubs as a kind safe space to "openly discuss my values." And as Tony told us about his campus, "Anybody that's doing anything in the conservative movement, I've met, because it is a small group." Networking is often facilitated by College Republicans, which serves as home base for many right-leaning students. While a few students, like George, swore off College Republicans altogether, it was more common for members to join College Republicans in addition to their other clubs. These joint members could be quite critical of College Republicans and the national party, but they still found it socially valuable and politically expedient to remain affiliated with them. Sandra put it this way: "I would say a majority of conservatives on grounds are members" of College Republicans, even if they might also be members of groups like Young Americans for Freedom or Turning Point. But, she assured us, College Republicans were still "the primary voice for conservatives. I, personally, don't envision that changing," because "we are established as the main conservative group. We have connections [and] clout in the community that other groups don't have."

Leftists at our four field sites have social ties akin to their conservative peers, derived from the solidarity of small numbers. And like their right-leaning counterparts, they exhibit a fair amount of cross-membership in far-left clubs. But one important difference on this end of the spectrum is that Democratic clubs are not a common denominator for progressives (leftists and liberals) in the same way that College Republicans are for politically engaged conservatives. This creates a sociologically significant chasm within left-leaning activist circles that does not exist for collegians on the right. Conservatives, despite their internal bickering, still exist within a single ecosystem on and off campus, attending each other's activities and even co-sponsoring events. While we see a similar ecosystem among those on the far left, we do not see it extended to liberals. For example, Georgia described the connection that identity-based clubs share at CU. "A lot of times we'll try to support each other. We'll have a People of Color potluck." They then added that their mantra when thinking about their varied memberships is " 'Bring back the coali-

tion!' We're trying more and more to make sure we're on the same page."
But College Democrats were conspicuously absent from the answers that
leftists, like Georgia, gave to our questions about the clubs they associate with on campus.

These things said, there is more variance in the types of coalition-
building happening on the left. While a good deal of what conservatives
do on campus consists of one thing—hosting speakers—progressives
are engaged in a more varied portfolio of activism. It is true that progressive groups partner to bring in speakers, as BSA, UMAS y MEXA, and
others did for Bobby Seale's visit to CU (as discussed in chapter 1). But
there are also specific campaigns covering a variety of environmental,
social, and economic issues, which means there are ample opportunities
for clubs to team up.

Liberal groups' disconnection from their far-left counterparts dilutes
the potential for substantively working together on many issues. Simon
provided a good illustration of how this plays out for Democrats. Initially,
he provided a long list of clubs and organizations UDems partner with.

> In terms of reliable working groups here at UVA [. . .] it goes back to the
> idea of networking within our community. [. . .] The Asian Student Alli-
> ance, we've co-sponsored a few events with them. We've got a group called
> Dreamers on Grounds for immigrants, and they do a lot of really good
> stuff. We've done a little bit with them. The Black Student Alliance, we
> have a good working relationship with [them . . .] . [Living Wage Now . . .]
> wants to make sure that all the workers at UVA are getting appropriately
> compensated. We have a really good working relationship with them.

But Simon followed up these comments by acknowledging, "It's interesting. Now that I've said all of this, while we have good relationships
with these groups, it's more of a façade, and it doesn't always turn into
tangible outcomes." Simon then shared examples of times that clubs
partnering with the UDems failed to attend a co-sponsored talk or provide volunteers for staffing phone banks and the like. At UA, meanwhile,
the Marginalized Students group, MSUA, had a lot of identity groups—
from the Adalberto and Ana Guerrero Center to the Women's Resource
Center—join the consortium, but the school's Young Democrats were
not among them.

Coalition-building is an essential aspect of any sustained struggle for social change. Infighting, on the other hand, can stymie activists. Within contemporary campus politics, we see—as is to be expected—elements of both across the political spectrum. Progressive clubs, just like the students within them, are divided between liberals and those on the far left. The right, in contrast, is more unified as a single bloc, despite tensions. While the groups on the right managed to hang together, they were riven by infighting—paradoxically, fueled in no small part by their proximity. That is, activists on the right were directly exposed to the ideological and tactical differences that characterized their various clubs, and members found in these differences reasons to argue among themselves over the real meaning of conservatism.[12]

SHAPING MEMBERS: CLUBS AS INCUBATORS

In the examples above, we see why students are attracted to some clubs and not others for ideological and tactical reasons, and why they are occasionally willing to work with other clubs on campus. But student groups are more than just organizations that welcome the fully-formed activists—with all of their preferences worked out—that are sorted into them. While we often assume that people have unfettered agency and information to craft their beliefs and practices, and that the groups they end up joining are just the sum total of individual members' choices, research on group interactions shows otherwise. Political clubs are, in fact, socializing agents, meaning that social groups have habits and customs that come to define people's relations within them.[13] The activism styles prevalent in different clubs, and the coalitions that young people participate in, can reconfigure the kind of political tactics that members ultimately come to view as appropriate and desirable. Thus, while pre-existing preferences initially attract or repel students to this club or that club, once they join, group styles normalize some actions while proscribing others. If students join a group that clearly clashes with their ideas or styles, they can leave. But when they stay, their practices can subtly or not so subtly be changed by the club. As incubators, therefore, political clubs play a powerful role in shaping personal and group identity and, by extension, campus-level political behavior. Clubs are socialization machines, churning out different iterations of student activism.

Abigail, who had participated in her school's Young Democrats group for years, offered an especially insightful take on how participation in her club shaped her personal views.

> I feel like it's hard for me to even separate, at this point, how much of my beliefs are just like my party identification and how much are things I actually believe. Because I think being a Democrat is such a big part of, I guess, my identity and what I've been doing. I agree with the party on most core issues, and there are some [issues] that I didn't used to [agree with the party on, but] my beliefs are now much more aligned with the party line than they were [before I came to UNC].

As Abigail implied, it is the time spent in her club that helped transform her into a more loyal party member. Warren described a nearly identical journey as a College Republican.

> I would say in high school I [was] a strong social conservative, having been raised in an evangelical community. That is how I came to college. Then over the last several years—from a mix of some education, political involvement, and observing elections in the last few years—I've become a "politically pragmatic conservative" [. . .]. I am not the kind of person that is going to go out and vote for a Tea Party candidate, unless I think they have the ability to win. [. . .] And then also, with the College Republicans, I think I was introduced to more establishment thinking. [. . .] I don't consider myself "establishment," but sometimes it makes sense to have standards of who you elect in a primary and that kind of thing.

In other words, while Warren still wanted to avoid being part of the "establishment," his time as a College Republican encouraged him to tamp down his social conservatism. Further, even when he might personally have agreed with a Tea Party candidate, he adopted his club's traditionalist orientation on electability over ideological purity.

If Abigail and Warren offer illustrations of clubs having a moderating effect on members and pulling them into the fold, Lydia's and Miles's experiences highlight how groups farther to the left and right nudge their participants into more extreme positions. Lydia, a member of the left-wing MSUA group, told us:

There were a lot of things that I [have always believed in], but I just
didn't have the words to describe [them], or I didn't have access to really
look into what [was happening . . .] . So, being in college, having my
community, and participating in activism, has maybe developed my
ideas more. I have a deeper understanding, and that has turned into
stronger beliefs. Before, I might've been [less offended by sexism on
campus]. Now I'm like, "No! Everything is fucked up! We have to really
change our thinking on that."

That is, while Lydia described a continuity in her beliefs before and after her involvement with MSUA, her interactions with fellow leftists
encouraged her to be more than slightly offended. Part of being a good
MSUA member was learning to acknowledge injustice and be a vocal advocate for change.

Miles's story is similar to Lydia's, but he described becoming increasingly reactionary in his politics, in no small part due to his membership in Turning Point. In his telling, he came to school as a "traditional
conservative," but felt shunned by his liberal peers in the buildup to
the 2016 election. During this time, Miles wrote a Facebook post in support of then candidate Trump, and his best friend of many years cut off
social ties in response. Hurt by this, Miles doubled down on his controversial, populist views. "That's when I actually started seeking out
Turning Point." Once in the group, Miles found a clique of equally fiery
classmates who nudged his political evolution forward. This encouraged
his growing desire to "take the underground conservative counterculture and put it above ground." To this end, Miles showed us flyers he
planned to put up around school as part of his job as his chapter's "min-
ister of propaganda." The flyers were all designed to offend progressive
sensibilities. The most provocative one mocked concern over police violence. This flyer, copied from a meme circulating in right-wing social
media, was a graph seeking to minimize the impact of police shooting
Black men and women by showing a higher number of "Blacks killed by
Blacks!" The headline read, "Black Lives Matter is Bitching about This?"
with an arrow pointing to the comparatively smaller number of deaths
instigated by police officers. Other images Miles had selected to put up
criticized gun regulations (via a cartoon ridiculing the notion that gun-

free zones will disarm terrorists) and social welfare efforts (a poster with giant letters: "The greatest social program IS A JOB"). Being an active member of Turning Point pushed Miles to dive deeper into confrontational representations than he likely would have done on his own or if he had joined a less combative club, like College Republicans.

Self-identified libertarians—as opposed to libertarian-leaning conservatives—tended to be uninspired by conservative groups on campus, whether College Republicans, Turning Point, or Young Americans for Freedom (even if they sometimes attended their events). They wanted to have a different experience, and to be shaped by different styles of engagement, within the groups they joined. As Ernest, a member of Students for Individual Liberty (SIL), told us, "The vibe I get" from clubs like Turning Point and Young Americans for Freedom "is more dogmatic." And such dogmatism is "getting away from the reasons" Ernest got into libertarianism, which for him begins with researching the issues and debating ideas. "I tried to arrive at what I thought was the right conclusion. When I look at those clubs, I get the idea" that it is more "dogmatic and less about reason and being open to new ideas." Ernest found that SIL allowed him to focus on the intellectual side of conservatism. Speaking of the events his club had held, he recalled that "Most recently, we had a speaker talk about the ongoing tension between the Kurds and the Turks" and how "Kurds are actually some of the libertarians' best allies." Another speaker, from the Cato Institute, "was basically in support of open borders." And the reason SIL hosted the talk "was to get people to come out and listen to him speak and get the facts on immigration." As we can see in this description, Ernest's libertarian group tended to emphasize ideological principles (and the policies to match). This can be contrasted with the partisanship of traditionalists (or even their libertarian-leaning conservative peers), as well as the reactionaryism of populist clubs interested in bringing in speakers like Milo and Gorka.

At the four campuses we visited, attending Democratic clubs and College Republican meetings generally steeped students in a rhetoric of incremental change and the centrality of elected officials in representing collective interests. Those on the far left and far right learned the opposite from their groups; they were inculcated in a rhetoric of extremes. Libertarians came face to face with members with seemingly contradictory ideas and learned to value debate. The key point here is that clubs exert pressure on their participants to adhere to their preferred styles and to distinguish themselves from those practicing other types of activism. We should note here that since 2016, some College Republican chapters have become increasingly provocative in the mode of Turning Point, mirroring the ascendancy of Trumpism in the GOP.[14] Indeed, at this moment in our nation's politics, campus conservative groups often work together to use their strength in numbers, even when they disagree. Our larger point is not that any particular ideological orientation is more or less prone to certain tactics; rather, we argue that once certain practices become normalized within a group, they become part of the membership's common sense of how politics should be done within the club. While motivated and charismatic students can drive their groups in new directions, and the consistent churning of members through college means that clubs' styles can evolve, groups strongly shape activism. Clubs are more than just the sum of their participants; they possess a power of their own to influence how participants think, feel, and act.[15] This becomes part of how students eventually understand their own political outlooks. Thus, expanding on our observations from chapter 1, clubs represent an important dimension of the college experience for the development of activists' political identities.

SELECTING TARGETS TO PRECIPITATE SOCIAL CHANGE

Aside from who can work together and who cannot, and what beliefs and styles student members come to hold, it is important to look at what club members wish to accomplish. All political groups are interested in promoting some form of social change on their campuses and, sometimes, in the larger world. The changes they want to see implemented, though, vary widely. There can be modest requests and there can be grandiose demands. Activism of any sort requires either targeting school policies or changing the overarching campus culture by persuading students to act or think in different ways. The former is concerned with university operations; the latter is focused on students' everyday lives. Activists make choices about which of these domains they primarily want to direct their energies. These decisions are coupled with their clubs' styles of activism. It is a bit of a simplification, but broadly speaking, at the four universities we studied, progressive clubs, especially leftist ones, tend to target school policies, while conservative clubs tend to target campus culture.

To formally alter how universities operate, clubs must home in on administrators. This approach is illustrated nicely by Levi, a leftist who, through Fossil Free CU, spent years pushing the university to use more environmentally responsible funding sources. They told us it is "not like there's direct antagonism" between conservatives on campus and Fossil Free CU. The reason for this is that "the targets of the campaigns that I've been performing are the administration, not other students." Alternatively, if clubs want to enact wider cultural changes—for example, to encourage complacent liberals and middle-of-the-roaders to consider conservative principles—they have their eyes on their peers. Which is to say, these activists aim to change the minds of other students. Administrative buy-in may be required in this domain too, but school officials are not the focus. Instead, this approach to activism is intended to unsettle collegians' own sense of the status quo. Trevor, for instance, did not describe any specific, tangible outcomes sought by his Turning Point chapter. He emphasized the group's more general mission of being "against campus leftist ideology." He then added, "We're trying to get the point across: you don't have to believe everything they tell you about social justice."

At all four of the universities we visited, leftist clubs—usually working in conjunction with ideologically similar groups—were involved in at least one (and usually several) major fights against their school's administration. At UNC and UVA, there were protests demanding the removal of monuments and building names progressives considered racist. The semester after our interviews at UNC, "Silent Sam," a prominent statue of a Confederate soldier, was literally toppled by activists. In spring 2017, Fossil Free CU occupied the chancellor's office for a week in an effort to demand that the school cut financial ties with the oil and gas industry. A year before our interviews, MSUA formed as a means of pushing university administrators to support a variety of issues affecting identity-based clubs and multicultural centers.

It is not that progressive activists are totally unconcerned with changing how the student body looks at things. Racial, gender, and sexual identity groups, for example, target the homophobia, transphobia, and racial microaggressions said to be invading young people's lives. Fraternities and college athletes have been the focus of interventions for their roles in "rape culture."[16] There are campaigns to get students to recycle more, drive less, register to vote, stand up for Deferred Action for Childhood Arrival (DACA) legislation, and the list goes on. But such efforts are generally coupled with direct policy demands made to administrators, like creating sensitivity trainings and sexual consent courses for incoming freshmen, replacing parking spots for cars with bicycle racks, and partnering with university leaders to train staff to aid students in a variety of causes. In other words, the objectives hinge on altering some aspect of how the school formally operates and spends its funds. Even the "White silence is violence" chant at the CU basketball game (discussed in chapter 1)—which was certainly provocative and aimed *at* the people in attendance—was attached to BSA's efforts to push the administration to direct more resources toward minority student retention. Which is to say, the students (or alumni and parents) in the audience for such efforts did not need to feel like "targets" for the campaign to work—although some probably did have the sense that they were under personal attack.

Student-led conservative activism, by contrast, is generally bereft of clear policy outcomes expected from administrators.[17] Our right-leaning interviewees complained very little about their schools' specific rules and procedures, aside from a few critiques of affirmative action. None, for instance, proposed quotas on hiring more conservative professors, even when they bemoaned the lack of ideological diversity among faculty. If anything, they said their schools should do a better job of following their existing policies, such as on speakers' rights, which are usually written in a politically neutral way. To the extent that their campuses seemed unduly progressive, activists on the right were apt to believe it was the fault of their fellow students. As Joaquin told us, "It's not the university that shuts students down; it's usually other students that try to shut other students down." Conservatives' take on liberal hegemony, therefore, means that university policies are less central to their desired social changes than is refashioning campus culture.

Clubs on the right appear most eager to offer "alternative viewpoints" to the dominant progressive discourses found at their schools, usually by hosting conservative speakers whose perspectives, they believe, are in woefully short supply on their campuses. Hearts and minds are pursued almost exclusively, although the goal is sometimes less about converting their peers to their viewpoints than it is about inciting them to outrage. The content and tone of these invited guests can be quite different—from rhetorical bomb-throwers to bookish intellectuals. Regardless, they all serve the same purpose. They produce events that rattle the taken-for-granted assumptions of the left. And, in this hegemonic disruption, we can make out a form of conservative protest. It is not a protest with picket signs and bullhorns, but bringing conservative speakers to campus is a means for those on the right to publicly air their grievances about campus leftist ideology all the same. Further, this speaker-as-protest model dovetails with the policy agendas of national organizations by generating talking points for conservative media and politicians.[18] It is not a coincidence that when right-leaning clubs do end up targeting administrators, it is often precipitated by their speakers getting disinvited or de-platformed.

CONCLUSION

Throughout this chapter, we have seen examples of how student-led groups go about the business of activism. Using the metaphors of the sieve and the incubator from the sociology of education literature, we have shown how activists are sorted and molded by their clubs. This depiction is also consistent with theoretical approaches in the areas of culture, organizations, and social movements, all of which demonstrate how groups' practices can become normalized and taken for granted, and how ideology and culture shape the selection of tactics. Whether conceptualized as group styles, cultural repertoires, or political culture, student clubs' influences make some types of coalition-building possible, particularly on the right and among leftists, but leave others—mostly liberals—without reliable partners.[19] Group members' ideological positions also affect target selection. For progressives, especially leftists, the focus is on changing university policies, and the primary targets are school officials, as they are the people pulling the levers of the bureaucracy. Conservatives, by contrast, zero in on their peers. Their drive is less on altering policies and more on unsettling the status quo. At the moment, controversial speakers are the tactic of choice.

Target selection is a linchpin of student activism. It helps explain the nature of the contentious political battles happening in higher education today. As we will detail in chapters 4 and 5, there are very different channels for student activism on the left and the right. Progressives are embedded within school structures. This is true even among the far-left activists who prefer to see themselves as dissenters fighting against the power structure. Multicultural centers are a major part of this story. Conservatives, on the other hand, lack the same level of institutional support on their campuses. So, they partner with organizations several steps removed from their universities. Right-leaning students, unlike their left-leaning peers, show little interest in changing university rules and procedures. They want to transform campus culture (a much more diffuse goal), and they are increasingly willing to engage in provocative tactics to move things in this direction. We hasten to add here, though, as we will see in chapter 4, that the conservative channel is not indifferent to policy. Instead, the right's bureaucratic focus is outsourced to well-funded national organizations.

CHAPTER 4

The Conservative Channel—Pulled Outside from the Right

with Zosia Sztykowski

In chapter 2, we briefly introduced Amanda, a moderate Republican at UA, and Ariel, a populist conservative at CU. In many ways, Amanda and Ariel have similar profiles. Both were raised in civic-minded families who discussed politics around the dinner table. Envisioning possible futures in conservative politics, each was highly involved in student-led groups at her school. In their pursuits, both benefited from national organizations on the right which offered training, funding, networking opportunities, and career mentorship. Yet, while there are many similarities in Amanda's and Ariel's experiences, important differences set the two women apart. First among these is that they disagreed ideologically. Amanda's moderate viewpoint aligned with the anti-Trump faction of the traditionalists, putting her at odds with Ariel's avid support of the president. Consequently, they gravitated toward distinct clubs on campus to support their activism, and therefore ended up connecting with separate segments of the conservative channel.

While the focus of chapter 3 was on how campus clubs draw in and then shape students like Amanda and Ariel, here we look at the well-funded organizations behind right-leaning campus politics. Deep-pocketed conservative donors have helped create a complex political ecosystem, which is contoured by an interlocking network of tax-exempt foundations, think tanks, and advocacy groups. Many of these organizations focus on policy-making, working behind the scenes to make lasting changes to American society based on neoliberal economic reforms and evangelical Christian values.[1] A subdivision of the varied landscape on the right focuses specifically on higher education and the students within it—whether law students supported by the Federalist Society, postgraduates mentored by the Institute for Humane Studies, or collegians fired up to resist the "woke" socialists supposedly overtaking academia.[2] We are interested in the last category having to do with undergraduates, since it represents the conservative channel for student activism taking place on college campuses. Within the channel are distinct segments. There are organizations supporting undergraduates that emphasize a refined conservatism, which seek to instill a set of civic values and principles connected with liberty and freedom.[3] Their preferred approach is to host seminars and sponsor speakers that do not inflame campus sensibilities. There also are activist-minded groups that rally young people to embrace highly partisan positions through confrontational tactics.

The idea that organizations recruit collegians into different styles of conservative activism has been explored before. It is part of the sorting and shaping discussed in chapter 3. In an earlier study of college conservatism, one of us used case studies of the Young America's Foundation, Leadership Institute, and Intercollegiate Studies Institute to explore the sponsorship of "provocative" and "civil" styles.[4] Since the time of that research, the available infrastructure for mobilization has transformed. Groups have expanded and contracted. Entirely new organizations have emerged. The familiar chapter and conference model, in which political club members are supplied with recruitment materials, organizational support, and subsidies to attend regional and national meetings remains popular. Other organizations continue to offer immersive internships and exclusive gatherings. But some now forgo local chapters and internship opportunities, and instead activate students through online content. As may be expected, much of the conservative channel blends bits and pieces of each of these mobilization strategies.

Differences aside, the organizations that comprise the conservative channel cohere in advancing the premise that the liberal hegemony of higher education shortchanges all students and is deeply unfair to those on the right. It is taken as an undisputed fact that the truly marginalized population on campus is made up of conservatives. One of the aims of these groups is to help right-leaning students connect with one another.

Many promise to link undergraduates with leaders in the policy-making and partisan spheres and to provide guidance for burnishing their résumés. Some of the most effective organizations may even be regarded as "employment agencies" or "career funnels" to future employers within the political ecosystem of the right. Savvy students—like those we interviewed—take part in the conservative channel with an eye toward how their activism can position them for well-paying political jobs after graduation.[5]

To illustrate how young people chart a course through the choppy waters of the conservative channel, we begin by looking at Amanda and Ariel and the range of national organizations they interact with. Then, we drill down on three different organizations: the American Enterprise Institute (AEI), Turning Point USA, and PragerU. There are many other advocacy groups and foundations, conferences and think tanks that we might have selected, but these three organizations allow us to explore a variety of activism models. As our data will show, the right is splintered in its approaches to mobilizing students, which is a good reflection of conservative politics in general.[6] Yet although infighting and ideological squabbles exist, the right has managed to build an elaborate, well-funded organizational space that galvanizes young supporters and grooms future leaders by pulling them outside the confines of campus.

TWO STUDENTS, TWO DIFFERENT SEGMENTS OF THE CONSERVATIVE CHANNEL

To understand the intricacies of the conservative ecosystem, it is useful to get a sense of students' everyday experiences with organizations aligned on the right. Amanda's trajectory exemplifies one route, in which students leave more sensationalistic, confrontational groups behind. In high school, Amanda was named an "Outstanding Teen Age Republican in the Nation"; as a college student, however, she could not stand Donald Trump or the politicians in his orbit. Asked if she cared for the president, Amanda responded, "Oh no, not at all, not at all, no." To the question of whether Trump should be defeated in 2020, Amanda replied, "Absolutely." Asked if she would be happy if Vice President Mike Pence took Trump's place, again she was adamant, "No, no. I mean like just *everything* about this administration. [. . .] I don't like Mike Pence. I can't stand anyone in the Trump family. Like, I really hope they're all gone." At the same time that she expressed contempt for the president, Amanda spoke admiringly about other Republican Party leaders. "I look for people who can work with both parties and are open and accepting to hear both sides." She pointed specifically to Marco Rubio, saying, "Something I liked *so* much about him is that he is just not a strict conservative and [is] willing to work with both parties. [It is] the same thing I love about McCain."

Although others may beg to differ about Rubio's willingness to compromise (and Rubio himself might dislike being characterized as "not a strict conservative"), Amanda said these things to emphasize that she cherished being "open to a diversity of viewpoints." Because of this, she said she was dispirited by the reactionary tone of many of the clubs at UA. She originally joined the College Republicans, but she ultimately left the group. "I came to campus and was so disappointed after my freshman year." This is because the chapter is "really ultra-right at this point." Her displeasure with the Turning Point chapter on campus was even more intense. To repeat her sentiments from the previous chapter, "I just want to make [it] really clear: I would *never* join Turning Point." The reason, she told us, was that "they like conflict" but "that doesn't appeal to me." At the national level, the ascendancy of populism also led Amanda to forgo attendance at the Conservative Political Action Conference (CPAC), an event she once loved. "I wouldn't even go to CPAC" anymore, she said. "The year [Trump] was sworn in, I didn't go."

Disappointed with Trumpism and UA's "ultra-right" clubs, Amanda nevertheless remained deeply interested in politics and did not want to forswear conservatism altogether. Rather, she sought new opportunities as she cultivated a more refined ideological perspective. She was getting her degree in the Philosophy, Politics, Economics and Law program (PPEL), a small interdisciplinary major that promotes analytical and critical reflection on the fundamental values that shape society. It is also a program known on her campus as a home base for conservatives.[7] Amanda was also a leader of the Executive Council, the student outreach program of AEI. She and five other carefully selected UA students took part in AEI's semiannual conferences and helped plan events for peers at their school, such as bringing in scholars to speak about topical issues.

On the flip side, Ariel was an enthusiastic Trump supporter. While she had some harsh words about what she felt was the president's undignified behavior on social media, Ariel thought that Trump's presidency was a much-needed corrective to the status quo of the national party. As we will recall from chapter 2, Ariel said, "I think he's good for the party, because I think the party needed some shaking up." In contrast to Amanda, who admired establishment Republicans, Ariel was unsure if she even wanted to identify as a Republican. Focusing her invective on precisely the politicians Amanda respected, Ariel complained that high-ranking members of the party, such as Jeff Flake and John McCain, went overboard criticizing Trump; for this reason, she said, "I feel like the whole Republican name has kind of lost its way."

Given her support for the president and her disregard for the never-Trump wing of the party, Ariel was not interested in a group like AEI. Nor did she bother joining the College Republicans, which she dismissively predicted would become less relevant with time. Rather, Ariel was the president of the CU chapter of Turning Point, a national organization whose founder, Charlie Kirk, regularly appears on Fox News, staunchly defended the Trump administration, and urges students both to stage events that provoke liberal classmates and to report their instructors' "leftist propaganda" on its Professor Watchlist website. Ariel was proud of the forty or so members on her campus who "talk about economics [and] fundamental core American values," and she appreciated "all this money" that the national organization sent to her club. This included help for bringing right-wing barn burners Ann Coulter and Milo Yiannopoulos to Boulder.

Unlike Amanda, Ariel still enjoyed attending CPAC. In fact, for Ariel, the conference had only gotten better in the Trump era. She found it energizing to see the celebrity pundits and populist politicians that got top billing after the 2016 election. Ariel also liked the "summits" hosted by Turning Point and the trainings offered by the social media–oriented PragerU. Ariel was a member of PragerU's outreach program, PragerFORCE. As she explained, "Turning Point was kind of my start," which then led her to PragerU. "And it's just a continuing domino effect of getting involved with these core groups." As Ariel saw it, her involvement with these organizations "opened up incredible opportunities." The most recent of these was a trip to Los Angeles to meet with other top PragerFORCE "ambassadors" and network with the group's director.

In considering how Amanda and Ariel navigated the conservative channel, what we see are two students carving two very different paths through the activist landscape. One was following a more civil path. This does not mean her chosen niche was without controversy—tensions are often so high at the intersection of higher education and politics that ideological clashes seem unavoidable. But it does mean that Amanda's preference was for engaging in what she believed could lead to bipartisan agreement. Ariel, on the other hand, sometimes paid lip service to dialogue and reaching out to the other side, but much of the mobilizing she took part in was explicitly designed to incite anger among progressives. This provocative path has become increasingly popular with conservative students, and it is one with a growing donor base behind it. Keeping Amanda and Ariel in mind, we now turn to the organizations themselves, so we can better understand how they operate, and ultimately how they influence the tenor of contemporary campus politics on the right.

THE AMERICAN ENTERPRISE INSTITUTE

The American Enterprise Institute, or AEI, is not an organization that typically comes to mind when thinking about college-age conservatism. It does not try to "own the libs," as more raucous organizations such as Turning Point do. Nor is it laser-focused on getting students to campaign for candidates, as College Republican chapters have done for decades. While AEI historically has sent speakers to CPAC each year, their presentations do not serve up the red-meat talking points which, at least since the start of the 2016 election season, attracted thousands of students to rally for Trump. Yet, quietly and methodically, AEI has taken its place in the conservative channel for a subset of nearly 1,000 right-leaning undergraduates each year.

Founded in 1938 and housed in a beautiful Beaux Arts–style building on Massachusetts Avenue in Washington, DC, AEI is one of the nation's oldest and most handsomely endowed right-of-center think tanks. Its board of trustees is disproportionately made up of the chairmen and CEOs of major investment companies such as the Carlyle Group. The Charles G. Koch Charitable Foundation, the Walton Foundation, and many other conservative donors supported AEI's $59.4 million in expenditures for 2019.[8] Committed to "expanding freedom, increasing opportunity, and bolstering free enterprise," the organization is home to scholars who have chosen not to pursue the academic route, but instead to focus on research with direct ties to policy-making.[9] For decades, the organization has made a big impact. President George W. Bush, for example, hired twenty AEI scholars to work in his administration. In 2019, its scholars were interviewed 730 times on radio and television and penned hundreds of op-eds. That same year, AEI scholars also gave testimony before Congress more than 30 times.[10]

But producing work by and for policy wonks is not the only thing that AEI does. In 2019, 5 percent of AEI's total expenses were spent on campus outreach, for a total of nearly $3 million in expenditures. With this level of commitment, the organization has become heavily invested in "identifying, educating, and developing our nation's next generation of policymakers, scholars, journalists, and business executives, who will fight every day for America's first principles," according to its website. AEI's former director of academic programs, Tyler Castle, told us the organization enrolls approximately 700 students each year through campus chapters, annual meetings, and summer seminars.[11] On top of this, 200 students have internships throughout the year. AEI may be, as Castle described it, a "university without students," but through its academic programs and internships, young people are equally incorporated into its policy-making mission. Donors are told such opportunities educate collegians to "know and understand the fundamental principles so that they are not easily swayed by false ideals." And, as they explain on their website, "Beyond graduation," members of the Executive Council "have gone on to the nation's top graduate schools and to work on Capitol Hill, for top consulting and financial firms, for presidential campaigns, for leading non-profits, and in other fields."[12] In other words, AEI is in the business of producing the next generation of conservative leaders.

FINDING AND REFINING TOMORROW'S CONSERVATIVE LEADERS TODAY

AEI sponsors what it calls "one of the most substantive and innovative campus outreach efforts in the nation," developing students' appreciation "for the competition of ideas and liberal democratic values."[13]

These pedagogical goals are aligned with the organization's non-confrontational approach to politics. As Castle put it, "We're not trying to build activists or people who are really engaged in day-to-day politics." Instead, he told us, AEI wants to foster concern for "bigger ideas." AEI's programs are not simply aimed at reaching "true believers" in the conservative movement, either. Castle assured us that AEI's academic programs and internships are available to any student who is sufficiently "open-minded." Such goals are a good fit for Chris, an Executive Council member at CU, who admired the organization for being "a nonpartisan" policy think tank. "They don't form opinions. They do the research." He then added, "Maybe their research does point to more conservative thinking, but they are completely nonpartisan, and everybody is invited to take part in these discussions." These articulated goals also resonated with Amanda and her desire to learn from diverse viewpoints.

Executive Councils are the backbone of AEI's academic programs. Each local council consists of no more than six students, recruited by AEI staff through an application and interview process. From their start in 2013 on 25 campuses, Executive Councils now have a presence at 100 schools, involving more than 400 politically engaged students across the country. Members serve as "AEI's informal representatives" on each campus, said Castle, and organizational staff work with these students to "foster conversations about public policy" with their classmates. The conversations themselves are undergirded by support for, among other things, bringing AEI scholars to campus to give presentations—a resource appreciated by UVA's Billy, who noted that "they offer quite a few speakers." At UA and CU, the two campuses where we met council members, the most recent AEI scholar to visit was Charles Murray. A few months prior to our interviews, Murray had been the subject of a contentious de-platforming at Middlebury College.[14] We will discuss Murray in greater depth in chapter 6, but for now we will just mention that his speaking engagements often make waves because his ideas are associated with theories supporting racial differences in intelligence.[15] Asked which speakers, besides Murray, AEI frequently connects with universities, Castle mentioned Arthur Brooks (the former president of the organization and "one of our biggest names"), Michael Rubin ("one of our scholars who focuses on Middle East politics and issues"), and assorted others ("there's probably 20 to 30 AEI scholars who we send to campuses"). Castle also pointed to how think tanks mostly aligned on the right collaborate with one another, noting that the AEI campus speaking events pull in people "from places like Brookings, Manhattan, Hudson, Hoover, all these different organizations that are in a similar space."

Executive Councils serve as a conduit for other AEI offerings too. These include all-expenses-paid student conferences. Held twice a year, the conferences are an intensive educational experience for the hundred or so students who attend; they hear from policy experts and have the opportunity to network with professionals in the field. According to Chris, the meetings offer not only opportunities to discuss such heady policy points as "California's Medicare and pension program" (the topic of conversation at a regional conference held on the West Coast), but also "leadership training," which is useful in equipping him to navigate campus bureaucracy on behalf of his AEI club. "I interact with" university administrators "every single day," said Chris. "I am always requesting funds and going in front of boards, going to meetings with campus representatives." So, as Chris saw it, AEI is "just as much of a leadership training as it is about discussing public policy."

There is also the Summer Honors Program, which attracts about 200 students each year. It comprises sixteen one-week courses taught by prominent (and sometimes controversial) scholars on the right. One of the courses is "Freedom, Progress, and Tradition," taught by Yuval Levin, an AEI scholar and contributing editor at the *National Review*. Another is taught by UC Berkeley law professor John Yoo, under the title "The Constitution: Original Meanings and Modern Times." Yoo is best known for developing a legal justification for torturing enemy combatants in America's war on terror.[16] Students apply to different courses, and those who are selected for this competitive program can receive funding for lodging, travel, and meals, as well as stipends. Castle explained that the courses are "kind of like an upper-level college seminar." But he also said that, compared to what students are learning at their colleges and universities, his organization's seminars are "more practical," because AEI scholars "are working day-to-day in the policy world," so they "are able to connect theory" to "how things actually work." As part of their hands-on education, students make in-person visits to locations around Washington, DC relevant to the issue they are studying, such as going to the House Ways and Means Committee or the Council of Economic Advisors.

AEI is explicit as to how it can help students segue into post-baccalaureate jobs—indeed, introducing students to jobs in the field is one of its calling cards. Most directly, AEI offers internship positions on both the research and the business side of the institute. The former are intended to appeal to students with a desire to eventually become scholars themselves, while the latter are for those interested in running a think tank one day.[17] In other words, through its internship program, AEI fosters the policy-making areas and bureaucratic functioning of the political ecosystem of the right.[18] Additionally, Castle told us, throughout the Summer Honors Program, staff convene "career professionals" who meet with participants in small groups of four to five students to "have a more personal conversation about their careers." There is even an internal career funnel toward the end of a summer course, in which "we'll usually have a member of our HR team come and just share about internships and job opportunities in a fairly informal way, just letting them know about the opportunity." Castle said that "a lot of these students have gone on to intern at AEI or get jobs at AEI. So, it's informally a recruitment tool [. . .] to get bright, good students to work for us in the future." In effect, what AEI provides is mutually reinforcing, student-centered programming, which strengthens commitment over multiple experiences.

AEI is currently at the forefront of organizations serving as a bulwark for the intellectual and civil side of the conservative channel for student activism. Chris indicated that he believes this legitimacy extends even to faculty perceptions when he said, "It is really nice to be tied to a national organization that is recognized," because "when we talk with professors, they will say, 'Oh, you are the AEI group on campus who is facilitating this event. Okay great, I've heard about AEI. I have read Walter Mead's stuff in *The Wall Street Journal*."[19] Yet, for all its high-mindedness, AEI is still in the fray of contentious campus politics—after all, it has the author of the "torture memos" teach its seminar on the Constitution. And AEI is the institutional home of scholars like Murray, who is frequently referred to by the left as a "eugenicist," and the philosopher Christina Hoff Sommers, who has written about feminists' "war against boys" and appears in a video that has been viewed millions of times on the more provocative PragerU website (as we will explain below).[20] In other words, even as it develops programming purportedly aimed at spanning the political spectrum, AEI is very much an active player in the agitations happening in higher education. And it provides an outside leg up to undergraduates interested in seeking employment in its version of conservatism.

TURNING POINT USA

Amanda, our traditionalist Republican interviewee who expressed alarm at efforts to "demonize" political opponents, was withering in her critique of Turning Point—the organization to which we now turn our attention. Amanda was joined by several other right-leaning students in our sample who spoke disparagingly of the organization. Tony, for example, told us that Turning Point comes "to campus and they want to trigger and disrupt and make a big headline." Chloe accused the group of being "bombastic" and "strident." Sandra summed up a lot of traditionalist, libertarian-leaning conservative and libertarian students' views by stating, "I, personally, don't think [their provocative] events are productive."

Ariel, on the other hand, as a populist, was a huge fan of the organization, and her enthusiasm was echoed by several of her peers. As we saw earlier in the book, Miles explained that his CU chapter wanted to "take the underground conservative counterculture and put it above ground." Trevor, another member, stated that Turning Point's national leaders "are the people you contact when you want to have any event and you need funding." These leaders will "send out activist kits." And they have people that will "give you ideas." At the time we talked with Trevor, he was finalizing his chapter's plans to hold a "socialist graveyard" event to coincide with Halloween—an action meant to call attention to the terrifying dangers of radicalism in the Democratic Party.

According to its website, Turning Point's mission is to "identify, educate, train, and organize students to promote the principles of freedom, free markets, and limited government."[21] In this respect the organization does not sound too far removed from the stated principles of free enterprise and individual liberty promoted by AEI. Both groups share in their disdain for command economies. But their organizational strategies are fundamentally different. Education about "big ideas" is replaced by tapping into the frustration of right-leaning students and sponsoring events on college campuses intended to fan the flames of the culture war. Where AEI has a long history of influencing US policy (and being willing to train students in the process), Turning Point has exploded onto the scene with a short, sharp shock to campus politics by using mobilization primarily as an effort to make headlines in conservative media outlets, as Tony (himself no stranger to making headlines) astutely noted.

Since its inception in 2012, Turning Point and its founder, Charlie Kirk, have become as close to household names as any organization or individual in the conservative channel for student activism. Kirk is celebrated as a charismatic Young Turk on Fox News; he was even the first speaker to take the stage at the 2020 Republican National Convention. He was also a prime source of information for the Trump White House. On a single day in April 2020, for instance, the former president retweeted eleven of Kirk's posts. This was a recursive process. Kirk and his followers gained credibility in right-leaning circles for being able to snag Trump's attention and for garnering appearances at national events. Trump got to bask in the adoration of the young fan base Kirk helped to mobilize.[22] Fox News pundits also appeared at Turning Point events and promoted them on their shows, which further enhanced Kirk's and his organization's relevance to Trump and his followers. And donors have made ever larger contributions to Turning Point as the premier group supporting the populist agenda on college campuses. Journalists in the "liberal" media have also noticed Turning Point's meteoric rise, seemingly out of nowhere.[23] In 2020, Turning Point claimed to have tens of thousands of members on more than 2,000 high school and college campuses.[24] Tax documents show that the organization's revenues tripled in 2018, up to $28.5 million. In just a few short years, then, Kirk managed to make a small fortune off his tax-exempt nonprofit and other ventures, including serving as the head of Students for Trump, an advocacy group set up for the reelection of the president in 2020.[25]

While Turning Point's overall budget is barely half that of AEI, Kirk's organization is singularly focused on student mobilization, and it does this mainly through a strong social media presence and catchy phrases like "Socialism Sucks," "Taxation Is Theft," and "Sunday Gunday," which get distributed on stickers, hats, T-shirts, and internet memes. On the campuses we visited, it is hard to overstate how ubiquitous Turning Point merchandise was among right-leaning collegians, even those who disliked the organization. As Chloe (a loyal College Republican member) told us, Turning Point has "cool stickers," and "they had fun signs" at CPAC. Beyond the swag, the students who actually joined Turning Point did so because they were drawn to the provocations championed by Kirk, and they enjoyed the glow of his fame. As Josephine put it, "Nationally, they're huge and well-known, and they have a figurehead behind them, with Charlie Kirk, [who goes] on the [television] networks and [has a] huge social media presence."

FIGHTING THE CULTURE WAR ON CAMPUS

Each of the four schools we visited had a Turning Point chapter, where members gathered for meetings, attracted new recruits, and hosted events. Other conservative clubs do these things too, but Turning Point makes galvanizing students the very essence of its goals, and it leaves the door-knocking for politicians and staffing campaign phone banks to groups like the College Republicans. A national field program oversees Turning Point's mission through a system of regional and field directors.[26] According to Ariel, her field manager "will help out with events or sometimes come to meetings or table with us," adding that he is available to help make sure events are "going smoothly." This was the person Trevor turned to for reimbursement for the supplies he purchased for events like the socialist graveyard. Turning Point employs around 200 such representatives.[27]

In addition to relying on the counsel and financial resources of field directors, students find guidance in the *Turning Point USA Chapter Handbook*, which gives instructions on how to become a registered student organization, contains tips on writing press releases and fundraising, and offers branding advice for campus clubs.[28] As members stressed to us time and again, grabbing attention is the name of the game. One suggestion is a "Drowning in Debt" demonstration, complete with a rented dunk tank and members donning swim trunks and bikinis out on the quad. The handbook also suggests doing an "Affirmative Action Bake Sale," where White and Asian students are required to pay more money for cookies and cupcakes than their Latinx, Black, and

Indigenous peers—all of which is designed to reveal an inherent unfairness in race-based policies. While the dunk tank is a lighthearted gimmick, many students of color feel attacked by the underlying message of the bake sale, as it insinuates that they have been given an unearned boost in the admissions process at selective universities.[29]

Turning Point's national organization requires chapters to put on at least one event per academic term. To fulfill this obligation, clubs are encouraged to extend an invitation to one of the 100-plus individuals on the organization's Speakers Bureau. Turning Point foots the lion's share of the bill to host these figures, but other national organizations and local donors are often willing to co-sponsor high-profile events too. As we documented in chapter 3, bringing right-leaning speakers to campus has become a form of conservative protest—a way for students to feel like they are countering liberal hegemony. Compared to AEI's scholarly lecturers, Turning Point has a stable of lightning rods: people like former Trump advisor Kellyanne Conway, reactionary filmmaker (and Trump pardonee) Dinesh D'Souza, former independent prosecutor Kenneth Starr (famous for his dogged pursuit of President Bill Clinton), and retired congresswoman (and one of the founders of the House Tea Party Caucus) Michele Bachmann. In other words, exactly the sort of people likely to upset left-leaning community members.

For conservative students, an additional perk of joining a Turning Point chapter is the chance to take part in its conferences. Once they cover their own travel costs, members can attend nearly for free. There are multiple regional conferences per year, promising to hone leadership skills, refine mobilization strategies, and provide networking opportunities with students at other schools. Trevor noted that the western regional meeting he attended was well worth the trip. "I've never been to any kind of conference or anything like that before," he said. "And it was interesting because you get to hear these really good speakers, talk to them if you want. Some people got contacts for them. And then on top of that, it's just a lot of mingling with other students. [. . .] I met people who run Turning Point at [the University of] Wyoming and they're going to link up with us now. So, it was very good; it was kind of a personal networking kind of thing."

Most importantly, there is the annual Student Action Summit (SAS), which is a national event whose attendance numbers rival CPAC's. Turning Point describes its summit as drawing more than 5,000 students between the ages of 15 and 25 to "hear from guest speakers, receive first-class activism and leadership training, and participate in a series of networking events with political leaders and top-tier activist organizations."[30] Speakers for SAS 2020 included Donald Trump Jr., Fox News anchor Tucker Carlson, White House allies like the former congressional representative and current South Dakota Governor Kristi Noem, and even Vice President Mike Pence.[31] Beyond SAS, there are smaller leadership summits designed for women and minorities. Of the Women's Conference she attended, Ariel reflected, "It's empowering women to find their voice." She continued by explaining that compared to other Turning Point events, the conference was "more focused on why we need women in the conservative movement."

Run by millennials in an effort to attract Generation Z, Turning Point has a strong online presence to complement its chapter and conference model. Social media "influencers" are encouraged to share the organization's talking points with their online followers. And through its stand-alone Influence Media Department, Turning Point has developed the infrastructure necessary to help magnetic young pundits establish themselves in a synergistic relationship with the organization. Alex Clark is one good example. She has a Turning Point–sponsored video series, "POPlitics," which "covers entertainment news and pop culture without the propaganda."[32] Despite the promise, what Clark actually does is shoehorn snarky partisanship into current affairs. For example, she begins her show from July 24, 2020, by mocking Dr. Anthony S. Fauci's ceremonial opening pitch for the Washington Nationals. By any standard, the septuagenarian's throw was comically off the mark, but in Clark's telling, the "mainstream media" glossed over Fauci's wayward pitch in order to "further their agenda"—although she does not clarify what that agenda is or why anyone should care that the director of the National Institute of Allergy and Infectious Diseases is bad at baseball.[33] Clark also leaves unstated that Trump supporters at the time were accusing Fauci of undermining the president's rosy prognostications about the novel coronavirus spreading across the globe, and that Trump concocted his own invitation from the New York Yankees out of jealousy over the attention given to Fauci.[34]

Most disconcerting to academics like ourselves is Turning Point's Professor Watchlist, whose goal "is to expose and document college professors who discriminate against conservative students and advance leftist propaganda in the classroom." This is a time-tested tactic of confrontational groups on the right, aimed not only at getting students to report their professors but also at prying money out of deep-pocketed donors who revile "tenured radicals." A decade before Turning Point got its start, the Leadership Institute sponsored CampusReform.org as an online database to ferret out "liberal bias and abuse on the nation's college campuses."[35] The Professor Watchlist is more of the same. However, it was built for the social media era, when attacks on academics can reach larger audiences by going viral.[36] And, never an organization willing to let a good crisis go to waste, Turning Point amplified the conservative message that students should be skeptical of their colleges' and universities' intentions just as faculty around the nation were rushing to prepare for the coronavirus pandemic in March 2020. Kirk himself tweeted, "To all college students who have their professors switching to online classes: Please share any and ALL videos of blatant indoctrination [. . .] . Now is the time to document & expose the radicalism that has been infecting our schools."[37]

While the long-term viability of Turning Point is unknown, its chapter and conference model, coupled with a strong social media presence, speakers events, and the Professor Watchlist, has been a resounding success in the short run. The organization has gained mainstream attention and attracted a wealth of donor contributions due in no small part to its founder's strong connections with the Trump family. As we noted in chapter 3, many College Republican chapters have adopted a more provocative style and a more populist ideology in the wake of the 2016 presidential election. But controversy has been Turning Point's bread and butter from the very beginning, and it has left mundane activities for other groups to perform—like actual campaign work for local candidates—while it established strong, headline-grabbing ties with the Trump White House. The members we interviewed were attracted to the energy that comes with being part of such a well-publicized group. Not unlike the conservative students in Amy Binder and Kate Wood's 2013 book *Becoming Right*, who cited the 1960s radical Yippie leader Abbie Hoffman as an inspiration, the Turning Point members we interviewed embraced the political theater that Kirk's organization staged.[38] Some also thought that their contact with the organization would help them down the line in conservative politics. To this end, Turning Point offers employment services, paid positions, and an alumni network for members, but it has nothing akin to AEI's career funnel into the political ecosystem on the right. Mainly, what Turning Point offers its members is a set of resources for "triggering libs," the opportunity to see the organization's leader hosted on national television shows, and the chance to join like-minded peers at conferences headlined by big-name, flame-throwing conservative speakers.

PRAGERU

A third model that exists in the conservative channel is PragerU, short for Prager University. Founded in 2009 by the radio talk show host Dennis Prager, the mission of PragerU is to "promote what is true, what is excellent, and what is noble through digital media."[39] Unlike other right-leaning organizations mobilizing students, it does not fund campus chapters or offer a robust internship program. And should there be any confusion, it is also not a university. PragerU holds no classes and grants no degrees. What it does do is produce educational online content. Specifically, PragerU recruits academic experts and conservative pundits to write and narrate highly polished five-minute videos from what it calls a "Judeo-Christian perspective."[40] And, like Turning Point and other outside organizations promoting an activist mindset, PragerU's messaging is urgent and oppositional. One of its videos, starring the University of Toronto clinical psychologist Jordan Peterson, is called "Dangerous People Are Teaching Your Kids." In this video, which has received 13 million views, Peterson explains that tuition dollars are funding professors seeking to "undermine Western civilization." AEI's Sommers is featured in "There Is No Gender Wage Gap!" which dismisses decades of academic research on structural pay inequity as instead the justifiable outcome of women's and men's individual career preferences. It has over 14 million views. At least one of those clicks was Ariel, who said she does not believe in the wage gap because "it's not so much about sexism, and it's more so about choice"—which is exactly the point Sommers drives home in the video. Scholars like Peterson and Sommers—firebrands in their own right—sit cheek by jowl with comedians and YouTube personalities like Dave Rubin (not to be confused with the AEI scholar Michael Rubin) and Steven Crowder. Dave Rubin contributes the wildly popular "Why I Left the Left," with over 28 million views. One of Crowder's offerings is "Democratic Socialism Is Still Socialism," boasting nearly 20 million views. Both lambaste progressives as omnipresent threats to American society.[41]

In addition to PragerU's usual five-minute explainer videos, there are longer takes on current events. Just after the police killing of George Floyd in spring 2020 set off demonstrations around the world, at least two 25-minute interviews were posted to critique the protesters and their cause: "Black Lives Matter Is a Marxist Movement" and "Black Lives Matter Is Not Helping Blacks." This is on top of several shorter videos, such as "The Media Pushed Lies about Ferguson," "The Mainstream Media Will Not Tell the Truth about Black Lives Matter," and an interview with Larry Elder (in which the Black radio host "eviscerates the myth of 'systemic racism' and leaves Dave Rubin speechless").[42] This anti-progressive tack is true of all of PragerU's videos, whether on the topic of race, gender, education, religion, or economics. The content is meant to provide "a counter perspective to some of the narratives on college campuses" and "to really educate people on different issues and provide easy talking points so it's digestible for anybody," according to Devon Mirsky, who leads the student outreach program at PragerU. Or, as one libertarian professor explained to us about Dennis Prager, he might be "a religious nutbag," but PragerU videos offer "a counterpunch" to unchecked progressivism. The same professor then told us that universities sometimes "deserve a gut punch."

If success is measured by the number of people reached, PragerU has found a winning formula. Its videos rack up millions upon millions of views—every day. By fall 2020, the organization claimed that its videos had been viewed four billion times.[43] But capturing eyeballs is just the start. Persuasion is the real goal. Here, too, PragerU claims to be making great strides. According to the organization, 70 percent of viewers report that a PragerU video changed their mind on an issue; 17 percent said the videos have influenced their behavior and actions; and 85 percent said they have referenced PragerU videos in political discussions.[44] Mirsky may have been correct, then, when she stated that "really leading the forefront of conservative politics with the youth, I would say, is PragerU and Turning Point USA. I think we're the two main organizations." What is more, the overlap between Turning Point and PragerU can be seen in the ascendancy of Candace Owens, the former communications director of Turning Point who now hosts *The Candace Owens Show* on PragerU. Kirk and several others from Turning Point's Speakers Bureau are also featured in PragerU videos.

The organization makes around four new videos each week. Producing slick content capable of attracting such a large audience requires extensive financial backing. Each of its five-minute segments costs in the ballpark of $25,000 to produce, and about the same to market. Fifty thousand dollars per video can add up quickly, but PragerU's coffers have plenty to keep the enterprise going. Its anticipated budget for 2020 included $25 million in revenue, up from approximately $6 million in 2016. This rapid growth resembles that of Turning Point. And, like Kirk's organization, PragerU has donors ponying up big money to support its programming. Major early contributors included some of the top funders of the right: the Lynde and Harry Bradley Foundation, the Maccabee Task Force (a pro-Israel organization sponsored by the late casino magnate and Trump backer Sheldon Adelson), and oil tycoons Farris and Dan Wilks. Smaller donations also come from content sponsorships, as well as ordinary viewers, who are encouraged to "help support our mission" on every navigable webpage. This latter source comprises fully 40 percent of PragerU's funding.[45]

STUDENT AMBASSADORS: PROMOTING CONTENT, CHANGING MINDS

Most of PragerU's focus is on content production. However, the organization maintains a rapidly expanding student outreach program—PragerFORCE—which the organization claims has more than 6,500 student "ambassadors" on 1,500 high school and college campuses.[46] The ambassadors' main task is to promote the viewing of PragerU videos at their schools. As Mirsky explained, PragerU operates "a little bit different from other organizations" because it does not support "physical on-campus clubs." Instead, PragerU enlists students to "help spread awareness throughout the internet, by sharing videos" in the meetings of other clubs and in the classroom. This approach lends itself well to crossover with previously established student-led groups. "We want to make sure that we provide these resources for Turning Point USA, College Republicans, Young America's Foundation. All those different groups can use our videos in their meetings, and that works in place of us having to start a national club." Ariel was a model PragerFORCE ambassador, on top of her role as president of her campus Turning Point chapter. "Pretty much what we do is just share videos so that you kind of monopolize on people seeing the videos" so that they "are familiar with the name." Leading by example, Ariel even succeeded in convincing her gender studies professor at CU to have a class screening of Sommers's wage gap video.

PragerFORCE members are also expected to "go out there and show support of our brand" on their own social media accounts, according to Mirsky. This helps increase PragerU viewership and is meant to counteract the policies on internet platforms, which occasionally restrict its videos. "Whenever we catch wind of the left colluding to de-platform our content, we initiate a swarm of PragerFORCE members who fight back online by up-voting our videos, reposting our censored content, or simply defending our ideas online."[47] This is said to be essential work, because when videos are "de-platformed" by so-called agents of radicalism (like the tech giants Facebook and YouTube), the organization is at risk of being "de-monetized," said Mirsky—cut off from ad revenues and potential donors. Such "de-platforming" events also add fuel to charges of a culture war, even though many videos from hundreds of creators are regularly put on YouTube's restricted list, and such action does not hinder most people's ability to view the videos anyway.[48]

Josephine, another ambassador we interviewed, spoke of how she promotes the program not just by "word of mouth" but also through "a lot of Instagram. We do a lot of Facebook Live." As a reward for this kind of work, Josephine, Ariel, and about fifty other top PragerFORCE performers get to travel to an annual gathering for PragerFORCE ambassadors in Los Angeles. As with Turning Point, these opportunities are relished by students as an opportunity to meet one another and get to know organization staff. Thus, while the model of mobilization is decidedly virtual, it still requires activists using their personal social networks and putting in work on their campuses to increase PragerU's audience size, donations, and profitable clicks.

Unlike at AEI, there is no clear evidence of formalized mentoring and networking at PragerU. However, a few of our interviewees suggested that participating with the organization can be a launch pad for their career pathways. Mirsky's own job history through the conservative channel of student activism provides an instructive example. A native of California, she began her career while in graduate school, interning for Meg Whitman's 2010 gubernatorial campaign. In that position, Mirsky was introduced to the Leadership Institute; four years later, she was briefly a field representative for that organization. Then, while working for the Leadership Institute, she became acquainted with the fledgling Turning Point, and took a job as a field director in that organization, eventually becoming the regional director for California. From there, Mirsky applied for a job at PragerU. As she explained, "Once I was in this conservative campus loop, it just kind of became one thing after the other pretty quickly." When we spoke with her, Mirsky was the director of PragerFORCE, and was in a good position to pay it forward by putting in a good word for students she has worked with, connecting them with the Heritage Foundation internship coordinator and other conservative groups. Although this does not constitute a deeply institutionalized career funnel, staff are happy to help students find pathways in the conservative sphere. Josephine also mentioned PragerU as a career building block. She used her travel to Los Angeles as a PragerFORCE ambassador as a means to network her way into a Fox News internship, having previously joined College Republicans and Turning Point "because I knew that that could launch me into more groups." Less formal than AEI's career funnel, but perhaps more personalized than Turning Point's employment services and alumni network, contact with PragerU—in some cases—can boost the job opportunities of young conservatives.

CONCLUSION

AEI, Turning Point, and PragerU are just three of a much larger pool of organizations constituting the heterogeneous conservative channel of student activism. Social movement scholars have debated the extent to which elites shape political contention, with many arguing that most movements depend largely on local networks rather than outside investors. Studying conservative student activism allows us to see that elites and movement professionals often do direct resources to particular constituencies and strongly influence their mobilization.[49] Indeed, the conservative channel would not look anything like it does today without resource-rich outsiders.

Considering these three groups' similarities and differences allows us to grasp several of the key features driving contemporary campus politics. These organizations understand student outreach to be an existential mission for the conservative movement. While attracting young, vibrant activists is a hurdle for the right, donors are willing to contribute heavily to these organizations, which gives them the resources to excel in their particular areas of focus. AEI supports right-leaning scholars and nurtures future policymakers. Turning Point mobilizes the culture war, especially the Trumpist brand, on campus. PragerU produces persuasive (and pervasive) online content to support the conservative agenda. Distinct as each organization is, together they cohere in fostering skepticism about higher education among the students they work with. In doing so, they pull undergraduates beyond their campuses as they encourage alternative knowledge sources and funding streams. At the same time, the similarities and differences between these organizations have consequences for the types of activism students on the right engage in. Of the three organizations we examined in this chapter, AEI stands out for its civil tone. Castle even balked at the term "activist" during his interview, preferring to emphasize the think tank's intellectual mission. Turning Point and PragerU—the upstarts—encourage their members and followers to take a different tack. They are greasing the wheels of contentious politics.

Overall, national organizations like AEI, Turning Point, and PragerU provide valuable resources to the conservative clubs we described in chapter 3. And, as we discussed in that chapter, student-led groups sort and shape their members by setting the norms and expectations of what college politics should and should not entail. What we have revealed in this chapter, then, is a bit of what the current landscape for those possibilities looks like. These national organizations' strength is in undermining the academy. The right considers itself so vilified by higher education that it has created an outside channel to bypass it. Thus, all three organizations are, in their own way, part of an insurgency against liberal dominance. Yet, while positioning themselves as underdogs offers certain tactical advantages—and certainly helps drum up donations—it also represents a weakness within the channel. Specifically, as organizations like PragerU and, even more so, Turning Point become emblematic of the right, an environment emerges primed for confrontation with students who operate from within the progressive channel. It is far from clear whether conservative provocations can truly usurp liberal dominance on campus in the long run, or even whether such tactics will have enduring effects in Republican politics outside the university setting. However, with the coffers for PragerU and Turning Point expanding, their odds of gaining ground are likely to increase.

CHAPTER 5

The Progressive Channel— Pushed Inside from the Left

In chapter 4, we learned that right-leaning students have access to an array of well-funded organizations at the national level. Although varied in their styles and offerings, the organizations in the conservative channel are laser-focused on pulling students beyond the campus, seeing academia as unfairly tilted to the left. Tactically, they provide a discourse about why students should be skeptical of higher education. Financially, they offer all-expenses-paid conferences, subsidized celebrity speaker stables, networking opportunities, and even—in the case of the American Enterprise Institute (AEI)—a defined labor market funnel via internships and summer fellowships. With their ability to tap these resources, conservative students often feel more connected to the national groups sponsoring their activities than they do to their peers and faculty on campus.

In this chapter, we focus on the progressive channel, where we find something quite different. Unlike outside conservative organizations that sow doubt about higher education's values and goals, national progressive organizations—such as foundations, advocacy groups, and individual donors—express their faith in academia by providing billions of dollars for research, financial aid, endowments, and centers that serve students and faculty. From the eighty-year-old Ford Foundation to benefactors like Bill and Melinda Gates, this philanthropic well is constantly replenished by charitable blue bloods and socially conscious new wealth. Counter to a video that Charlie Kirk recorded for PragerU, in which he browbeats viewers to divest from colleges and universities because they are liberal indoctrination mills,[1] well-heeled progressive donors give abundantly to postsecondary institutions.

While these deep pockets have done much to keep the academic enterprise afloat, particularly in the modern era of state funding retrenchment, they do not generally extend their largesse to left-leaning student activism to nearly the same extent that we see among conservative organizations. While critics on the right "have long championed the cause of conservative undergraduates, who, they say, suffer on college campuses," left-leaning philanthropists assume that higher education serves students' best interests.[2] Where conservative organizations realize that the current Republican voting bloc of older Whites is demographically doomed unless organizations activate young voters, progressive organizations have largely taken collegians' politics for granted, assuming that the overwhelming majority identify as liberal (an assumption belied by HERI national surveys of incoming freshmen, as we saw in chapter 2). And where for decades outside conservative groups have fused the ideological doctrine of economic freedom, limited government, and Christian values to fire up support, progressive organizations—much like the Democratic Party—are more fragmented into separate issues, leaving their funding base less concentrated for left-leaning campus politics overall. From the top down, in other words, progressives have been organizationally out-maneuvered by the right for decades.[3]

This organizational deficiency is mirrored from the bottom up when it comes to student activism, with left-of-center collegians expecting less than their conservative peers from outside groups. Since the 1960s, progressive social movements that involve undergraduate mobilization have not sought out rich networks, relying instead on organic coalition-building to achieve their goals.[4] This can be a point of pride, as when Levi explained that for leftists organizing today, "There's really not a lot of funding." As Levi stated, "Being an activist is usually out of your own pocket." In this way of thinking, self-funding is virtuous because leftists and liberals rely on the motivations of ordinary people, not the assistance of elites. But a dimmer view also can be taken. For decades, progressives have been relatively complacent about galvanizing the next generation of activists and voters—a net negative when resource mobilization is a crucial factor in movement success.[5] To this point, Isaac proved less sanguine than Levi, explaining that the UVA club he belongs to, Students United, "operates on a shoestring budget, as do other small organizations within Charlottesville. It's not this system where someone like Charlie Kirk has managed to get angel investors to spend millions on their organizations that then trickles down to students like us." Conservatives among our interview sample were also aware of the disparity. For example, the faculty advisor to the Turning Point USA chapter at UA echoed Isaac's observation, saying that "The proliferation of national [. . .] organizations sponsoring clubs? I don't see that on the [. . .] left."

Those on the right might argue that any gaps in outside funding for student activism are irrelevant, since the underlying priorities of colleges and universities are already aligned with progressives' goals. Left-leaning collegians, by these lights, do not need outside organizations to advance their causes. There is more than a glimmer of truth to this description, as we will outline in detail below. Instead of being "pulled outside" of their campuses by lavishly funded national groups, leftist and liberal students are better described as being comfortably "embedded within" university structures—inside academic departments, student affairs offices, multicultural centers, and peer networks. These on-campus opportunities—or what we call the progressive channel—anchor students to the internal workings of their schools and lead to a greater sense of belonging with peers, faculty, staff, and administrators than conservative students feel.

Yet, as much as students on the left experience being in the ideological swim of things on their campuses, we find downsides to their inside connections and relative lack of resources obtained from the outside. Students sometimes grow weary of their activist-oriented work in college, coming to suspect that their demands for greater social justice are met not with administrators' genuine action, but merely with superficial support. They may feel like insiders, but only to a degree. Students can become cynical when school officials seem largely to outsource their diversity-minded initiatives—such as recruiting and retaining historically underrepresented populations—to Black and Brown students.[6] Such experiences shape mobilizing efforts, often turning progressives' sights on the very administrators who might otherwise be taken as allies. And, as students near graduation, some realize that a lack of connection with outside organizations limits their pathways post-college. Where left-leaning students enviously point to their conservative peers' seemingly easy entrée into the political sphere, they describe their own routes into full-time progressive jobs as clunkier and more do-it-yourself. No less than the outside organizational channel on the right, the embedded channel on the left has positive and negative consequences for students' framing of the issues that matter to them, and for their subsequent activism.

THE MORE LIMITED OUTSIDE ECOSYSTEM ON THE LEFT

Before looking at the on-campus dynamics that give structure to the progressive channel, it is important to take stock of a few of the many organizations that lend outside support to left-leaning students' political engagements. Our claim is not that such organizations do not exist—indeed, the full list of progressive outside groups is likely much longer than the list of conservative organizations—but rather that they play a smaller role in progressive student activists' day-to-day lives. We pay special attention to these outside groups' mobilization tactics and financial resources, comparing them to players in the conservative landscape. Just as we saw on the right, organizations use a variety of approaches to connect with students—some have chapters on campus, many host training conferences, and (specific to the left) one group funds voter mobilization at a large scale. Unlike what we discovered on the right, however, all but one of the operations we profile has less access to financial resources. The relative lack of outside funding creates a more insular relationship in progressive student activism: the lower the financial support for students from the outside, the more young activists turn to campus units to accomplish their goals. The more connected students become with campus units, the fewer ties they forge with outside actors.

STUDENT PIRGS—A MODEL INSIDER

One national organization worth considering is US PIRG (US Public Interest Research Group) and its associated state-based and student PIRGs—a multilayered group whose name and clipboard-toting members may be familiar on many campuses, but whose structure, goals, and financial model are poorly understood. Students involved with the organization have opportunities to work on issues that are generally progressive. However, for reasons that will become clear later, members are neither explicitly cultivated for careers in policy-making (as is true for conservatives who are connected with AEI) nor given a bullhorn to articulate political ideology (as is the case at Turning Point and PragerU).

National, state, and student PIRGs form a federated system of regionally based Public Interest Research Groups which "have delivered results-oriented citizen activism, stood up to powerful special interests, and used the time-tested tools of investigative research, media exposés, grassroots organizing, advocacy, and litigation to win real results on issues that matter."[7] To mobilize students on behalf of its causes, the organization sponsors a network of thirty-seven campus chapters in eight states, including at three of the universities we study: UA, CU, and UNC. Approximately 500 students nationwide get course credit for participating in PIRG campaigns, on the logic that the organization serves a pedagogical function by connecting collegians to "real world problems" and teaching them how to work "within the system to make change," according to Student PIRGs executive director Andy MacDonald. PIRG members attend state- and national-level conferences to learn about issues and mobilization techniques, using money that they have raised on campus to support their travel.

The precursors to state-level PIRGs were student-run efforts springing from "Nader's Raiders," a group of undergraduates working in the 1960s and 1970s with the consumer advocate Ralph Nader on such issues as regulating pesticides and pressuring car companies to install airbags. Since the 1980s, the group has grown substantially larger; as of this writing, the PIRGs have nearly 400 organizers, policy analysts, scientists, and attorneys lobbying the US Congress and state legislatures.[8] US PIRG offers approximately twenty full-time campus organizer jobs for recent graduates, and many dozens of paid summer jobs to canvass in the community. MacDonald expressed pride that his organization offers employment to students, although he noted ruefully that PIRG's assistance with careers is "less formalized" than what occurs on the right. "Conservatives have a much more definitive thing," he said.

For those familiar with Nader's political stances, it may come as a surprise to learn that the organization is officially nonpartisan. Its website calls the issues "neither progressive nor conservative"; they are "just problems that our country shouldn't tolerate in an age of great abundance and technological progress."[9] Yet, when reviewing a partial list of campaigns sponsored at UNC—increasing recycling, saving bumblebees from extinction, and discouraging the use of antibiotics in farming—one could be forgiven for assuming a progressive bent. Indeed, the students we met who worked with Colorado's and North Carolina's PIRGs identify as left of center. Nevertheless, the issues that UNC's club has *not* taken up (because they are "too charged" and have "too much of a partisan lean," said Kristen) include mobilizing to defend Deferred Action for Childhood Arrivals (DACA) and backing the protests to tear down the Confederate memorial on her campus—two hot-button issues at the time of our data collection. Deciding not to engage on these topics at all, or even to encourage voting for Democrats who are likelier to support their causes, puts the student PIRGs at a remove from other progressives' mobilization activities. Not a single student in our sample who was not already a member of the campus PIRG chapter mentioned the organization as a potential ally.

Student PIRGs are careful to avoid issues with "too much of a partisan lean" partly because the organization's livelihood depends on it. In a distinctive twist on how outside groups fund student activism (certainly from the standpoint of donor-based conservative organizations), Mac-Donald told us some of the money from the contributions gathered by student chapters flows up and into the hands of US PIRG, not the other way around. What is more, this unusual funding source is made possible because it is universities that collect money for the PIRGs through tuition and fees. At many participating schools, unless students know to opt out, a part of the fees that every student pays to their college each year supports the PIRG chapter on campus and higher levels of the organization.[10] Overall, this funding model generates "a couple million dollars" a year for the entire system, said MacDonald—a small sum when compared to the reserves available at the three organizations we profiled in the conservative channel. But such funding has been critical for supporting professionals and training students in the organization.

As one might imagine, the PIRG financial and pedagogical model is not viewed favorably by right-leaning critics, who argue that these hidden fees are used to lobby legislators for progressive causes. In a Fox News essay, the libertarian author Radley Balko calls out Nader's "hypocrisy" in demanding greater transparency in hidden ATM fees while simultaneously "mandating, tricking, or manipulating college students into donating to leftist activism."[11] And, according to MacDonald, critics have tried to shut down PIRGs by cutting off their funding, while university administrators—stung by conservative critiques—are enhancing student fee autonomy, which makes it harder to run things the way the organization has grown accustomed to. While we remain agnostic about whether the PIRG funding model is deceptive, we were surprised to learn how it works. The way we make sense of it is this: the PIRG model illustrates how at least one organization in the progressive channel (even while it remains technically nonpartisan) works closely with partner universities, anchoring students' activism inside the institution rather than pulling students off campus to accomplish their officially nonpartisan goals.

ELSEWHERE IN THE PROGRESSIVE CHANNEL: PLANNED PARENTHOOD, COLLEGE DEMOCRATS, AND NEXTGEN AMERICA

Planned Parenthood—the long-standing advocate for reproductive freedom—is another organization that directly sponsors progressive students' political activism, although it does not have an inside funding track like the PIRGs do. The Planned Parenthood Action Fund is the organization's advocacy arm, and it commands a large annual operating budget—just over $35 million.[12] This number may sound like enough to provide ample resources to student activists associated with the organization. However, the money is used to sustain a wide variety of activities, including supporting the national organization and local affiliates in their efforts to defend abortion rights and access to other medical care at Planned Parenthood branches. The sum spent on collegiate activism is likely far smaller.[13]

We interviewed a handful of collegians who were involved with Planned Parenthood Generation Action, the group's student activism branch, which has representation on more than 350 campuses across the country.[14] Alexa was one student who attended a Generation Action conference, where she learned practical skills for mobilization. "They trained us in organizing. They trained us in phone-banking, how to organize our own things" and "how to talk about issues." Applying this training to her "own things," Alexa wrote a blog about reproductive justice, authored an op-ed essay published in the student newspaper, and collaborated with other groups to raise awareness about sexual assault on campus. This was highly rewarding work, Alexa reported. But the lack of adequate funding from the parent organization took a toll, and she ended up stepping away from a leadership position after spending two years as the club's president. As Alexa explained, "It was very straining on myself, like financially, just having to put my own money into things" and "not getting credit or paid" for the work being done—"It was a lot." At odds with what we heard from conservative students who were well resourced by outside organizations, this was a common refrain among progressive students working with outside national groups.

Complaints about inadequate funding were raised not just about organizations mobilized around particular issues like reproductive health, but also about clubs supporting Democratic priorities overall. College Democrats of America (CDA) is the outreach arm of the national party, and CDA's mission statement commits the organization to "educate students about the philosophy of the Democratic Party, work with Democrats across the country to achieve the goals of CDA and the Democratic Party, and work to bring more young people into the political process."[15] Such substantial goals suggest that CDA would provide sufficient financial and networking resources for its student clubs on campus, but in fact this is not the case. The governing body of the Democratic Party, the Democratic National Committee (DNC), has largely failed to coordinate much student activism, said our interviewees. According to a past president of the CDA, the national organization's entire operating budget for each year is $50,000, and the organization is staffed by students serving in unpaid positions.[16] This interviewee could not conceal his frustration leading up to the 2018 midterm elections. "Fifty thousand dollars is not enough money to run a national organization," he said glumly. As for what he would do if CDA had more resources, he juxtaposed his organization to the College Republicans. "One of the things we're trying to [improve] this year is the merch, but, as I said, it's hard to get anything out on a $50,000 budget." College Democrats, he pointed out, were still using old banners and Obama logos in the 2018 midterm elections. He contrasted this with College Republicans chapters that "get a lot more resources to recruit than we do." Anthony, a member of UNC's Young

Democrats, complained that the lack of support extends beyond money, citing a dearth of national networking opportunities. "I think a lot of times the College Republicans tend to be more tight-knit on a national level" than CDA. "I don't really know what the reasoning is," but Republican students "know a lot of the big players on a national level," whereas the College Democrats he knew tended to rely on local networks.

One notable exception to the low-dollar investments in mobilizing college-aged voters is NextGen Rising, the youth corps of NextGen America—the organization founded by the billionaire and (for a brief moment, in 2019) Democratic presidential candidate Tom Steyer. Launched in 2013 as NextGen Climate, NextGen has since broadened its focus to a range of issues, including supporting DACA, bail reform, and clean drinking water.[17] Since its founding, the organization has zeroed in on citizens under the age of 35 who, leaders say, have the potential to form the largest voting bloc in the country. In order to identify, engage, and mobilize this segment of the electorate—which has the lowest voter turnout rate in the nation—NextGen runs polished digital campaigns out of its central office in San Francisco. For the 2020 election, it claimed to have 10,000 workers committed to registering 300,000 young people in upcoming elections, establishing networks between progressive politicians and their constituents, and disseminating information on where and when to vote.[18] In addition, NextGen is a grant-making organization: in 2018, the organization awarded $40 million in grants to progressive organizations and sustained an operating budget of approximately $14 million.[19]

What makes Steyer's group stand out in the progressive channel is the amount of funding it directs toward collegians, and the networks it builds among them. Rather than being an organization that has a student *arm*, NextGen is dedicated to being a youth-focused national organization, full stop. To activate voters, the organization has created hundreds of paid positions for college student workers, making NextGen Rising resemble the organizations we detailed in chapter 4—at least in terms of dollar amounts and number of collegians reached. During a 2018 interview, Ben Wessel, who was then the political director of NextGen and later the director of NextGen Rising, contrasted his organization's goal of motivating young people "around the issues that are most pressing to them in their own communities" to the College Democrats' goals, which, he said, "always tended to be a little bit more of like the nineteen-year-olds who like to wear suits" and meet politicians.[20]

NextGen America aside, outside progressive organizations did not appear to devote nearly as much time or treasure as conservative organizations did to the student activists we met. For example, outside groups on the left have been largely absent in providing resources to help collegians respond to contentious campus speech controversies—the number one issue that roiled much of higher education in the Trump era. And the weak links connecting progressive students to such resources are apparent to leaders of national organizations. Molly Nocheck, the campus outreach and internship coordinator for the Foundation for Individual Rights in Education (FIRE), a campus speech organization, explained that every year liberal students apply to FIRE's internship program and summer conferences, even though her organization is perceived as leaning to the right. The reason, Nocheck says, is that progressive students lack opportunities elsewhere. "From my experience working in outreach, there's a lot of different conference opportunities for conservative and libertarian students. But I haven't really seen as many for more liberal students." If progressives are serious about mobilizing young people, they may want to take a page out of the conservative playbook and start placing a higher priority on sponsoring activism at the collegiate level.

THE PROGRESSIVE CHANNEL: MINIMALLY PULLED OUTSIDE, BUT EMBEDDED WITHIN

If students on the left lack comparable resources from the outside, what they do have going for them are strong ideological connections within the campus. Although not to the caricatured extent of "indoctrination" that conservative critics would have us believe, progressive ideas prevail in higher education, particularly in liberal arts disciplinary fields and administrators' initiatives.[21] Students on the left take classes with professors who produce frameworks for understanding social inequities. University events boards invite speakers who advance left-of-center viewpoints. Liberal and leftist activists request meetings with administrators to air grievances about campus policies. And because students on the left—particularly those from underrepresented populations—

contribute to school diversity, administrators frequently respond positively to those requests. School officials may even ask for those students' help to advance their goals. Progressives are also able to make use of multicultural centers, such as for Asian-American, Black, Latinx, women, or LGBTQ+ students. These centers are university spaces that often amplify the viewpoints found in particular academic departments, and they provide institutional backing for progressive initiatives on campus.[22]

This does not mean that students to the left of center—especially those on the far left—have no complaints about their schools, or that their institutional power matches that of faculty and administrators. But there is a distinct and potent channel for progressive activism that is created *through* the formal and informal structures of higher education. All of this leads left-leaning activists to have a sense of embeddedness on their campuses. Ironically, such close ties can blind progressives to the myriad ways their ideological orientations are actually supported day in and day out at their schools. Fish are unaware of the water in which they swim, as the essayist David Foster Wallace wrote.[23] This taken-for-granted sense of belonging is a far cry from how conservatives describe their experiences in academia.[24] The flipside of students on the right often feeling alienated on their campuses is that progressives feel at home without thinking much about it—that is, until, in frustration, they may push for greater change than faculty and administrators are willing to entertain. In the sections below, we note the various cultural and organizational arrangements on campus that naturalize progressive students' experiences there.

PROFESSORS, PEERS, AND ADMINISTRATORS

Unlike their conservative counterparts, few progressives believe faculty to be adherents of far-left ideologies. However, they do regard professors' worldviews as left of center. Jerod, a self-identified liberal, told us, "I would say that the issues discussed in class tend to be more left-leaning." He then added, "When you're looking at issues of racial justice and poverty, those tend to be things that the left generally focuses on—issues of equity and social and economic justice." Iona attributed her own burgeoning leftism to learning what she felt were indisputable facts in her social science and humanities classes. "A lot of my views align with history," she said. In her political science and history courses, she told us, professors "talk about how the United States has caused problems because they interfered" in other nations' affairs. Faculty's liberal views are on display in the natural sciences too. Levi, a biology major who identifies as a socialist, told us, "Professors aren't supposed to politicize the classroom, but a lot of the folks in [my classes] are very liberal, so there are many offhand comments that are dropped, and everybody is pretty much on the same page in the classroom." Levi acknowledged that "Republicans in the classroom can feel isolated," but Levi rationalized this as an inevitable outcome of needing to critically discuss social issues. Talking about wildfires and floods exacerbated by global warming, or the racial disparities in exposure to environmental pollution, might not be politically "neutral," but such topics need to be addressed. If that is political, they said, "then it's political. It's also talking about" important aspects of "people's lives." As Levi and other students attested, it is easy to find support for progressive ideas in the college curriculum.

Then there are classmates' politics. The students we spoke with—activists on the left and right—characterized most of their peers as an apathetic lot. As they saw it, the average student is just not energized by political issues. But our progressive interviewees also felt that their classmates were casual ideological allies, despite their overall complacency. As Jamison reported, "Definitely, in many of my classes, especially the more discussion-based ones, when you have the opportunity to hear people's comments, you size them up a little bit." And, in doing so, Jamison concluded, "Most of the comments are liberal-leaning, left-leaning. So, sure, maybe part of that is that conservatives [are] less likely to speak," but he insisted there is a progressive "consensus within each classroom. The median person is definitely on the left." Although Jamison's estimates do not comport with the Freshman Survey data we examined in chapter 2, assumptions of progressive dominance on campus were a common view. Marco, for instance, told us, "In a discussion-based class, you're going to get pretty liberal vibes," while Jace explained that "the average American college student, I would say, is probably right around where I am—maybe even a little more on the left." Kristen described how she came to believe that most students at her school lean to the left: "look at the student groups on campus." In doing so, she assured us, you can see how many progressive clubs there are. And these left-leaning groups "are much bigger on campus" than conservative groups.

In addition to feeling aligned with faculty and peers, progressive students feel linked to campus through the imperatives of administrators. Several of the students we interviewed worked together with admissions directors, or with staff in student affairs offices or multicultural centers, whose goals dovetail with progressives' priorities. This was especially true for members of identity-based clubs. In fact, much of the activism done by these groups coalesced around making their schools more diverse and inclusive—which involves not only targeting administrators, but also working with them as allies. Policy initiatives emerging from such efforts are frequently anathema to conservative desires for a "color-blind" system.

The Black Student Movement (BSM) at UNC was one example of this dynamic. August, a liberal student, explained that BSM has been working with the Office of Undergraduate Admissions "to do direct contact for every student of color that gets admitted." The goal is to "expose them to UNC" and "the community" to show them what is available to students and "what could be offered to them academically, professionally, socially, and then, what kind of support they could have financially to attend." With resources provided by administrators and activated through students' on-the-ground legwork, BSM members tried to keep themselves and younger cohorts of underrepresented populations connected to campus. Similarly, Sheridan worked with the Office of Admissions at UA. Asked about her efforts, Sheridan, herself a working-class student of color, said, "I really try to help [. . .] the lower-income population, that first-generation, the marginalized groups to go and get a college education." She described this work as "very fulfilling" because it allowed her "to actually go out and work" with underrepresented populations. Not only did Sheridan talk with prospective enrollees; the university sought her advice on how best to reach new students. "What's really cool" is that staff and administrators trust minority students, "because a lot of the student recruiters come from lower income areas" and "have faced adversity. So, they ask us, 'What would work for you, if you were still in high school? [. . .] Do we need to start [. . .] translating [informational materials] into Spanish so that parents can understand?' So, by having us there, we're able to figure out what's the best way to get students to understand how they can actually take advantage of the different opportunities."

Beyond admission goals, there are myriad ways administrators are aligned with left-leaning students. In a 2018 op-ed for the *New York Times*, Samuel Abrams, a political science professor at Sarah Lawrence College, argues that offices of diversity support a range of issues supporting progressive worldviews.[25] At his school, for instance, administrators sponsored a "'liberation summit,' whose topics included liberation spaces on campus, Black Lives Matter, and justice for women as well as for lesbian, gay, bisexual, transgender, queer, intersex, and asexual and allied people." The prevalence of these types of events and programs was apparent to us as we visited our four campuses too.

In short, if much of present-day academia conforms (at least in part) to left-of-center ideologies, administrators cannot be separated from this. After all, they are the ones who ultimately approve commencement speakers, fund hiring lines, and give resources to a variety of campus units and initiatives. And, as Abrams's research suggests, "student-facing" administrators' political leanings tilt further to the left than those of faculty. Kristen's positive description of UNC is illustrative. "I think we have support from most of the administration. We've never had a meeting where [someone] was like, 'We totally disagree with you. [. . .] Stop being active on campus.' Nothing like that has ever happened. It's more just, 'Okay, we agree with you. Can this actually get done? Can we make it happen here?'" And in general, Kristen felt the answer had been "yes."

At the same time, it is important to add that colleges and universities are not a leftist's nirvana. Faculty research advances military technologies and propels corporate profits. Over the past several decades, academia has been restructured by a market logic that undermines the citizenship goals of a liberal arts education. The actual function of American higher education, in other words, is far from radical.[26] These sorts of critiques are top of mind for many progressive students, and there is often little love lost between far-left activists and school officials. Nevertheless, higher education operates from within a liberal framework—one that can even tolerate extreme elements operating within it. To go back to David Foster Wallace's parable of the fish in water, the far left's frustration with academic institutions only reveals just how taken-for-granted progressive viewpoints have become on most campuses.

AFFILIATIONS WITH MULTICULTURAL CENTERS

In addition to feeling ideologically aligned with a variety of people at their schools, progressive students are connected to their universities through multiple institutional spaces that support their identities and worldviews. This was particularly true of the leftists we spoke with. Multicultural centers are valued places where students can comingle and learn leadership roles under the guidance of supportive staff. Universities have a wide range of such spaces. Typically under the purview of student affairs offices, these centers can be hubs of progressive activism on campus.

Lydia told us about several UA programs and centers with which she had been involved, and how that involvement had led to her forming deep connections at her school. Taking us step by step through her affiliations, Lydia said, "My freshman year, I was an intern in the Women's Resource Center," and "I also have done stuff for Housing and Residential Life. There is one program called Advocates Coming Together. I was the co-director for that, and that was kind of like general social justice education for some residents who are part of that group." Lydia's list went on, including a stint as a peer advisor in the dorms, a program coordinated by the Office for Equity and Student Engagement. After her sophomore year, Lydia moved from the Women's Resource Center to the LGBTQ Resource Center, where she became acquainted with a network of students forming the advocacy group Marginalized Students of the University of Arizona (MSUA). Lydia also worked for the campus Safe Zone program over the summer, "which is a training program about LGBTQ identities." Although Lydia was unusually involved on her campus, her experiences showcase how institutional spaces on campus are plentiful, interconnected, and animated by issues progressives care about.

Vanessa's description of the Cultural Unity and Engagement (CUE) Center at CU was also telling. "That's where the BSA has our meetings [and] UMAS y MEXA has their meetings. And that is a really, really nice space. Usually, when you go in there, it's mostly people of color." Vanessa saw the Center as much more than a meeting site for clubs; she sometimes used the CUE's couches to take naps—a true sign of her comfort level there. She contrasted this with her sense of alienation from other areas of CU. As she told us, "Think about how many dorms on campus are all White." The CUE, in other words, was—in the broadest sense of the term—a "safe space" for Vanessa and other members of underrepresented populations at CU.

Beyond providing an appreciated haven, multicultural centers help students mobilize for activism in two key ways, particularly when it comes to targeting administrators (as we discussed in chapter 3). First, these centers serve as the crossroads where students meet like-minded peers. This is important for building the coalitions essential for successful mobilization. Atlas pointed to the role of multicultural centers in the formation of MSUA, the group representing marginalized students mentioned by Lydia. "MSUA is a coalition of all the different cultural centers and a lot of the different politically active groups," and its goals are "just kind of spelling out for the university what is needed from them in order [for students] to feel successful and feel like we had a place at the table." As Sheridan, another member of MSUA, explained, the original point of the coalition was to "come together to create a list of demands from every center" on campus. To this end, "The students of the Adalberto and Ana Guerrero Center, African American Student Affairs, Asian Pacific Student Affairs, the LGBTQ Resource Center, Native American Student Affairs, the Women's Resource Center, and our allies" joined forces to compel UA to make changes.[27] Lydia spoke of the social ties shared by members of these groups: "There were students [in MSUA] from the different resource and cultural centers, [and they] are the ones who got together because we already had that established relationship to each other." Although leftists may not be as well-connected nationally to one another as conservatives are through outside organizations, they are networked on their campuses.

Second, beyond serving as hubs where students become acquainted with one another, multicultural centers are spaces where activists can seek direction from staff on how to frame their demands to school officials. Alexa pointed to the delicate balance required in these relationships, saying that staff "didn't want to step on our toes" by being too directive, but "sometimes it was helpful when there was staff at our meetings to give us advice when we wouldn't know what to do." Further, the fact that many of MSUA's demands were requests made *on behalf of* multicultural center staff underscores the synergistic relationship between student activists and the people who work in the centers. Sheridan elaborated on the request made to administrators for additional support for the Women's Resource Center. "A lot of those demands focused on increasing funds for victim advocates," she said. "So, for sexual assault, we [. . .] want a counselor in the space who is specialized in that type of trauma." The students also pushed for paid internships "that focus on topics like consent and sex ed." She then added, "There are different things like that, where we could increase either funding or manpower in these spaces to better the center."

Often, staff in the multicultural centers were progressive activists during their student years, and they see their current positions as a way to help shepherd undergraduates through the process of mobilization— much like how field representatives in the conservative channel mentor and advise young activists on the right.[28] Yet the employees of the centers also must be careful to calculate their roles. On the one hand, the institutional capacities of center staff give them significant power in campus politics compared to outside conservative voices—a fact that lies at the heart of Abrams's critique about administrators skewing to the left.[29] On the other hand, our interviews with Jeri and Sam at CU's Environmental Center illustrate the tension between staff's personal political views and their occupational obligations when working inside the university. "I don't want to say ['student activism' is] a dirty word," Jeri said, at which point Sam interjected that "We can't do that anymore," and then explained that the Environmental Center's emphasis is now on "supporting student leadership." "We are student affairs people," Sam assured us.

All that is to say that in the progressive channel, a sometimes awkward relationship exists between administrators' and staff's own ideological orientations and their professional positions. The sensitive terrain that staff must navigate can lead students to feel jaded and distrustful of the progressive channel because those at the helm frequently seem to be pumping the brakes on institutional change, mindful of what their schools can and cannot do without losing the support of stakeholders above and below them. By contrast, the conservative channel—funded from the outside—is free from such conflicting priorities. Rich, right-leaning organizations can advocate for student activism unhindered by overarching institutional norms of nonpartisanship or fear of hurting the reputation of higher education in the eyes of the public.

Marginalized Students of the University of Arizona (MSUA) may be an extreme case of sustained student mobilization, but it provides a useful illustration of the progressive channel's successes, as well as its challenges. Working with a variety of multicultural center staff, activists involved with MSUA notched several accomplishments over two academic years spent targeting school officials to change university policies and practices. Students met many times with administrators; they crafted stronger and clearer articulations of their progressive priorities; and they succeeded in pushing administrators to hire new staff for the centers. Nevertheless, the years-long experience left many students feeling deflated. Reflecting on the consortium, Alexa said that MSUA "made some progress. But all the progress that's made is the non-controversial stuff, like adding more mental health counselors, adding more financial aid counselors, creating more staff positions, and making some trainings more creative. Those are pretty easy to do." The harder stuff that students demanded—moving the university away from a neoliberal model of education; mandating (not just offering) cultural sensitivity courses for all faculty, students, and staff on campus; eradicating inequities in the college experience—were never successfully addressed, according to Alexa, as administrators fell far short of students' expectations. Lydia made an even sharper charge, accusing university leaders of strategically using bureaucratic tricks to stall potential gains. "The administration's response to the list of demands was to have a diversity task force—which was the most student affairs thing ever," she said derisively. And according to Lydia's and Alexa's classmate Alex, the problem was death by a thousand cuts. Administrators "set up committees, and they set up working groups. And then, suddenly," MSUA is not as effective as it once was, "because all the people-power has just kind of been drained out of it and given to a select few to work directly with the administration."

We heard similar accounts from students at other schools. When asked if CU's school officials had been supportive of BSA, Vanessa agreed, but said "it's very shallow support in that they'll arrange a meeting with us where they say they want us to voice our concerns, and then *they* talk the entire time." And, worse, "then they ask for a photo op, and they put it on their website. And they're like, 'Ooh, look at us. We're meeting with the Black Student Alliance. What a great conversation.' But it *wasn't* a conversation; it was a lecture." Alejandro, also at CU, pointed out that the administrators making cuts to resources like the CUE "have mainly been Black and Brown women, so women of color in these powerful positions. From my perspective, they have been tokenized" by administrators above them "as a strategic move." As Alejandro saw it, this gave higher-level administrators bureaucratic cover for taking resources away from underrepresented populations by allowing them to claim, "Well, they're *your* people making these cuts." In other words, for progressive activists, especially those on the far left, the existence of multicultural centers is considered a given. Having an audience with administrators is assumed. Yet from these baseline expectations, students grow cynical about what is *not* being accomplished, thinking that universities do little more than pay lip service to progressive nostrums.

In sum, leftist and liberal students are in the thick of things on campus. Multicultural centers are built in the name of minority groups, and student affairs offices lead initiatives confirming progressive priorities. Although school officials' words usually exceed their deeds on such matters, members of leftward identity-based clubs, especially those representing underrepresented populations, are granted an audience with administrators much more frequently than those operating in the conservative channel. Such bureaucratic connections help build students' advocacy and leadership skills. Leftist and liberal activists also consider professors and peers to be at least somewhat like-minded allies. And yet, despite this embeddedness, those on the far left understand themselves to be dissidents fighting against the power structure of their schools. Much of their concerted activity in the progressive channel still leads to skepticism about administrators' motives and cynicism that adequate changes will ever be enacted.

THE PROGRESSIVE CHANNEL'S IMPLICATIONS
FOR STUDENTS' LAUNCH OUT OF COLLEGE

There is one additional facet to progressives' inside activism that is worth mentioning: students' thick ties on campus do not translate into apparent pathways toward gainful employment in the outside political sphere in the same way that their right-leaning peers' activism is rewarded by the outside organizations that support and mentor them. Much like their conservative classmates, several of our leftist and liberal interviewees said they were interested in pursuing some form of politically engaged work after college. The problem is that students on the left could not see a clear path with identifiable steps for converting their activism into an occupation. In chapter 4, we saw that AEI makes an impressive commitment to connecting undergraduates like Amanda to its scholars and outside policymakers, while Ariel and Josephine were confident that their involvement with Turning Point and PragerU could be stepping stones to careers as pundits or campaign operatives. We did not hear the same optimism among progressive activists.

Madeleine, a leader of UA's Young Democrats, thought the problem lies with her party not providing enough funding to cultivate the next generation of leaders. The DNC "doesn't have enough money" and "they can't pay their interns enough," she told us. When asked if she thinks conservatives are better positioned than she is for jobs directly out of college, she said that she believes the right is "more organized, and I think it's because they're paying their people more," and they run their organization "more like a business than a volunteer organization. I mean, the president of the College Republicans, from what I'm aware, makes almost $80,000." Shaking her head, she repeated, "The national president makes almost $80,000 a year. [. . .] Like, that's his career!"[30] Growing more annoyed, she added, "The president of College Dems, nationally, is a good friend of mine, and it's a volunteer position." She is "doing that from the goodness of her heart."[31] Madeline's concerns echo those of the past president of CDA we interviewed. As we already saw, he also expressed concern over next steps for liberals, a situation that even he—with his connections to the DNC—was grappling with. "There aren't employment opportunities for me," he said. From his vantage point, the DNC needed to start helping "funnel people into employment opportunities" after they have spent "four or five years working" for the party while they were in college.

Coming from the far left, Isaac spoke of his personal experience not making ends meet, and wondered how he, and especially low-income activists, will put food on the table and afford rent in the future. "I'm planning on staying in organizing," he said. But "right now, it's hard to just do grassroots organizing all the time because I am 20 years old, and I am broke. It's infeasible to spend all of my summers just doing organizing." Expanding on this theme, he told us that radical organizing is "very inaccessible to those who can't support themselves on their own. A lot of the national-level organizers I know that live in DC, half of them come from families with trust funds. Who can afford to just work for free for a year? No one can do that unless you were born with money." Madeleine and Isaac put their fingers on what other progressive students also noted: leftist and liberal students who cannot afford to work without pay are being cut out of the deal. We did not hear this on the right; in fact, we heard the opposite. Several of the right-leaning students we talked with were bullish about jumping onto a career track provided through the conservative channel. Even in volunteer posts such as PragerFORCE, they felt confident that they were making connections that could be parlayed into salaried positions once they were out of college. Whether the opportunities on the right will actually pay off for these students is not something we can confirm with our data. But the fact that conservatives believe so deeply in the benefits of the outside conservative channel, while leftists and liberals do not, helps us understand students' relationships with the inside and outside channels to which they have access.

Aside from worrying about a shortfall in paid positions, progressives have a harder time identifying what a career pathway in politics looks like in the first place. Jerod said he is "heading to DC to work for a Jewish social justice organization" as a "one-year legislative assistant" directly out of college. But when asked what he would be doing after that first year, Jerod responded, "No clue." Dexter shared his frustration about not being able to get his foot in the door in the policy world. "I've been interviewing for a couple of political communication jobs, which look super interesting because of my political experience," and "they fit in well" with his interest in voting rights. But when those applications failed to go anywhere, possibly because he had only a bachelor's degree, Dexter began to consider going to graduate school. "It's one of those catch-22s," he said, "where the grad schools want students with experience in policy," while "the think tanks in DC really want graduate students." Making matters worse, from his point of view, is that there are "a lot of openings right now with conservative-leaning or Republican think tanks" in the DC area. He added, "I feel like they always do a better job at getting younger students engaged in the policy process. For Democrats, I don't feel like there's that much available." Piper told us that she had applied for "foreign policy think tank positions in DC," but had not "gotten any offers yet." She then went on, "I'm also looking at some intelligence career options and maybe a political campaign, I don't know. I wish I knew what to tell you. I've got a month before I graduate, but, yeah, I'm still trying to figure it out." More of the conservatives we talked with believed that they could rely on the outside channel to jump-start their careers immediately after they completed their bachelor's degrees; leftists and liberals felt little such assurance.

One career avenue mentioned by a few progressives, which we see much less frequently among conservatives, is returning to their universities after graduation, filling positions in such units as multicultural centers and student affairs. Although we have very few cases to point to, our data suggest that some undergraduates who worked as interns in these institutional spaces during college translate that experience into their early adult careers. Jeri and Sam, at CU's Environmental Center, are alumnae of the university, and they were activists involved with the center as undergraduates in the mid-2000s. While both Sam and Jeri were happy to be back on campus (during our interview they drolly cited the lyrics from the Eagles' "Hotel California": "You can check out anytime you like, but you can never leave"), this is far from a guaranteed pathway for undergraduates wishing to follow in their footsteps, since the number of activists dwarfs the number of available positions in university centers. A few progressive students pointed out another way of heading back to campus, saying that they might seek doctoral degrees, as seen earlier in Jerod's comments. As the sociologist Neil Gross shows, it is students on the left who are disproportionately attracted to the professoriate, especially in the humanities and social sciences. Conservatives, by contrast, are less likely to entertain the option of academia.[32]

Overall, looking at our data, we see activists on the left as having to craft more of a do-it-yourself pathway into politics, advocacy, and policy-making. Whereas some of our most active recent graduates on the right expected to continue to make their way in the interlocking outside organizational terrain of the conservative channel—through both internship and summer job opportunities, and eventually onto career ladders in government, policy, politics, or punditry—there is less certainty for progressive students.

CONCLUSION

In this chapter and in chapter 4, we have used our outside-inside approach to examine the conservative and progressive channels of student activism. On the right, national organizations are unified in a sense of urgency for recruiting and grooming young political talent. And, armed with formidable financial resources, they enjoy considerable success in pulling students off campus. Through internships, summer programs, conferences, social media content, and the promise of career possibilities, organizations give students experiences that lead to a sense of closeness with higher education's critics and breed cynicism about their own universities: that their college neglects their interests or, worse, tries to indoctrinate them to a progressive worldview. This creates tension on campus, which is particularly apparent when students involved with national organizations like Turning Point or PragerU try to agitate peers through provocative tactics.

Progressive students, on the other hand, have less access to well-funded national organizations. Collegians' support for progressive causes, along with a willingness on the part of activists to personally finance their own training and mobilization efforts, are generally taken for granted. But this organizational deficit is offset by left-leaning students' embeddedness on their campuses. Because of this, Greg Lukianoff and Jonathan Haidt warn us, progressives no longer have their perspectives challenged in academic settings. Rigorous intellectual debate has given way to "coddling."[33] As we have seen in this chapter, students on the left do assume that most of their professors, peers, and school officials agree with them politically. Staff help guide them to think about the goals of their activism and the means to achieve those goals. They participate in meetings called by administrators. Having talked with progressive students, however, we find the coddling perspective to be an oversimplification. There are strengths and weaknesses in both channels.

When compared to right-leaning students who benefit from national networks of richly resourced organizations and donors, activists on the left—as entrenched on campus as they may be—often come to believe that faculty and administrators are willing to work with them on their forward-looking projects, but not beyond the point of minimal institutional change. Specifically, because they must rely on actors operating from within their university for support, student demands often run into dead ends or are rerouted in less radical directions. In this respect, we might think of progressive students not so much as coddled, but as oddly isolated in their channel. This is compounded by the fact that much of the outside organizing on the left is geared toward voter registration drives, electing candidates, and supporting a variety of referenda. This type of work on college campuses is vital to the progressive movement, but it is very different from the multifaceted approach we see among conservative organizations, which builds identities and allegiances well beyond electoral politics.

What is more, leftists and liberals are often on their own when it comes to developing political careers after graduation. While they can find internships with national organizations and may take positions in multicultural centers and student affairs offices, or even aspire to become professors, their pathways outside the university—both while they are enrolled in college and when they enter the post-college labor market—are murky and financially precarious. There is a glaring irony in the left adhering to a mobilization model that so clearly disadvantages collegians unable to self-fund their activities. This has consequences for the long-term stability of the progressive channel for student activism, since participants would ideally have an easy path into work that is both politically purposeful and reasonably compensated. Would-be leaders of the next generation of leftist and liberal activists are not being ushered into careers by their elders to the same extent as their conservative peers, nor do these politically engaged students feel they are truly being listened to by administrators. Often, they feel adrift. And, as a consequence, a lot of talented young activists are cast aside.

CHAPTER 6

The Politics of Speech on Campus

Less than a week after the 2017 presidential inauguration of Donald Trump, professional provocateur Milo Yiannopoulos gave a presentation to a near-capacity crowd in the 400-seat auditorium of the Mathematics Building at CU. At that point, Milo had already been making waves in American popular culture for quite a while.[1] His status as an outspoken editor at the right-wing website Breitbart News catapulted him to stardom in youthful conservative circles. Milo is known for revving up his fan base by heaping vitriol on feminists, immigrants, the LGBTQ+ community, Muslims, and many more. While his proponents describe him as a biting satirist, Milo's numerous detractors claim he is a threat to civil discourse. In the weeks leading up to his talk at CU, multiple petitions circulated among students, faculty, and staff demanding that the school cancel the event. More than 2,000 people signed on to these initiatives, but Chancellor Philip DiStefano stood by what he felt was the university's obligation to the First Amendment.[2]

Milo's visit to Boulder would turn out to be tranquil compared to some of his other, more infamous speaking engagements. At the University of Washington, five days before his CU date, angry demonstrators threw bricks, and a man was critically wounded by a gunshot during the melee. Then, a week after he left CU, a violent uproar canceled Milo's talk at the University of California Berkeley. Among conservative pundits, the scenes of black-clad protesters in masks setting fires and clashing with authorities serves as a continuing reference point in critiques about higher education. At CU, Milo's presence brought out a couple hundred demonstrators and a cadre of police officers in riot gear. However, there were no arrests, and only three people were ticketed for minor offenses.[3]

Milo's fame has faded significantly since the days surrounding the 2016 election.[4] At the time we were interviewing activists, however, he was *the* figure on everyone's mind when it came to issues about speech on campus. While the college clubs that invited him to their schools rarely (if ever) supported all his controversial talking points, many right-leaning students were energized by his gleeful dismissal of propriety in defense of "Western culture." Progressives, on the other hand, saw him as an exemplar of how the First Amendment can be used as armor in a direct assault on historically underrepresented populations.[5] Milo's significance—for those who love him and those who loathe him—comes from his cheeky ability to pit the virtue of free expression against the grace of inclusion. Of course, the underlying tension between these two deeply held cultural values (and the fierce battles over which side to favor) is nothing new.[6] The ways in which students engage with provocations and discuss speech rights in relation to diversity, though, are pivotal components of campus politics. These struggles represent how young people are trying to define the appropriate boundaries for participating in our democratic society.

In this chapter, we explore how activists conceptualize the right to "free speech" on their campuses. We focus on Milo—along with similarly inflammatory figures on the right such as Ann Coulter, Dinesh D'Souza, Sebastian Gorka, Charles Murray, and Ben Shapiro—because of what he (and others) represented during the early years of the Trump administration. These firebrands make otherwise amorphous philosophical positions tangible, and the intricacies of what free expression and inclusion mean for college-aged activists are revealed in such talk. For conservatives, this is about maintaining a position in which speakers are given wide latitude in their expressions, no matter how noxious the content. For progressives who contemplate the physical and psychological consequences of "hate speech," this can mean favoring formalized restrictions on certain words and symbols. While these divisions are already well-known,[7] our interviews show how the collegians on the front lines of these debates conceptualize the stakes and think about the consequences. Even with the Trump presidency over, we see little reason to believe that these controversies are behind us.

WHAT IS FREE SPEECH?

Before getting to how our interviewees chewed on speech issues, it is important to give a brief outline of the legal debates on the subject and how motivated reasoning muddies the ideological waters. For starters, the US Supreme Court has spent decades removing speech restrictions.[8] The prevailing assumption in American legal thought is that the rights of speakers to express themselves outweigh most counterclaims about the potential harm caused by derogatory or hostile words and symbols. Public universities are bound by these court rulings because they are state-run institutions. While private schools have greater legal flexibility,[9] they often follow precedent set elsewhere. The requirement that public universities adhere to the First Amendment holds true even if a majority of the campus community wants some speakers or forms of speech curtailed. Erwin Chemerinsky and Howard Gillman are two of the nation's preeminent thinkers on constitutional law, as well as co-directors of the University of California National Center for Free Speech and Civic Engagement. They bluntly affirm what can be called an absolutist interpretation of the First Amendment. As stated in their aptly titled book, *Free Speech on Campus*: "Our central thesis is that all ideas and views should be able to be expressed on college campuses, no matter how offensive or how uncomfortable they make people feel."[10]

The Supreme Court's widening protections of freedom of expression derive from the position that democracies cannot function without autonomous citizens endowed with a right to openly debate controversial issues. Since censorship stifles debate, absolutists claim, people must be able to pursue knowledge and state their opinions—even when such inquiries and viewpoints are unpopular or taboo. Further, absolutists tell us that unfettered speech within the public sphere trains citizens to recognize bad arguments and gives people the ability to offer reasoned retorts. Ultimately, an unencumbered exchange of expressions (good, bad, honorable, or despicable) is supposed to lay the groundwork for fully developed, critical individuals. These views are most notably summarized in Justice Oliver Wendell Holmes's glowing depiction of the First Amendment creating a marketplace for the "free trade of ideas."[11]

For all the purported benefits of free expression, there is also a long line of scholarship critiquing First Amendment absolutism. According to many legal thinkers, American jurisprudence simply gives far too little credence to how words and symbols can reinforce social injustices. The law professor Charles Lawrence, for example, argues that in the face of ongoing structural inequality, the court's recent deference to bigoted uses of the First Amendment (as opposed to considering the intentions of the Fourteenth Amendment) is nothing short of state-sanctioned racism. Thus, against absolutism, there is what the critical race scholar Richard Delgado calls First Amendment legal realism. Realists assert that expressions degrading or humiliating to others because of some essential part of their identity (that is, "hate speech") fall outside the realm of ideas worth protecting. Such words and symbols, we are informed, should not be circulating freely in the public sphere.[12]

In contrast to absolutists, who see unfettered expression (even vile forms of it) as part of the democratic ideal, realists hold that hate speech represses civic participation through intimidation and degradation.[13] To this end, the philosopher Jeremy Waldron proposes that the court consider hate speech as a type of group libel, making it unprotected by the First Amendment.[14] The underlying assumption is that the good of the collective must be given greater consideration than the wants of individual speakers. Further, from this perspective, colleges and universities—public or private—have a moral obligation to prevent their campuses from becoming "hostile educational environments" for students most at risk of the negative consequences of noxious content.[15]

While the debates over speech rights among lawyers and philosophers will help shape future judicial rulings, such abstractions inevitably take a different form in the court of public opinion. That is, absolutist and realist positions on the First Amendment become part of ordinary people's legal consciousness,[16] and are thus incorporated into the political disagreements dividing the nation. In the process, high-minded ideals get dragged into the self-serving goals of partisanship. Intentionally or not, politically motivated reasoning will tilt activists toward seeing constitutional affordances in a manner that benefits their mobilization efforts while understanding constitutional limits in a way detrimental to those they are organizing against.[17]

In the not-so-distant past, for instance, First Amendment absolutism was associated with progressives. The Free Speech Movement of the 1960s—an amalgamation of collegiate leftism and civil rights foment centered in Berkeley—is the archetype. Then, as the once radical perspective of the Free Speech Movement became mainstream, conservative activists began refashioning their arguments within a framework of individual expression protected by the First Amendment. Following that, many on the left began seeing the First Amendment as a reactionary tool and started to conceptualize expansive speech rights as antithetical to promoting inclusiveness in society. At the far edges of radical activism today, the journalist P. E. Moskowitz describes a "fuck free speech movement" emerging on college campuses as a response to the divisive tactics of speakers like Milo. The upshot here is that, following the legal scholar Stanley Fish, any discussion of speech rights is more about how individuals make use of convenient symbols to support a broader set of ideological and partisan preferences, and less about foundational constitutional concerns.[18]

In the following pages we look first to how the conservatives we interviewed made sense of speech rights, and we then turn to progressives. We finish by considering how the different channels of student activism have carved the matter of free expression and inclusion into the contemporary political landscape.

CONSERVATIVES AND FREE EXPRESSION

Chris, the American Enterprise Institute (AEI) Executive Council member we met in chapter 4, sat down with us in fall 2017. This was a little less than a year after Milo's CU talk. Chris was in the midst of finalizing plans for a visit by Charles Murray and was keenly aware that the event could spark outrage, or possibly violence, at his school. Despite his vaunted post at AEI, Murray has never outrun the controversies surrounding his role in supporting theories of racial differences in intelligence. Eight months prior to our meeting with Chris, for example, Middlebury College students—furious that a "eugenicist" was on their campus—temporarily halted a lecture by Murray. Fearing further disruptions, the school had Murray finish his talk via a live video stream broadcast from a locked room without an audience. Later in the day, Murray and his companions were physically attacked by a smaller group of protesters as they were leaving the school.[19]

Mulling over why Murray was a good choice to bring in as a speaker at CU (especially with many students at the school still smarting from Milo's visit), Chris bundled together several ideas. "You don't learn new things by staying within your own little bubble, you truly don't." He continued, "I hope that students realize" they would be "shutting down the cornerstone of American freedom, which is free speech—not hate speech, but *free* speech" by de-platforming Murray. "This gentleman," Chris added, "is not saying anything hateful. It is just something that people disagree with." Chris then indicated his openness to protesters. "You can, of course, shout down the speakers. Fine. You have free speech too." Then he issued a warning: "But what is going to happen is your tuition is going to be raised" to pay for exorbitant security fees, "because we are going to keep bringing these people, and we are going to keep broadening [your] minds. If you want to have this hold-your-hand—you know, really lovey-dovey, 'Kumbaya'—college education, I don't think a big university [is] your place to be. So, I would hope that students here recognize that." In the end, Murray's CU talk went off without a hitch. It did, however, involve extra security measures and a police detail.

Chris's retort to the hypothetical protesters at his school hit on the key issues for nearly all of the conservatives we interviewed. First, Chris made it clear that he believed free expression is a nonnegotiable right— the "cornerstone of American freedom." Second, he wanted to interject rightist perspectives into college life. This was about exposing students to heterodox viewpoints—which would force progressives out of their ideological bubbles and would broaden their minds. Third, Chris denounced an expansionist definition of hate speech. Murray saying something people disagree with (such as his analysis of race and intelligence) does not, to Chris's mind, make it hateful. Fourth, he saw de-platforming as an occasion to reaffirm commitment to the First Amendment, not to back down from it ("we are going to keep bringing these people"). Each of these issues warrants further discussion.

For conservative students, like Chris, political identities are now pinned to free expression. Of our 35 right-leaning respondents (including 2 center-right moderates), 29 spoke directly about Milo. The controversies surrounding him did not arise in 6 interviews. Although one of these 6, Jessica, specifically supported regulating hate speech generally, she was the only conservative in our sample to do so. Tony and Steve were 2 activists who rejected Milo by name. They did this by drawing distinctions between the desired intellectual atmosphere of a university and speakers only interested in "triggering" students. However, both said they would support other provocative figures (like Coulter, Murray, Shapiro, etc.) coming to campus. The remaining 27 conservative students pulled no punches on the matter: Milo had every right to speak at their schools—even as some claimed to personally dislike him and would prefer that their clubs not invite him.

This shows the resonance of what can be called a rightist script for free speech among our interviewees—a script that has been produced by outside organizations such as Turning Point USA and the Goldwater Institute (a libertarian think tank), media outlets like Fox News, individual politicians like Trump, and of course pundits such as Milo. In fact, Milo has tried (only half-facetiously) to bill himself as the leader of a new free speech movement.[20] In Milo's rendition, it is the voices of conservatives being muted on campuses, the result of a blind faith in "social justice" that is intellectually stifling. Our interviewee Miles, for example, saw his own populism combining "conservative slash libertarian" values. When asked about these two ideological strands, he explained, "The two movements are being pushed together because, all of a sudden, conservatives are becoming *very* concerned with free speech, and, for libertarians, that's the number one issue." As Layla told us, "Republicans believe in free speech," and having speakers de-platformed is "why Republicans have felt as though we have been under attack on college campuses." Or, in Billy's words, "I have a fundamental belief that every person should have the right to say whatever they want." Likewise, Audrey told us, "Even if you disagree with this person, even if the things he is saying actually are abhorrent," he has "a right to say it."[21] For all of the tactical differences separating the conservative ideological strands (see chapter 2), speech rights are an area where libertarians, traditionalists, libertarian-leaning conservatives, and populists stand united for a common cause.

PROMOTING A MARKETPLACE OF IDEAS

Underpinning right-leaning students' First Amendment absolutism is their understanding of how speech rights can be used to promote unpopular (that is, conservative) viewpoints at their schools. This, of course, is the primary justification for supporting free expression, whether from the left or the right. For truth to be revealed and for ideas to be robust, divergent perspectives must circulate throughout the public sphere. To limit speech only to prevailing wisdom and current sensibilities suppresses intellectual advancement. We see such Holmesian sentiments in our data. As Ava told us, "The point of college is to educate people and bring other people's ideas to the forefront of students' minds so they can view all there is to the world." Ava said this in defending College Republicans at UC Berkeley inviting Milo to speak. Similarly, Joaquin explained why he would support Milo giving a talk. "One reason [my clubs] would be interested in inviting him is just to hear his point and to get his point out there, whether we agree with it or not." Joaquin concluded by stating, "I think it would be a good way to facilitate conversation at UVA."

As a corollary to wanting divergent views offered at their schools, none of the right-leaning students we talked with claimed they had an interest in censoring progressives. To the contrary, they purported to have an interest in hearing what the other side had to say. As Sofia told us, "If I don't agree with a speaker, I'll go to the event, then I'll ask questions. I don't try to shut them down by yelling at them," adding "I think I probably go to more events that I disagree with than I agree with." Or, as Silas said, "I have no love for Black Lives Matter. I think it's a pretty bad organization"; but if a Black Lives Matter activist like DeRay McKesson wanted to come speak at UNC, Silas continued, then he felt McKesson should be allowed to do so. "I would even be very interested in listening."

Following the rightist script for free speech, our interviewees positioned themselves as being open to dialogue with the other side—no matter how different or wrong they might believe their interlocutor to be. At the same time, a few also expressed a desire to show their disagreement with some speakers who have, or might eventually, come to their schools. To a hypothetical visit by McKesson, for example, Warren told us, "If I thought I could get the numbers, I would have a very respectful, probably quiet, protest across the street." Further, he assured us, "I wouldn't try to shut them down. I don't care." He followed this by stating, "Obama came here. I didn't protest." But even if a protest were to happen, as when members of Turning Point held signs outside former Black Panther Bobby Seale's talk at CU (see chapter 1), that was not the same thing as asking the chancellor to disinvite him or using force to try to de-platform him.

This is not to claim that conservatives never seek to stop figures on the left from giving talks or to silence professors they consider to be radical.[22] They do, and over the last handful of years there have been numerous progressive faculty who have been scrutinized on Turning Point's Professor Watchlist and, for many years before that, on the Leadership Institute's Campus Reform "watchdog" site—whether it be for the content of a lecture or a post to social media. Tenured positions have been threatened and jobs have been lost. Disinvitation efforts from the right (while less common than those coming from the left) are also more successful.[23] But in the free-form interview setting we created for them, this is not how right-leaning students chose to frame the issues and construct an idealized image of themselves. The rightist script for free speech claims to champion nearly all forms of expression, and this is very different from how progressives discuss these same issues.

HATE SPEECH AS A RED HERRING

The preceding two points about free expression (that it is nonnegotiable and there needs to be a robust marketplace of ideas) lead into the third—and most contentious—issue in how conservative students conceptualize the politics of speech on their campuses. This is about the operationalization of hate speech. In his description of Murray, for example, Chris intimated that *real* hate speech might warrant regulation. However, he did not believe that even a firebrand like Milo, much less a scholar like Murray, qualified for such disapprobation. Likewise, when we asked Charlotte about talks sponsored by her clubs upsetting progressive students at UNC, she replied, "Well, I think, depending on who you ask, the definition of hate speech is going to be very different. I believe many things liberals [label as] hate speech are not hate speech. It might flare you up a little bit, but it's not instigating violence." She went on to state that she believes "the definition of hate speech is very ambiguous, and I definitely believe in the right to free speech." As long as you are not advocating the physical harm of others, she explained, "then you should be able to say what you want to say."

Charlotte's point of view was representative. Whatever hate speech might actually be, conservative activists insisted it must be narrowly defined. Further, a few of our respondents on the right went so far as to dismiss the existence of hate speech outright. Maxwell, for instance, asserted, "Hate speech isn't a thing." Similarly, Silas, the same student who said he was interested in hearing McKesson speak at UNC, doubled down on the marketplace metaphor by telling us, "I don't have a problem with racist comments." They are part of "the free market of ideas," Silas said. And, as alluded to already, the Supreme Court has decisively come down in support of how conservative activists approach the concept of hate speech. That is, expressions degrading of or humiliating to others because of some essential part of their identity remain protected speech. Further, parsing out where legitimate intellectual inquiry ends and an attack on another's dignity begins is, as Charlotte implied, subjective—with students on the left and right drawing very different conclusions on the matter.

PROTEST BEGETS PROVOCATION

Finally, because of their broad interpretation of First Amendment protections, their belief in promoting heterodoxy in higher education, and their doubts about the validity of labeling speech as hateful, most of the right-leaning students we spoke with were contemptuous of the disinvitation and de-platforming strategies of progressives. More to the point, they told us these efforts only fueled their interest in hosting more incendiary speakers in the future. Audrey, for instance, found Milo despicable. She had previously argued against her College Republican chapter hosting him. But at the time of our interview, she said she was warming to the idea. "I feel like I'd be more receptive to it now, just because I feel like the [campus] culture has gone so heavily [toward] suppressing free speech."

Audrey then explained that if UVA students were to protest someone like Ben Shapiro, she might respond by ramping up the controversy. Shapiro, a youthful Harvard Law School graduate, founder of the right-wing website The Daily Wire, former editor-at-large for Breitbart News, and host of an eponymous podcast, was extremely well-regarded by conservative interviewees at all four campuses we visited. His brash style of argumentation has also resulted in a litany of controversies.[24] As Audrey quipped to us, "I'd be like, 'Yeah? If you're going to think someone like [Shapiro] is an awful, terrible human, let's bring someone that's actually awful and terrible!'" (by which she meant Milo).

Not long before our visit to North Carolina, the UNC College Republicans hosted Sebastian Gorka, a former deputy assistant to the president and strategist in the Trump White House who went on to become a frequent Fox News commentator. Gorka has been tied to far-right groups in his native Hungary, and he has generated outrage for comments that conflate Islam with terrorism.[25] Andy offered an insightful (and extremely tepid) review of his club's recent guest. "Gorka was a more expensive speaker than we would perhaps have liked. But because of his national recognition, and because he is a controversial speaker, he appealed to a lot of members of College Republicans, so that's who we ended up going with." Andy recalled that the event was protested by progressive groups, and that "there were a lot of angry responses leading up to it as well," which he conceded were "pretty legitimate grievances. He wouldn't have been my first choice as a speaker." However, Andy supported the event, because "I think he did provide some insights in coming to campus, not because I agreed with anything he said, but because he is sort of a representative of the administration that we have right now." He then added, "I think you have to listen to people like that, even if you really don't like what they're saying and what they stand for."

In this statement, Andy pointed to the fact that he did not personally agree with what Gorka represents, but that the club's desire to invite him derived in part from the fact he was certain to generate an angry response from progressives ("because he is a controversial speaker, he appealed to a lot of members"). And Silas, another UNC College Republican, was transparent on this matter. "I enjoyed [Gorka] speaking here. That was fun because we had a lot of protesters show up."

With our UNC interviews coming on the heels of that talk, it seems clear many conservatives at the school were dismissive of "hate speech" claims because of how progressives responded to his invitation. Right-leaning activists (even those who, like Andy, were not enamored of Gorka's résumé) felt students on the left were cynically leveling invectives for political gain. As Warren explained, "Folks were like, 'He's a Nazi.'" But Gorka "spent a good amount of time in that speech talking about why he's not a Nazi. Anyway, two years before, we had Ben Shapiro" on campus, and "folks were like, 'He's a Nazi.'" In other words, for Warren, Shapiro is a respectable figure (who is also Jewish), and so Warren found the accusations against Shapiro absurd[26]—which then deflected the power of any critique against Gorka as engaging in hate speech.

PROGRESSIVES AND INCLUSION

Carte blanche support for free expression was rare among the left-leaning students we talked with. Progressives were also much less certain than their conservative peers about the protections afforded by the First Amendment, despite the fact that civil liberties have long been seen as a progressive cause. Instead, activists on the left were split over figures like Milo having a legal right to speak at their schools. Some, like Donato, were positive that the Constitution does not protect hate speech. "These people: 'Free speech! Free speech! I want to hear their opinions!' Yeah, well, their opinions cause distress and harm to members of the student body. Why are [administrators] letting them on campus?" Donato went further: "Their free speech should not be protected," because "it is hate speech." And, he asserted, talks by controversial figures are "not protected by the Constitution," because they are "causing distress to our students." Other students felt certain their schools could not simply ban incendiary speakers like Milo. Many were unsure.

Beyond the issue of legality, there was often a sense of moral ambiguity over giving individuals unchecked free expression. Even if left-leaning students acknowledged that the courts routinely protect the use of derogatory or hostile words and symbols, a few still insisted that it needed to be prohibited on their campuses anyway. In discussing these matters, progressives frequently bounced between contradictory preferences in how administrators and political clubs should approach the thorny topic of hate speech. This makes it much harder to stake out a definitive progressive position about free expression on college campuses. And, while the First Amendment was given support in abstract terms by most of those on the left, nearly every progressive we interviewed placed caveats on their generic endorsements of speech rights. The political scientist Jeffrey Herbst disparagingly refers to this as "the right to non-offensive speech."[27]

We propose that this lack of certainty (along with the impulse to place a variety of restrictions on First Amendment protections) is due in part to the fact that national progressive organizations, generally, have only been reactive to campus speech events sponsored by the right. The same could be said of the leadership of colleges and universities. Collectively, they have not been proactive in helping students think through freedom of expression issues. While organizations such as the American Civil Liberties Union (ACLU) and PEN America have for decades been on the front lines fighting for civil liberties, until very recently they have not shown the same dedication as conservative organizations to outreach programs and messaging for undergraduates. Colleges and universities, for their part, send conflicting messages, with speech codes and principles of community encouraging respectful speech on the one hand, and statements of academic freedom and open inquiry promoting unfettered free speech on the other. The lack of clarity around speech issues has left progressive students without an equivalently deployable cultural and political script compared to the right.[28] What is more, the off-and-on close-knit relationships administrators forge with progressives—and particularly with underrepresented populations—may be perceived by those students as an implied promise from school officials to provide protections from hateful speech. So, when that assumed protection is seen as missing during a contentious event, it amplifies the feelings of harm experienced by the campus community.

AMBIGUITY, NOT ABSOLUTISM

In total, 33 of our 42 left-leaning students (including a center-left moderate) weighed in specifically about Milo's right to speak at their universities. Our other 9 interviews with progressives relied on different speech controversies, or respondents avoided concrete answers. Of those discussing Milo, 16 claimed his expressions are allowed by the Constitution (no matter how vile). Another 8 asserted that he has no such legal protections. Five of the remaining 9 were unsure what the law affords, and 4 gave contradictory answers by simultaneously deferring to an expansive definition of the First Amendment and indicating that they believed administrators were empowered to overturn Milo's invitations. Among those affirming Milo's speech rights, Katherine still implied that school officials had the jurisdiction to disinvite him. The other 15 discussed it as an unfortunate reality with which activists had to contend, and not the "cornerstone of American freedom" proudly touted by conservative-minded Chris.

Free expression and inclusion are additional places in our data where liberals and leftists distinguished themselves from each other. Liberals were more likely to affirm the constitutionality of speakers' freedom of expression than were those further to the left. While none of the progressives we interviewed discussed First Amendment issues in the absolutist terms of conservatives, leftists were more pessimistic about the utility of allowing free trade in noxious content. Instead, they framed expansive speech rights as a threat to social equity. In fact, none of the far-left students we talked with about Milo were certain he had constitutional protections to speak at their schools (by comparison, 70 percent of liberals said Milo did have that right). Among leftists, 7 out of 10 wanted him banned from campus; only 5 out 29 of liberals felt that way. These differences represent a significant rift among progressives concerning how activism should be done. For example, we can think back to chapter 3, when Melissa rebuked the far left for trying to de-platform a Republican congressman, as opposed to just holding a "peaceful counter-protest."

We spoke with Pierce in spring 2018 and asked him about Gorka's visit to UNC the previous semester. He told us that his group, Young Democratic Socialists of America (YDSA), was part of the opposition. YDSA "felt we really had to go out and oppose" Gorka, because he supports "an extreme right-wing neo-Nazi group in Hungary." As a result, YDSA (and many others) showed up at the venue and "made a lot of noise." When asked what the goal of the protest was, Pierce indicated that he would like to have prevented the talk from happening. At the same time, though, he did not think administrators should have formally disinvited Gorka. Instead, Pierce appreciated his peers having the opportunity to mobilize against the event. He described such confrontations as the essence of democracy. As Pierce explained, "That's my free speech, to show up with a sign." When we pointed out that YDSA did not quietly hold signs, but had hoped to shout over Gorka, Pierce quickly retorted, "Yeah, and free shouting as well. This is part of it."

Pierce's comments reveal the two key aspects of how today's progressive students are processing free expression. First, there is an assessment of whether certain words and symbols are too odious to be allowed into the public sphere at all. This is why Pierce linked Gorka to neo-Nazis—it implied that Gorka is a person who traffics in hate speech.[29] By extension, it justified efforts to de-platform him. Where to draw the line between free speech and hate speech is debated among progressives, but the potential of derogatory or hostile words and symbols to cause serious harm is not in doubt. This can be contrasted with the rightist script that dismisses such claims as antithetical to the mission of higher education.[30] Second, there is the matter of how properly to respond to incendiary speakers in one's midst. Some progressive students take a stance not terribly different from their conservative peers. They believe in strong constitutional protections for speech, and they argue against efforts to silence unpopular expressions. Others appear to consistently support limiting the types of speech currently covered by the First Amendment. A sizable portion of the progressives we talked with, however, cannot be easily slotted into either of these two camps.

We will explore in detail both aspects of limiting free expression brought up by Pierce. However, while our conservative interviewees presented a more or less united front on this issue, there is less agreement among progressives, and quite a bit of internal contradiction. Students like Pierce, for example, acknowledge others' legal speech rights while simultaneously championing efforts to physically block such speech from happening. This is technically in line with the First Amendment, since it does not rely on censorship from the state. But it falls well outside the spirit of a Holmesian vision for a marketplace of ideas. Pierce also ruled Milo uniquely out of bounds, and said he would support administrators' intervention in such a case. Further, it was quite common to hear left-leaning collegians voice paradoxical preferences—simultaneously asserting the democratic virtues of expansive speech rights and wanting those in authority to use their powers to curtail a wide range of words and symbols. Edward, for example, first claimed that Milo, or anyone looking to "cause an uproar," should not be allowed on campuses. Yet, a few moments later, Edward shifted gears and asserted that civil debate was the best way to counter noxious content. Likewise, Donato also transitioned from outrage over the lack of administrative oversight to implying a preference for dialogue and peaceful protest.

PLACING RESTRICTIONS ON VILE SPEECH

The absolutism of the rightist script for free speech has caused confusion on the left. Polls show that free expression, as an idea, remains sacrosanct for most students, but progressives also feel that using derogatory or hostile words and symbols is wrong.[31] Which is to say, the leftists and liberals we talked with liked the principle of protecting all speech, but most had a compunction to prevent some iterations of it. Such contradictory impulses are underscored in many colleges' and universities' principles of community, such that a statement like "We affirm the right to freedom of expression" might be followed by "We are committed to the highest standards of civility and decency toward all." Left-leaning students also disagree on how to define hate speech, as well as how to respond to its existence. Even legal experts fail to provide clear guidance on where *exactly* to draw the line on the use of derogatory or hostile words and symbols.[32] This often seems to be an intractable problem, so it is no wonder collegians wrestle with it. The complexity of this issue only serves to affirm the potency of conservative activists using incendiary speakers as a means for opposing the liberal hegemony at their schools. Such a tactic not only disseminates rightist ideas, it also disrupts progressive cohesion, and unsettles cultural sensibilities by dividing opinions over free expression and inclusion.[33] The ensuing controversies make college students, faculty, and administrators look like bad-faith actors—an image that plays well with other right-leaning discourses castigating higher education.

Thinking about the need to prohibit certain types of expressions, Vanessa offered an instructive take on the matter. When asked about the diversity of viewpoints at CU, she said, "I think the liberal perspectives outnumber the conservative perspectives," which she felt might explain why conservatives "feel that they're being silenced. But sometimes they're being silenced for justifiable reasons." Building on the last point, Vanessa concluded, "If you say problematic things, you're going to get silenced." Taking these points to the extreme, Donovan argued that even traditional Republican positions on taxing and spending could be a form of hate speech. He discussed this in reference to a recent visit to UA by the reactionary author and filmmaker Dinesh D'Souza. Donovan told us, "Even though he doesn't overtly [claim] 'Black people are awful,' he supports economic policies [that] reinforce the stereotype that Black people are awful."

Similar to Donovan, Isaac insisted that some "rhetoric is inherently violent and inspires violence against minorities, against queer people." In keeping with this idea, he told us, "I think the limits of free speech are definitely stretched" by Milo. Likewise, Jamison pronounced, "If what you're talking about is borderline hate speech and threatening, then I think you lose the right you have to that speech." The point being, whether odious expressions are defined broadly or narrowly, there is a line beyond which many progressives believe First Amendment protections should not apply. Most importantly, fighting against those operating beyond the pale is understood as far more pertinent than questioning where the boundary itself should be placed, and this sentiment is especially apparent among the far-left activists we interviewed.[34]

THE MESSY WORK OF CENSORSHIP

When it comes to what to do about derogatory or hostile words and symbols, things get complicated. Stepping away from the absolutist position of conservatives means that progressives must contend with greater ambiguity. Milo was especially problematic because he frequently singles out specific individuals for harassment—such as his infamous Twitter assault on the comedian Leslie Jones, which precipitated his permanent ban from the platform. On college campuses, he has used photographs of ordinary people (some of whom have been in his audiences) to berate groups and causes he does not support. Such antics are the low bar set by the law professor John Palfrey for speech undeserving of tolerance. This fact influenced how at least a few left-leaning students weighed Milo's legal rights to speak on their campus.[35]

Anthony, a member of UNC's Young Democrats, explained that he did not think every "conservative speaker is a hate speaker. I think that's a fault on the left." But "I wouldn't support Milo speaking here because he does have a track record of inviting harassment onto students." For progressives like Anthony, short of personal-level attacks, incendiary speakers should be allowed. And members of the campus community have the right to peacefully voice opposition. Likewise, referring to Gorka's UNC talk, Dexter told us, "That was fine. I think what ended up happening was students protested outside." Dexter liked this approach. "It's good to protest that and be active in that, but he should have the right to speak. If somebody was against that, I'd disagree" with them.

There are many leftists and liberals, though, who were quite dubious of any legal or moral justification for conservatives giving talks at their schools. And most progressive students did not couch their objections in terms of personal-level harassment. Instead, what they found abhorrent was the political content of Milo's speeches—his criticisms of Islam, support for a border wall, disapproval of feminism, critiques of gender fluidity, embrace of White male privilege, and so on. The same holds for other speakers as well. Donato, for example, was unsure if it was even fair to distinguish between giving a platform to Murray and his data-based views (dubious as some his conclusions may be) and the unvarnished White supremacy espoused by the alt-right impresario Richard Spencer. "They have different views . . . not different views, they have different messages. [. . .] But they have similar ideas, I guess. Charles Murray just might talk a little more like a professor, and Richard Spencer fires up crowds."

In such conflations, it is not surprising that leftists like Vanessa could claim that conservatives are being "silenced for justifiable reasons." The expressions of a wide swath of speakers from the right can be suppressed because, as Isaac and Donovan explained, they *inspire* violence—not directly with their own words, but indirectly—by reinforcing existing inequalities, normalizing marginalization, and encouraging the prejudices of others.[36] As Georgia stated, Milo "crosses that line" where his message is clear. As Georgia saw it, Milo "hates these people" and he "wants them to not exist. Their existence is in some way offensive" to him. "With bringing Milo, it sets a standard." Fearing that Milo's talk amounted to a university endorsement of hate speech, Georgia went on, "So, what I'm saying is, it's all about what [should be] acceptable on this campus." Milo was not the only speaker Georgia considered out of bounds, either. Ann Coulter was another Turning Point invitee Georgia felt was "saying crazy, off-the-wall shit that doesn't translate into 'Let's have a conversation. Let's have a dialogue.' It is, 'Hey, you see that guy? Fuck that guy!' That's literally all you can glean" from what Milo and Coulter are saying. Georgia concluded their comments by telling us that when "people are emboldened by" hateful messaging, "I'm scared."

In short, a variety of conservative views (not just the overt bigotry of the alt-right) were ruled off-limits by leftists, as well as some liberals—regardless of whether these ideas were packaged in the academic language of Murray, the populist politics of Gorka and Coulter, or the caustic mockery of Milo. Further, progressives of all stripes frequently seemed internally conflicted over what should be done about the problematic speech they identified. There were some left-leaning students who exuded confidence in their positions, and several of those we talked with made eloquent arguments for and against administrators banning incendiary speakers. Leftists like Isaac and Donovan knew exactly what they believed: hate speech does not warrant protection, Supreme Court be damned. Liberals like Anthony and Dexter, on the other hand, stood firm in their general support for free expression, making moderate concessions for the potential harm created by derogatory or hostile words and symbols. Others, however, were unsure how to reconcile generic support for First Amendment principles with their desire to restrict hate speech when confronted with concrete scenarios.

Progressives often started out arguing one position only to switch their stance minutes later. The principle of free speech was widely supported in general terms. Few people wanted to identify as being "pro-censorship." Usually, preferences for restrictions only arose in non-abstract discussions—Herbst's "right to non-offensive speech." Alexa, for example, granted cultural legitimacy to free expression. But when asked about Milo, she explained, "I would say the university should say no," because "he is so poorly aligned with [our] values." And his mere presence would "incite hate." Alexa continued, altering her position slightly, "I guess the best-case scenario would be to let" speakers like Milo come, but the administration "can't actively support it." But then, a few sentences later, Alexa again claimed, "They shouldn't allow those speakers to come." Further, Alexa couched her comments about Milo in an argument for why UA should set up a student-led panel to adjudicate grievances over prospective speakers. And "if there are large amounts of outcry against any speaker," the administration should not allow the talk.

Like Alexa and many other students, Sasha initially described a hypothetical visit to UVA by Milo as "his right to free speech." He explained that he would not want to ask the administration to disinvite Milo. However, this was immediately followed by the rejoinder, "But I would hope they would do it anyway." Withholding our own judgment, we asked him if he felt these two positions were incompatible. He replied, "That's a good point. I guess I can't believe both." And after a bit more contemplation, he decided that Milo's "hateful ideas" make a disinvitation "reasonable." But then Sasha thought some more and explained that speakers should only be banned if they are a "clear and imminent danger" to the campus community. He left unstated whether Milo would or would not meet this final criterion.

MANUFACTURED DISCONTENT

Over the past five years, there has been no shortage of hand-wringing among politicians, the media, and academics over the politics of speech on campus. Some, like Herbst, have sounded alarm bells over the supposed disinterest students have in protecting free expression. This fear is what prompted Greg Lukianoff and Jonathan Haidt to write *The Coddling of the American Mind*. Others, like the political scientist Jeffrey Sachs, claim that tales of collegians turning their backs on the First Amendment are a figment of conservatives' imagination. Much of this disagreement hinges on how the different sides parse the data. Generation Z is, perhaps, uniquely intolerant of opposing viewpoints, and very few researchers have separated this group from older millennials in their surveys. The proper interpretation of support for the First Amendment in fixed-response questionnaires is equally in dispute. The cultural significance of numerically rare but highly publicized events like Murray's shout-down at Middlebury or the violent protests in Berkeley and Seattle over Milo is also unclear.[37] To this we would add the importance of distinguishing political identities. While liberals are much more reserved in their views on speech rights than conservatives, it is the far left who are really pushing to redefine the limits to the First Amendment.

What the current speech debate does make clear—and what we can see in our qualitative interviews—is that young people are grappling with how to balance living in an equitable society with speakers' freedoms, which can include individuals using their constitutional protections to undermine inclusion and diversity. Progressives are willing to limit the use of derogatory or hostile words and symbols at their schools. Conservatives, on the other hand, firmly tilt the balance in favor of speech rights, even vile instantiations of it. At the same time, none of the right-leaning students we interviewed championed objectively unfettered speech, such as granting people permission to yell "fire" in crowded theaters, slander others, or taunt their peers into fistfights. Which is to say, there was consensus between the left and the right on the necessity of restraining at least *some* words and symbols. And we heard time and again from the leaders of the conservative clubs hosting incendiary speakers that they did not personally agree with much of the inflammatory rhetoric used by their guests. To repeat Andy's reticence about his College Republican chapter paying a sizable sum of money toward Gorka's UNC visit, progressives had "pretty legitimate grievances. He wouldn't have been my first choice as a speaker." Or as Trevor, with Turning Point, told us about bringing Milo to CU, "Personally, I've never been a fan of Milo." Trevor found Milo's talks to be intellectually vacant, relying mostly on "shock tactics," which are "dumb."

The question to ask, therefore, is: how did particular types of vile speech (and the pundits engaging in it) become emblematic of collegiate conservatism? Clubs are bringing in speakers who direct their provocations toward underrepresented (and thus, uniquely vulnerable) populations. This is the free expression activists on the right have become particularly concerned with protecting, even (or especially) at the cost of offending a sizable portion of their campus communities. The link between their prerogative to support this type of speech and their conservative activism more generally burned bright in our interviews. To recall Layla one more time, "Republicans believe in free speech," and having speakers de-platformed is "why Republicans have felt as though we have been under attack on college campuses." This sentiment held true even among the members of clubs that generally avoided hosting incendiary speakers themselves.

The answer to why supporting vile speech has become such a ubiquitous part of college-level conservatism is that student-led groups are operating within a larger outside channel of activism. Many national organizations on the right see the First Amendment as a valuable tool for disrupting liberal hegemony in higher education. Ultimately, it is the influence of outside players—such as the Leadership Institute, Turning Point, Young America's Foundation, PragerU, and Young Americans for Liberty, as well as local donors helping to fund their preferred campus clubs—that make speech uniquely effective in reactionary mobilization. Some of these organizations, like the Leadership Institute and Turning Point, maintain a stable of speakers ready to headline events put on by student-led groups.[38] There is also ample help to subsidize the costs of hosting such figures. Milo's campus tours, for example, were underwritten by the hedge fund billionaire Robert Mercer. These organizations can provide legal counsel when necessary, too.[39]

Perhaps most importantly, national organizations and wealthy benefactors set the tone for what types of activism are appropriate for club members, and they provide a ready-made and consistent script that right-leaning students use to defend their provocations.[40] The incentive structure in campus politics is increasingly oriented toward confrontation, especially on the right. One faculty advisor to several conservative clubs at UA explained the multiple components of the strategy, from initially causing a stir to eventually presenting a burnished résumé that looks good in the realm of right-leaning politics:

> Press is always good. You always want that. [. . .] If somebody's going to do something, [the clubs] want to get it on YouTube. [. . .] So, you pick speakers that [are] creating something that will be explosive. [. . .] It's not even about issues anymore. There's a conflict, and [students are] behaving in that field of conflict, and that helps to get press. [. . .] You go to your donors and it's very easy to show them, "We're on CNN. Give us more money." [. . .] Visibility is *huge* for national organizations. [. . .] Students are trying to find money, so they're willing to be utilized [by national organizations] in that manner. [. . . Students are] also looking down the road. These kids are looking at internships. They're looking at training. [. . .] These are the [students] that are going to end up in politics. [. . .] And they know that by doing these

types of events, especially if there's some visibility [it's] all the better for them.

Such tactics are not without precedent, but the appetite for stoking outrage, as this faculty advisor saw it, was expanding on the right, as were efforts to capitalize on the negative responses such provocations precipitate from the far-left flank of the progressive movement.

OUTRAGE OVER THE OUTRAGE

The Goldwater Institute, a conservative think tank, is of special note here. We interviewed Jim Manley, one of its lawyers, who worked to develop model legislation which allows state lawmakers to force public universities to penalize students who engage in efforts to disrupt speakers at their schools. The model legislation has been roundly criticized (even among some conservatives, including at the Koch Foundation) for infringing on school autonomy. Regardless, numerous bills have been drafted, and several have been passed, based on the Goldwater model, including in two states in our study: Arizona and North Carolina. Colorado and Virginia have also passed laws related to campus speech. Colorado's is the least controversial, banning free speech zones, thus allowing protected forms of expression in all public areas of universities. Virginia passed a bill based on the right-leaning American Legislative Exchange Council's (ALEC) Forming Open and Robust University Minds (FORUM) Act. This legislation requires annual reporting on university compliance with speech rights, and it has raised concerns among both free speech organizations and university groups.[41]

According to Manley, Goldwater introduced its model legislation at the end of January 2017, "and then, I think, it was three days later Berkeley was on fire because of Milo Yiannopoulos." For Manley, it was fortuitous timing, as the "bill was the only thing that was there that addressed this issue of shout-downs and violent protests." Goldwater, in Manley's estimation, "ended up with a solution to a problem that was really becoming a crisis." Further, he told us, "The reason people on the right are ginned up about free speech is because their speakers are the ones that are being disinvited and shouted down. So, yeah, they love free speech right now, because it is helping them to keep their message alive."

To Manley's last point, several national organization leaders on the right whom we interviewed emphasized the importance of maintaining the broad protections currently afforded by the First Amendment. Jenna Robinson is the president of the James G. Martin Center for Academic Renewal, a public policy institute funded by the conservative Pope Foundation. The Martin Center was one of the main groups working to get a version of the Goldwater model adopted in North Carolina (the center's home state). Robinson explained that the Martin Center would bring speakers to university towns "to talk about the importance of protecting free speech on campus." The goal was to raise "awareness to this issue," so that audiences could "learn about why it's so important to protect free speech on campus." Even more importantly, the Martin Center hoped their talks would get "stakeholders on that issue" to "move forward" with passing legislation—and they did.

Young Americans for Liberty (YAL) considers itself the largest mobilizer of collegiate activism on the right, and its leaders perceive progressives protesting their speakers as a dire threat. As YAL's then president, Cliff Maloney, informed us, "One of the things that happened when I took over" was that "we kept getting our speakers shut down, and our students were getting redirected to free speech zones." This, Maloney explained, became "a barrier for our students," because for YAL "to be successful we have to be able to speak on campus. We have to be able to recruit. We have to be able to engage with students." Maloney then added that "the root" of the problem was "unconstitutional speech codes and policies that campuses can use to shut anybody down." In response, YAL started its "National Fight for Free Speech" campaign. Maloney touted the campaign's successes, saying, "We've overturned 51 unconstitutional speech codes." He conceded that such success does not guarantee students will hear different viewpoints, but "it means they have the ability to. They're not going to be coddled, and certain ideologies are not going to be shut down on campus because we've now made it so that free speech and differing opinions have the ability to reach students." Similarly, Devon Mirsky, who organizes PragerU's outreach to college students, told us, "I think, for all of us, it actually comes down to something very simple. And that's just to have conservative voices not be completely disregarded and criticized and demonized."

Unlike the Goldwater Institute, the Martin Center, YAL, and PragerU, which actively embrace libertarian and conservative causes, the Foundation for Individual Rights in Education (FIRE) is a group that eschews overt partisan identification. However, FIRE was founded in 1999 by Alan Kors and Harvey Silverglate, the authors of *The Shadow University: The Betrayal of Liberty on America's Campuses*—which is now a canonical work in the conservative library about higher education. Thus, it is an organization popularly identified with the right, much to the consternation of its CEO and president, Greg Lukianoff. FIRE has several initiatives aimed at "protecting the individual rights of students and faculty members at America's colleges and universities," including a speech code rating system that affixes red, yellow, and green labels to university policies, and an arm of the organization that litigates speech policies.[42] Lukianoff explained in his interview with us that although FIRE takes up cases supporting the expressions of leftists and liberals, these do not generally attract media attention, since they do not fit the "culture war narrative." Far from being an organization known by all students in our sample, FIRE was mentioned only by conservative students—all of them commending the organization for advancing free speech.

Whether new to the issue, or having been on the scene for many years, organizations on the right (and one that is widely interpreted to be right-leaning) cultivate a script about the squelching of unpopular speech on liberal campuses—a script that is easily picked up by conservative students. This is a cultural text produced in the conservative channel that right-leaning collegians use to think about the politics behind free expression, which they then apply to their club activities and university contexts.

PROGRESSIVE ORGANIZATIONS: SLOW TO THE ISSUE

Unlike conservative organizations, which have been producing a transportable script about speech issues for decades[43] (albeit with renewed vigor in the Trump era), civil liberties groups commonly identified with the left have been slower to generate such resources. Caught up short following conflagrations at Middlebury, UC Berkeley, and other schools across the nation, a range of organizations have begun to refocus on campus speech issues—but not before considerable damage had been done to higher education's reputation, particularly among Republicans.[44] One such group is PEN America, a long-standing advocate for free expression for writers. In an interview with us, Jonathan Friedman, the program director of the Campus Free Speech program at PEN America, conceded that a more "proactive" stance is now needed. That is, schools should take "a more constructive approach to educating people about free speech rights, about how to have difficult dialogue on campus." For Friedman, this is about "modeling disagreement." Projecting into the future, it was important, he said, that university administrators put "systems in place for how they might react to situations involving speech, think about ways that they can teach incoming freshmen, for example, about free speech and inclusion issues, and other ways that they can announce their values very clearly."[45] This is necessary "so that in the moment of a crisis, where there is something that is bringing a lot of emotion to the floor, it's a situation that they are a little bit more prepared for, and one that they have anticipated a little better." Implicit in such a description of PEN America's current Campus Free Speech program is an acknowledgment that universities and their students have largely been left on their own to react to provocative speakers, without a widely available set of precepts to depend on. "Our entry point," Friedman said, is "teaching people the value of free expression, and why it is a bedrock value of an open democratic society."

PEN America is not the only nonpartisan organization that has stepped up efforts in the speech arena in the past few years.[46] In the wake of First Amendment controversies in 2017, the American Sociological Association, for example, released "Sociology-Focused Resources on Campus Speech" with the intent "to better understand what comprises free speech on campus and find the tools to help protect it." During that same year, Janet Napolitano, then president of the University of California system, funded the National Center for Free Speech and Civic Engagement to "explore in a thoughtful, deliberative way the current state of free speech on our college campuses, our relationship with the First Amendment, and what the future holds for free speech."[47] Led by Chemerinsky and Gillman (discussed earlier in this chapter), the Free Speech Center sponsors several initiatives, including #SpeechMatters annual conferences and a fellows program for scholars and other professionals working on issues related to speech and engagement. In this respect, the center is positioned to fill a space left conspicuously bare for many years—a space which we think has left many progressive students with few resources to contend with the complexities of speech on campus.[48]

THE POLITICS OF CAMPUS SPEECH

To summarize, conservative organizations (and their wealthy patrons) promote and fund speakers that sometimes upset many of the people on the campuses they visit. Occasionally, progressive reactions catch organizers off guard, as appears to have happened with Murray at Middlebury College.[49] However, provocations are often very much part of the design—as is the case with any of Milo's speaking events. Elliot Kaufman, a former conservative activist from Stanford University, for example, acknowledged in an op-ed for *National Review* that "The left-wing riots were not the price or the downside of inviting Yiannopoulos—they were the attraction." Or, to repeat the words of the UA faculty advisor to conservative groups we interviewed, today's activists want "something that will be explosive." In promoting such tactics, right-leaning organizations are creating a context in which the First Amendment—and a willingness to stand up for even utterly toxic content—has become conceptualized as a crucial aspect of what conservatism means.[50] These organization leaders understand that free expression is a wedge issue among collegians, and conservatives have learned how to deftly use speech as a weapon against liberal hegemony.

Our data also highlight progressives' ambivalence about the First Amendment. When they discuss free expression, it is mostly in terms of how those on the right use it to undermine equality on their campuses. It is the most marginalized students—racial and religious minorities, members of the LGBTQ+ community, undocumented immigrants—who are forced to pay the heaviest price of free speech, as it is their identities that are criticized and pathologized.[51] But the uncertainty and internal conflicts on the left over how to respond to incendiary speakers reveals both the efficacy of the rightist script for free speech and the lack of preemptive framing on the part of progressive organizations to help students muddle through difficult speech issues.

Of course, we cannot prove that progressives' ambivalence about speech lies in the organizational absence of a handy script. Even if the UC National Center had existed when Milo first showed up on college campuses, or if PEN America's Campus Free Speech program had already been up and running when Murray visited Middlebury, progressive students might or might not have embraced the permissive views on speech that each of these organizations is trying to deliver. But, in the absence of either organization, and with the presence of conflicting messaging put forward in colleges' and universities' principles of community, progressive students have had untidier tools to work with than the unambiguous free-speech cudgel put forth by the right. Overall, left-leaning students' views on constitutional limits do not lend themselves to a simple narrative. This is because finding the appropriate balance between individual autonomy and the needs of the community involves negotiating complex philosophical grey areas. While all meaningful expression presupposes normative restraints, old boundaries blend into the background of "common sense."[52] Any imposition of new borders, though, can seem tyrannical. Inchoate as their positions may have been, new boundaries are what our leftist and liberal interviewees appeared to want. And those on the far left were willing to go to extremes in their project of redefinition. The vast majority of our conservative respondents, by contrast, were unified against any new limits.

CONCLUSION

The disputes on campuses over incendiary speakers have cooled from their hottest moments in the wake of Trump's election in 2016. The underlying tensions between free expression and inclusion, however, are far from resolved. Perhaps because the meanings of freedom and dignity are ever evolving, this friction will never disappear. And progressives have long been divided over liberal and more left-wing interpretations of free speech. There are ways for the most pugnacious of these battles to be mitigated, though. In fact, constitutional scholars often bristle at the notion of free expression and inclusion being in opposition.[53] The hope is that they are actually synergistic values. Additionally, colleges and universities can be structured in ways that facilitate all participants feeling safe and welcome.[54] Firebrands are most explosive when introduced to schools already primed to ignite over contentious issues, and especially on public university campuses, where conservative state legislators are quick to call foul. Meanwhile, provocative forms of activism are less appealing in the first place if all students—including leftists and conservatives, as well as underrepresented populations—are better integrated into campus life.[55]

Understanding how activists frame the issues of speech rights and diversity is essential to unpacking the ever-growing complexity of campus politics. Collegians of every ideological stripe are struggling to set the proper terms for democratic participation in an equitable society. But students are not taking these issues on alone. In looking at speech on campus, we see a prime example of how the insurgent strategy enacted through the outside conservative channel has undermined aspects of the liberal worldview within academia. The resources provided through progressive embeddedness—so far—have offered little support in countering the harm leftists perceive to occur when their schools provide platforms to incendiary conservative speakers. We do not know the long-term viability of the speaker-as-protest model, but we do know that another strength of the right's insurgent strategy is adaptability. Outside organizations have no reason not to move fast and break things. The institutional components of the progressive channel, on the other hand, must be more restrained. What happens on university quads can come to shape social norms and legal thinking. Thus, whether righteous or wrongheaded, today's collegiate quarrels over free expression and inclusion are likely to refashion the boundaries of the public sphere in the decades to come.

CHAPTER 7

Genuine Openness in Polarizing Times and a Look toward the Future

Throughout the previous six chapters, we have explored students' ideological orientations, their on-campus political mobilizations, and the various ways outside organizations and institutions within universities shape collegiate activism. We have seen that polarization and strife often run deep, not only between students with oppositional worldviews, like Georgia and Tony (whom we juxtaposed in chapter 1), but also between students with similar partisan identifications. In chapter 2, for example, we highlighted disagreements between leftists and liberals and divisions between the strands of conservativism. In subsequent chapters, we compared different activists' trajectories, tactical preferences, and strategic outlooks. Just as American politics is increasingly bitter and contentious,[1] we can see these fault lines even more clearly on campus. Such divisiveness is, unfortunately, what we expect to see continue in the future.

However, we want to start this chapter by noting that partisan bickering and provocation is not all we found when talking with undergraduates in the two years following the 2016 election. College students of *unlike* mind sometimes come together to transcend their differences in ideology and policy preferences. During our time on campus—amidst one of the most disruptive presidencies in American history—we discovered a growing number of students across the political spectrum choosing to leave behind feelings of animus and the tactics of hostility, in favor of talking with one another to build a sense of mutual understanding. Their numbers are small, but some politically engaged students are taking part in what we call trans-partisan dialogue groups. They are diving headfirst into social interactions very different from those occurring in most college activists' ideologically sorted clubs.

This desire for empathetic discussions is not a phenomenon that sprang up *ex nihilo* in the heat of the Trump era. More than twenty years ago, Daniel Yankelovich, a renowned pollster and social scientist, published *The Magic of Dialogue*. In his book, Yankelovich lays out strategies for better communication in politics, business, and elsewhere. His argument is that common assumptions about dialogue—that it is intended to yield mutual understanding and harmony—gets it only half right. This is because successful dialogue can be *dis*harmonious. Through engaged dialogue, Yankelovich contends, it is perfectly reasonable for participants to "come to understand why [they] disagree so vehemently with someone else." In other words, unlike ordinary conversation—where comity is a desired outcome—or debate—in which the goal is to persuade others of a particular side—Yankelovich writes that through dialogue, "each of us internalizes the views of the other to enhance our mutual understanding." These ideas, which are derived from philosopher Martin Buber's classic work on I-Thou interactions, imply what Yankelovich describes as "genuine openness of each to the concerns of the other."[2]

It might seem that such genuine openness would be difficult to pull off at a time when so many Americans cannot stand to be around those affiliated with the opposing political party, express deep skepticism about each other's news sources, and fundamentally disagree about scientific truth. For this reason, we were intrigued by the students we met who joined trans-partisan dialogue groups to do just that. Their efforts reveal the sincere work some collegians are willing to put in to fix what they believe is wrong with American democracy. They are doing it by starting on their own campuses, reaching out to the peers they disagree with most.

BUILDING BRIDGES THROUGH CAMPUS DIALOGUE

Broadly speaking, the philosophy and practices of dialogue have been embraced by any number of national organizations in recent years. For example, there is Living Room Conversations, which was started in 2010 and is geared toward helping regular folks at home talk more peaceably about current events. For academics there is Heterodox Academy, which was co-founded in 2015 by the psychologist Jonathan Haidt (whose ideas we discuss throughout this book), along with the legal scholar Nicholas Rosenkranz and the sociologist Chris Martin. The intention of this organization is to promote a diversity of viewpoints, specifically addressing the absence of conservative ideas in academia.[3] And, aiming to involve college students directly, there are a variety of national groups that partner with school officials or campus clubs to encourage listening and understanding between members of their communities. At the universities where we teach, for instance, there are "Campus Conversations" and the "Diversity Dialogue Series."

One of the best-known models intended to get students involved in such conversations is Sustained Dialogue. Around the same time that Yankelovich published *The Magic of Dialogue*, the American diplomat Harold Saunders was on a similar mission—in his case, to translate his knowledge about international conflict resolution into cooperative action in the domestic sphere. Using the principles he developed in security talks with global leaders, Saunders assisted students at Princeton University, his alma mater, in addressing the school's growing racial tensions in the late 1990s. Shortly thereafter, he helped create chapters at other colleges and universities; and he established a campus network to aid in the coordination of these clubs in 2003. There are now sixty-four colleges and universities that use the tools associated with the model. From the "high-impact experiences" that students gain in Sustained Dialogue, the goal is for participants to "develop a diverse set of leadership skills, including strong personal identity awareness, knowledge of social justice, empathy, facilitation, and conflict resolution skills."[4]

As it turns out, one of the universities we chose to study, UVA, was the second school to create a Sustained Dialogue chapter.[5] The group has maintained a highly active presence on campus since its inception in 2001—plunging into the topics of race, class, religion, gender, sexual orientation, and politics. To handle such potentially volatile discussions, student moderators (or "mods") use three norms which, Piper told us, "are pretty much the reason dialogue can happen." First and foremost on the list "is to assume best intentions." Mods encourage participants to look past their first reactions—to pause, reflect, and not take personally other speakers' beliefs that conflict with their own. The second norm "is to lean into discomfort" by very intentionally not tuning out or getting angry when disagreements arise. "You don't *not* speak," said Piper, just because an issue makes participants uneasy. Group members are encouraged to stay present and engage in the discussion, even when the urge for fight, flight, or freeze kicks in. The third norm— familiar to anyone who has gone through couples therapy—is to "speak from 'I' statements" to avoid generalizing and *ad hominem* attacks. As a trained moderator, Piper said your job "is to continuously remind the group of those norms" so that the dialogue "can be worthwhile." Between 300 and 400 regular participants, alongside 50 mods, are involved in Sustained Dialogue in any given year at UVA, according to our interviewees.

BridgeUSA is another trans-partisan dialogue group working with college students. It is a newer and smaller organization than Sustained Dialogue. But, while Sustained Dialogue takes on a variety of social issues (from faith to gender identity), Bridge is more focused on the matter of political polarization. The national organization was launched in 2016 after the student leaders of independent peer-led dialogue clubs at the University of Notre Dame and the University of Colorado learned of each other's activities fostering mutual understanding among collegians. Joining forces, they developed a plan to take their "bridge" model national. Four years later, with chapters at thirty schools and more on the horizon,[6] Bridge had managed to get sizable donations from benefactors on both the right and the left of the political spectrum. Bridge's leaders are highly cognizant of the need to avoid any hint that their organization has an ideological tilt. The social entrepreneur and "San Francisco Republican" Bill Shireman is a mentor to the group, as are the past Obama administration official and CNN commentator Van Jones and the political centrist Jonathan Haidt. Each of these mentors has pushed ideas about viewpoint diversity that have shaped the group's strategic approach.[7]

We first heard about Bridge at UNC, where Blaire estimated that her chapter averages around fifteen people at its weekly meetings. In the spring of 2018, we went to Dallas to attend the second annual Bridge-

USA Summit to see if we could learn more. Approximately a hundred students from around the country attended, including at least three students from the four universities we focus on in this book: Bishop and Maxwell from UNC, and Gregory from CU. At this event, we also got the opportunity to meet a number of other young people deeply committed to the dialogue concept. Over the summit's two days of programming, we heard a lot about the three pillars of what the group has branded the "BridgeMindset"—championing ideological diversity, promoting a solution-oriented political culture, and teaching constructive engagement.[8] These pillars share much in common with the norms of Sustained Dialogue, and bear a strong resemblance to the ideas of Yankelovich. As Shireman told the summit audience, "the keys to radical transformation" are combining courage and honesty while extending courtesy to those who express alternative ideas.

Organizational ideals, such as the BridgeMindset, are one thing, but hearing how students hash out the tenets' meanings with one another provides insight into how they make sense of the challenges at hand. We found their engagement to be impressive. Speaking to the importance of ideological diversity, one student at the summit described the value of exercising "epistemological humility," pointing out that "not absolutely trusting your own beliefs is a way to be more flexible, to not be doctrinaire, to not harden and hunker down and mistrust the other side." Further, the BridgeMindset teaches adherents to refrain from advancing their own perspectives by looking for chinks in others' rhetorical armor—or, as another student said, "learning from others is uppermost." That is to say, the goal is not to view fellow members as intellectual combatants whose beliefs can be defeated through superior debating skills. Instead, the aim is to understand what people with different ideas believe and to learn from them. It is only through taking this stance that constructive solutions—the second pillar—might be realized. Finally, to the third pillar, students and speakers at the summit repeatedly confirmed the need for civil discourse, not "dominance disputes," as our interviewee Maxwell called them. Appreciating ideological diversity, not ossifying into one's positions, and staying civil allows participants to recognize the complexities behind people's political positions and to refrain from reducing them to just their party affiliation.

THE NEED FOR DIALOGUE ON CAMPUS IN THE TRUMP ERA

Setting aside for the moment the conceptual tools these groups use to promote mutual understanding, the reasons students gave for having gotten involved in trans-partisan dialogue groups in the first place are interesting and instructive. As Musa Al-Gharbi, a Heterodox Academy member who works closely with Bridge, told us, there is "a widespread perception among a lot of students that there's something afoul in the way that institutions of higher education are working today," and that "we need to be able to find a way to bridge these divides." Blaire, for example, described how the tensions around the 2016 election inspired her to adopt the BridgeMindset. According to Blaire, supporters of Donald Trump at UNC were hiding their political allegiances from their peers. Even though she is a committed Democrat, Blaire felt that "not being able to speak openly about" the presidential candidate you support is "one of the main problems" on her campus. She told us she wanted to be part of a club "where anyone could feel like they could express their ideas and actually be heard, instead of being marked [by] who [they] voted for." This need really hit home once Blaire realized that her best friend had voted for Trump, which left her "really kind of shocked." Without a sincere commitment to mutual understanding, Blaire thought even the closest of relationships could be in danger of falling apart. At UVA, Mae said something similar. Sustained Dialogue mods, she recalled, heard a lot of students saying, "I feel really isolated about this. I don't tell my friends [I voted for Trump]. I feel like once I say something, I'll just get ridiculed, and no one will talk to me about it and help me learn." Like Blaire, Mae was eager to help foster an inclusive community for those of all ideological stripes.

Bishop, who describes himself as a moderate, is exactly the sort of student who has benefited from taking part in trans-partisan dialogue. "After the 2016 election season," he said, "I was very confused about where I stood politically, because I had been shifting away from my more left-leaning views." Following his instincts to try to learn more about conservative ideas, he first joined Turning Point USA—a decision that, in hindsight, he described as misguided. After attending a few meetings, he felt uncomfortable with its populist messaging and confrontational style. He was relieved to eventually find Bridge, a group in which it is "hard to tell where everybody in the club actually lies on the political spectrum, which I think is really great. Because we're just talking about what we believe as individuals and not putting ourselves into categories." In a similar vein, Jessica, a Christian conservative, got involved with Sustained Dialogue because, after the election of Trump, she explained, "I don't feel perfectly at home with other conservatives." In response to what she felt were the provocative tactics of her peers in Turning Point and College Republicans, Jessica helped spearhead Converge, a subsidiary of UVA's Sustained Dialogue chapter focused specifically on political issues and on "decreasing polarization" and "increasing mutual understanding and empathy towards the political Other through one-on-one conversations."

Members of both Bridge and Sustained Dialogue insist that students should not have to compromise their political convictions to participate in their groups. During the BridgeUSA Summit, this topic came up several times. Students were adamant that the point of the BridgeMindset is *not* to bring students to the ideological center or to push them into being moderate independents. As one student at the summit stated, "We have a pro-disagreement message, and that makes people like Bridge better than [if we were just trying to achieve] unity." Another member chimed in: "We are not talking about reaching consensus; we are talking about talking about disagreement." A third participant said simply, "We are not trying to get people to be bipartisan." Because the center is not the goal line, students from different ideological poles feel comfortable staying in the groups. For example, Jessica told us that neither her bedrock pro-life stance nor her desire for conservatives to stay in the White House were changed by joining Sustained Dialogue. On the other end of the political spectrum, when asked if Sustained Dialogue had caused her to moderate her liberal views, Piper said, "I don't think my location on the political spectrum has changed very much." But what has changed significantly is her "ability to take in" the entirety of "people who disagree with me."

Piper's last comment speaks to the primary goal of trans-partisan dialogue groups: citizens (college students especially) should try to discover what the sociologist Arlie Hochschild calls people's "deep stories"—the emotional roots behind ideological orientations and political preferences.[9] Understanding where others are coming from leads to a diminished urge to demonize them. As Gregory explained about his decision to join the Bridge chapter at CU, "Seeing the political climate that we are in, it just seemed obvious to me that the solution to this problem was having both sides talk to each other more. Because it seemed like both sides saw the other one as evil and just irredeemable, essentially." Likewise, Maxwell insisted that it is important "to represent the opposition's ideas fairly and think about them" by putting "yourself in the skin of other people."

We should add here that, according to our interviewees, the empathy championed by Bishop and Maxwell is good not only for "the opposition," but also for the individual. Participants viewed dialogue as providing an opportunity to explore their own political beliefs and, beyond that, to perhaps undergo personal transformation. These themes can be seen in Piper's comments: "You learn a lot about who you are and your identity." Or, in Maxwell's words, "Everyone is sharing their wisdom with everyone else, and, I think, through dialogue, we find more truth than if we were just by ourselves." Additionally, Gregory described dialogue as a way to build a sense of community. "I just feel good about the message that we're based around, the principle of the group." And he liked having the sense that he was "doing my part in forwarding dialogue and making people more open to it. It makes me feel that I'm on the right side."

The sense of purpose touted by Gregory, along with the excitement members recounted from some of their dialogue sessions, resemble what the psychologist Abraham Maslow calls "peak experiences"—moments of euphoria that can accompany self-actualization.[10] Marco, a frequent participant in his school's Sustained Dialogue chapter, for example, reported that he was "super into" the discussions he had been involved with. For Piper, the whole thing was "kind of addicting" when all the pieces snapped into place. "Sometimes you have a dialogue" and "it just felt like the time flew by and you learned a ton about other people, and you engaged with questions you've never thought about before and, when it's over, everyone is just smiling and in a great mood, because they are glad they spent that time doing what they did." She summed up by noting that such moments are what "I really live for." Of course, not all efforts at dialogue produce such transcendence. "The flip side of the coin," said Piper, is a "stagnating dialogue" when participants give only "shallow" responses, and "another person wouldn't elaborate, and no one else would build on it." Reflecting specifically on a disappointing discussion about patriotism in relation to professional football players kneeling during the national anthem in protest over police violence, Piper complained that all of the session's participants held back. When this happens, "you miss out on that moment at the end where you feel like you really heard what everyone thought, and you are able to humanize the other side. You can't do that if the other side doesn't feel like they can be the other side."

Beyond personal growth, members of trans-partisan dialogue groups have higher aims, including developing political leadership skills for the future. Gregory, for instance, thought of his participation on campus as one small part of the ultimate goal of having "better political conversations" in society at large. "And what comes from that, I think, will be good in terms of real change that we see in policy." He then added, "If you're able to come to more of an understanding, then you'll be able to have a bigger coalition of people behind a certain idea, and that will create change." Maxwell saw the end game in starker terms. "Dialogue is required to keep a peaceful country peaceful. Otherwise, people drift apart." He did not want "polarization to continue," because "the end of polarization is war, and I would like to avoid that." To the extent that these students felt learning genuine openness was part of future political involvement, they were already gaining firsthand experience at their schools, as administrators have leaned on Bridge and Sustained Dialogue chapters over the years to help smooth over political divides on their campuses.[11]

A BRIDGE TOO FAR: THE CHALLENGES FOR TRANS-PARTISAN DIALOGUE GROUPS

As much promise as trans-partisan dialogue groups hold, members also face formidable challenges. The most glaring of these is simply getting people to set aside their distrust and anger. While members of Bridge and Sustained Dialogue exhibit courage in discussing divisive issues with one another, some chapters have found certain topics to be too hot to handle. During the BridgeUSA Summit, for example, we heard some participants explain that abortion was off-limits in their campus clubs because that "is just a gridlocked issue. I don't think that we can move the needle on that one." At UNC, where Bridge members did manage a conversation about abortion, talking about Trump was considered the no-go. According to Blaire, "We did, at the beginning, talk more about politics and Trump, but it got kind of old because the people in our group" felt that it was "a divide that you can't really" cross. Obviously, our nation's fundamental rifts remain just as intractable when trans-partisan dialogue groups are unable to tackle the really tough issues.

Additionally, many of these groups' efforts are likely to be most appealing to less politically committed students—individuals with self-identities not already consolidated along party lines. Indeed, two of the three moderates in our sample felt most at home in Bridge chapters. This is far from a bad thing. We already heard Bishop (a center-right moderate) speak of his positive experiences with Bridge members not revealing their party affiliations. Blaire described this as making sure her club is welcoming to those not "necessarily interested in all the nitty-gritty politics of it." But the inverse of this is that many of the dedicated activists we interviewed for this book—that is, the collegians really pushing the envelope for social change on their campuses and beyond—may not be so eager to participate. Politically engaged students often *do* want to get into the "nitty-gritty" of advocacy and activism. As Anthony told us, he joined the Young Democrats specifically because he was looking for the "nuanced debate-type thing." In other words, participation in trans-partisan dialogue groups, as with other clubs, is the result of students sorting themselves according to pre-existing aspects of their identities. So, while Bridge and Sustained Dialogue will nurture group styles that shape their members' outlooks and preferences, this can only happen if they first get students through the door to attend meetings and become personally invested in the clubs.

We can add to this critique that many students from historically underrepresented populations increasingly feel burned out by much of the "dialogue" being organized in the primarily White settings of the universities we studied.[12] Resigned to the mathematics of the problem at a school with UVA's demographic composition, Piper explained that if fifteen Black people show up to participate and "you have enough overall participants for fifteen groups [. . .] you could put one Black person in every group, or you could clump them and have totally White groups, and then a group with three Black people, and then [a] totally White [group], and a group with three" Black people, and so on. Piper was aware of the downsides associated with either solution. An option that includes all-White groups means some groups will lack racial diversity. But the problem with the first way of grouping is "tokenizing Black people in each individual group [. . .] where they try to talk about race and someone says, 'What is the psychological impact of feeling like your race colors people's perception of you?' And everybody turns and looks at the Black person." Devin Willis, an anti-racist counter-protester during the Unite the Right rally, summed up his frustration with UVA administrators' "empty gestures" of dialogue, telling a reporter for the *Chronicle of Higher Education*, "I don't exist to enlighten privileged young White people at a university. [. . .] I'm not the curriculum."[13] We heard a similar theme voiced by Sasha, an Asian trans student at UVA. "There is always one" dialogue session "about sexual orientation and gender identity," he said. The majority of participants are "straight and cisgender," so "I got a little tired of it" because the sentiments expressed are always, "Oh, I'm straight and other people aren't, and I have so much privilege, and I feel so bad for them." Although Sasha continued to participate in Sustained Dialogue, he questioned whether it was worth his time to help the "majority group wake up to what other people are experiencing."

Finally, the path from practicing genuine openness in dialogue sessions to actually mobilizing people for social change is a rocky one. During the BridgeUSA Summit, which was held in conjunction with EarthX (an environmental exposition), discussion about climate change was at times hampered by participants' inability to agree on the parameters of the topic, as well as by their skepticism over whether members in their clubs back home would want to collectively support any one collaborative solution. This is a matter made all the more perplexing for participants because progressives and conservatives have such different starting points. To what extent are humans causing climate change, and is it a problem? If it is a problem, and humans are the cause, should Bridge chapters be advocating carbon taxes? Or, really, is it about phasing out oil and gas usage altogether? And, from there, participants may disagree on whether any political activism should be a goal of the organization at all.

During the summit, participants expressed only mild interest in co-operating on joint civic action requiring policy convergence. While students throughout the two-day event avidly discussed the norms and expectations required for mutual understanding and civil discourse, the connection between the action goals of the group and the subject of environmentalism (or really, any other policy area) ebbed and flowed, despite efforts by organizers to focus participants' minds on the issue of potential mobilization. Perhaps organizing to propose policy solutions will just take time, and, since Bridge chapters have a great deal of autonomy, it may be something that clubs will follow on some campuses but not on others. Whatever the case, the second pillar of promoting a solution-oriented political culture appears to be more aspirational than the other two tenets, although several members did express their commitment to future advocacy. During the summit, Manu Meel, one of Bridge's leading figures at the national level, put it this way: "Step one is to create that critical culture through facilitating dialogue and discourse." And then the "logical next step" is to ask, "How do we [. . .] actually work on something together?"

The takeaway here is that, so far, trans-partisan dialogue groups fall short of reliably creating what the philosopher Jürgen Habermas famously called the "public sphere"—an intersubjectively shared space for debate and political action.[14] Of course, creating such an idealized forum is a big ask of any group, and the remedies for polarization cannot be laid solely at the feet of today's collegians. Regardless, discovering the intricacies of how one feels about same-sex marriage or gentrification through dialogue with someone who thinks differently about those matters is not the same thing as developing good arguments or policy solutions, or putting the weight of a club's membership behind a candidate whose policies they believe in. We already know partisans shouting over one another does not lead to shared answers, but dialogue that cannot confront our nation's most pressing issues head-on—and ultimately offer workable solutions—may be equally ineffectual. While members of trans-partisan groups are some of the few people on campus who seem to be doing the kind of personal growth work we hope students will engage in during their college years, these groups may funnel students to nowhere, and perhaps even lead them away from overt political involvement.

Even so, members of these groups have shown their dedication to curiosity, vulnerability, and a willingness to disagree without hostility—no small feat in these contentious times. As Al-Gharbi said in his address to the BridgeUSA Summit, "We live in a polarized environment and it's risky to reach out. If you work across the lines, you are seen as a traitor or a villain. You might be called a sell-out to your side." Many in the audience seemed to know from firsthand experience the accuracy of his words; we watched as heads nodded in agreement.

We believe, following Yankelovich, Saunders, and Haidt, that genuine openness can help college activists succeed in ways not accessible through the traditional tactics of campaigning, debate, and protest. This is especially important now, when so many students can be set off by seeing someone wearing a Make America Great Again hat or a Black Lives Matter T-shirt, or simply by hearing someone mention support for a candidate from the other party. As Evan Mandery, a criminal justice scholar who uses dialogue techniques in his undergraduate ethics classes, writes, "Curious things start to happen to people when [students] listen generously. [. . .] One hears the sincerity of people's convictions, the authenticity of their experiences, and the nuance of their narratives. Being open is transformative because, almost inevitably, one finds that the stories they've been told about what people believe oversimplify reality."[15] Dialogue may not be the endpoint at this critical juncture in American democracy, but it presents an important alternative to the explicitly partisan forms of activism that we have seen throughout the earlier chapters of this book.

THE OUTSIDE-INSIDE APPROACH FOR STUDYING FUTURE CAMPUS POLITICS

It is tempting to end on a high note, with a prediction that college-level trans-partisanship will help lead the country out of darkness. But we are not overly optimistic in the short run, despite the sincere efforts by some students. The Trump era and its aftermath have embroiled American colleges and universities in political controversies in a way not seen since the 1960s.[16] In the face of presidential threats to deport immigrants, administrators declared their universities sanctuary campuses. Social media posts of faculty, guest speakers, and students accused of making all manner of offensive statements went viral over and over again. Legal scholars, politicians, and media pundits debated at length the meaning of academic freedom and free speech on campus. State legislatures, following the blueprints of conservative think tanks, threatened to cut funding for institutions they deemed elitist and indoctrinating, and to expel students who repeatedly protest speakers. At the student level, disruptive political events occurred at an incredibly fast pace. On the four campuses we studied, there was the Unite the Right rally and counterprotest at UVA; the toppling of a Confederate monument at UNC; controversial visits by Ann Coulter, Bobby Seale, and Milo Yiannopoulos at CU; and battles over funding choices at UA, including rancorous critiques of the influence of the conservative philanthropist Charles Koch at the university. In short, the years 2016–2020 were ones for the record books.

As of this writing in the fall of 2021, Trump has been voted out of office, and while many may hope that the turbulence at colleges and universities will subside during the Biden presidency, it is unrealistic to think that ideological divisions will be quickly mended. COVID-19 has brought renewed attention to gaping inequities in higher education and far beyond. The killings of George Floyd, Rayshard Brooks, Breonna Taylor, Adam Toledo, and so many other Black and Latinx individuals at the hands of police ignited international protests against systemic racism, with many college students leading Black Lives Matter protests on and off campus.[17] At the same time, far-right extremism is wrenching apart the Republican Party, with likely downstream effects on the political clubs we focus on in this book. And well-funded conservative critics will continue to blame an overly liberal academy for indoctrinating students into progressive worldviews. Indeed, if history is any guide, organizations on the right will expand in response to a Democratic administration retaking the White House.[18] Meanwhile, as colleges and universities grapple with the fallout of an extraordinary confluence of economic, social, and political crises, activists in the progressive channel may become increasingly wary of faculty and administrators who are unable to meet their demands for greater diversity in admissions, further inclusion in the curriculum, and student debt relief. On top of this, there are the longer-term effects of the remote learning that was enacted during the pandemic. Progressive critics will join collegians to decry what they see as the corporatized, neoliberal, and racially insensitive system of higher education.[19] Mainstream journalistic accounts will continue to cover dramatic school events or the foibles of student protesters because colleges and universities have become central tropes in the culture wars.

The outside-in/inside-out analytical approach we adopt in this book provides a model for making sense of the inevitable political controversies that lie ahead. Like journalists, future researchers should paint a vivid portrait of students' lives, but they should also contextualize those lives through an analysis of social structures. Like critics on the right, scholars should not shy away from looking at the largely leftward skew of colleges and universities—but they should avoid hyperbolic generalizations based on extreme cases. Academic researchers might use traditional survey-based educational research on social backgrounds (as we did by looking at students in the aggregate using the CIRP Freshman Survey), but then add a deep qualitative analysis to understand how their student subjects actually conceptualize their identities, school experiences, and civic participation. And, following scholars who use an organizational perspective to study higher education,[20] those interested in collegiate activism should emphasize the importance of institutional goals and resources in shaping the activism taking place in higher education. They also need to look at the outside organizations attempting to guide the content and direction of contemporary campus politics.

Using these tools, our research reveals how those on the right are pulled outside of campus by national organizations. This influence—which we have called the conservative channel for student activism—tends to promote a discourse hostile to the academic enterprise. And it provides alternative sources of knowledge and funding for participants. It also offers a more developed career funnel into policy-making, politics, and punditry. The progressive channel for student activism, on the other hand, pushes its participants further inside their campuses' institutions through student affairs offices, multicultural centers, and academic disciplines. And while it is a dominant aspect of college culture, the progressive channel does not provide a clear route out of school and into post-baccalaureate avenues for paid forms of advocacy and activism. It also frequently champions a dissident identity that helps to sour politically engaged students toward their erstwhile partners in administrative positions, and, potentially toward faculty as well. Thus, there are costs to how both the left and the right have built up their political foundations.

As we conclude this book, one crucial question to ask is: who is winning in these polarizing times? From one point of view, leftists and liberals clearly have been successful at dominating campus politics. As we pointed out in earlier chapters, there are many times more progressive faculty than conservative professors, and numerous academic disciplines (particularly in the social sciences and humanities) emphasize left-leaning worldviews.[21] In addition, university administrators and staff promote (in words, if not always in deeds) the liberal agenda of multiculturalism, equity, and inclusion. From the inside out, then, progressive students have enjoyed a position of power and comfort on campus. Yet, for all the ideological heft the left holds, the right enjoys advantages of its own. The insurgent strategy found in the conservative channel for student activism—maligned as it may be among much of the professoriate and a plurality of students—has the financial backing and the strategic acumen to negate the structural advantages of progressives. Despite resistance from the campus community, Turning Point chapters and other clubs of their ilk will continue to bring highly controversial speakers to their schools (or find other equally disruptive practices), because members will be motivated from the outside to do so. The ensuing acrimony directed toward the clubs will then be harnessed into a narrative that conservatives are a stigmatized minority.[22] Our interviews with those on the left show there is often not a coherent counter-narrative to conservative positions, particularly in the area of free speech.

Another crucial question to pose as we wrap up our argument concerns the implications of our findings. The sky is not falling for progressive education; we are not arguing that the collapse of liberalism in higher education is nigh. However, it would be equally foolish to brush aside the leverage conservatives have gained, and are likely to continue to gain, in academia. This will matter for the civic life all of us can expect in the coming years. While we are critical of some of the tactics and policy preferences circulating in the progressive channel, we are also very much champions of the overall objective of the progressive project in higher education. If the right continues to pummel the left—that is, if state and federal governments retreat further from their obligations to foster an informed citizenry, if the Republican Party mistrusts expertise and scientific data, if scholars are hampered in critically teaching their knowledge in the classroom, if underrepresented populations are limited in their ability to obtain the same degrees from public universities as those from privileged classes—we, as a society, lose.

Society also loses if campus politics ceases to be about exchanging ideas and becomes simply a battle over which side can scream the loudest to generate the most social media attention. Tamping down what we see as negative forms of mobilization (practiced by the left and the right) will require school officials understanding how students make sense of their ideological orientations and then appreciating the outside-in/ inside-out dynamics at play on college campuses. More than this, it will mean committing to real-world change—often in the face of opposition by activists coming from one or the other end of the political spectrum. It will be a tough line to walk. Thankfully, there is a plethora of existing scholarship on how to do this, and we have referenced a lot of it in the preceding pages. There are also working models already up and running, like Harvard's Institute of Politics or the Stavros Niarchos Foundation Agora Institute at Johns Hopkins University. We hope that the findings presented in this book can help inform future efforts at facilitating productive interactions between all members of the campus community.

While our expertise is not in the area of policy, our time studying this topic has brought us to a few conclusions. First, conservative donors have a particularly important role to play at this historical moment. They need to be pushing the organizations dependent on their largesse to encourage civic responsibility over sensational encounters. Second, university leaders need to heed the call from leftists to develop tangible solutions to the very real social inequities that currently exist in learning outcomes. But that is not all. As many others have advocated, we would also like to see administrators lead the charge in finding better ways to embed their right-leaning matriculants in the campus community. Likewise, professors (ourselves included) need to stop missing the opportunity to help expose students to the depth of intellectual thought found on the right side of the political spectrum. A college curriculum bereft of conservative ideas does not make everyone a liberal, just as abstinence-only education does not prevent people from having sex. In the realm of ideology, one-sided teaching will only make some curious students more open to the illiberalism of right-wing populism.[23] Finally, a unique implication from our project is that progressive organizations outside academia need to build up a national infrastructure comparable to what we find on the right. If nothing else, this will help provide opportunities for leftist and liberal undergraduates to more seamlessly move into political careers after college.

Of course, we know none of these calls for action are easy. Some suggestions—like endowing nonpartisan centers—are expensive, especially for public universities. Other suggestions—when viewed through a partisan lens—are at cross purposes, because it can be hard to simultaneously appease warring parties. Thus, the odds are that our suggestions might fall on deaf ears. We suspect that neither the Bill and Melinda Gates Foundation nor Turning Point is going to change its organizational agenda because of this book. Kirk is not going to stop calling universities indoctrination mills, and liberal philanthropists are unlikely to start pumping millions into a career funnel for progressive activists. But taking the steps we suggest would go a long way toward allowing the young activists within the progressive and conservative channels to think of campus politics as something other than a zero-sum game. Such changes would not guarantee that we all win, but they would make us all a little less likely to lose.

Acknowledgments

We would like to thank our interviewees for generously giving their time. So many of the students, organization leaders, and members of the campus community that we talked with went above and beyond in sharing their insights and helping us to connect with additional respondents. Quite simply, without them this book could not exist. We also benefited greatly from working with a large number of people who have read, funded, transcribed, administrated, or otherwise supported us on our four-year journey researching and writing for this project.

We would like to thank the Division of Social Sciences and the Academic Senate (both at UC San Diego) and the Spencer Foundation for their generous financial support. Erin Leahey, Andy Perrin, and Josipa Roksa—at the University of Arizona, UNC-Chapel Hill, and the University of Virginia, respectively—helped us find space to conduct interviews. Loretta Sowers and her team of transcribers—Dorothy Tuzzi, Anita White, Elizabeth Lanni, and Janine Martin—took great care translating 114 audio interviews to electronic paper. Kristen Walker, Ana Minvielle, and Jesse Martel at UC San Diego, and Andrea Buford, Kristin Bigelow, and Kellie Dyslin at Northern Illinois University handled our grants.

Having talented research assistants helped advance our project. UC San Diego undergraduates Sara Abumeri, Alyssa Hawkinson, and Zoey Meyer were a great team. Zosia Sztykowski, a UC San Diego doctoral student, helped us do a deep dive into national conservative and progressive organizations, and also helped write portions of chapter 4. Ellen Stolzenberg of UCLA's Higher Education Research Institute not only crunched numbers and helped write the start of chapter 2 for the edification of others, but also assisted us in seeing how our findings fit into a larger national context. Additionally, Edgar Romo at HERI provided quantitative analysis.

Colleagues across the country gave us meaningful feedback. Thanks to Jonathan Friedman, Jonathan Zimmerman, Tom Cushman, Evan Mandery, Michèle Lamont, and anonymous reviewers for the University of Chicago Press for pushing our work in productive directions. We would also like to thank Henry Farrell at the *Washington Post*, Chris Quintana at *USA Today* (formerly at the *Chronicle of Higher Education*), Dominick Doemer at Scholars Strategy Network, and Inga Kiderra in UC San Diego Communications for helping get media coverage for early versions of this research. A shorter version of chapter 6 appeared in *Sociological Forum*, and we are grateful to editor Karen Cerulo and anonymous reviewers for enhancing those ideas. Claudio Benzecry and anonymous reviewers at *Qualitative Sociology* shaped our ideas about conservative students' attitudes toward Trumpism. Mitchell Stevens and Emily Levine invited us to include a portion of our findings in *Change* magazine.

Colleagues at UC San Diego and NIU were a great boon for us both. Lauren Olsen, a UC San Diego doctoral student at the time, held our hands as we took baby steps learning to code with Dedoose. Jeff benefited from a department and college that allowed him a year-long sabbatical from teaching and service obligations. Mike Ezell helped make that possible, and he kept things running smoothly behind the scenes. Amy would like to thank Eric Bakovic, Mary Blair-Loy, John Evans and Ronnee Schreiber, Kelly Gates, Robert Horwitz and Libby Brydolf, Akos Rona-Tas and Judit Hersko, and Jeff Haydu for walks, talks, and meals. Her Friday Zoom office writing group members, Yasemin Taskin-Alp, Mariana Lopez, Richard Pitt, Gershon Shafir, and Karina Shklyan, lent their support to push the book over the finish line. Continuing conversations with former graduate students Daniel Davis, Kelly Nielsen, and Lisa Nunn were also delights for Amy. During the early stages of writing, carpool conversations with Emma Kuby and (heated debates with) Andy Bruno helped keep Jeff grounded. At UC San Diego, Shanley Miller, Brenda Guzman, Jillian Tracy, Teresa Eckert, Shavonne Holton, and Rick

Clarke helped clear time in Amy's busy schedule as department chair so that she could get writing done. The Binder clan—particularly sister Elizabeth and mother Lois—kept Amy from going bananas during the pandemic. And Amy thanks Edward Hunter for his friendship, love, and expert grilling techniques. Jeff has cherished his socially distanced Catan meetings with Christina Raine, Jonathan Raine, Josh Loney, Lia Newman, and Chris Gannon (even though they never let him win). As always, Keri Wiginton has been a shining star in Jeff's life. Not only did she tolerate years of bloviation about this project, but she inexplicably remains Jeff's teammate in online Catan despite his abysmal track record at earning victory points.

Finally, we owe a huge debt to many people at the University of Chicago Press. Elizabeth Branch Dyson has been a constant source of hilarious quips and enthusiastic support; but much more than that, she lent her incisive eye for seeing which arguments worked and which left something to be desired. Mollie McFee, Dylan Montanari, Christine Schwab, Carrie Adams, and Eleanor Ford expertly handled our manuscript's movement through the publication process, while Chicago's copyeditor, Evan Young, did a wonderful job cleaning up our prose.

Notes

CHAPTER ONE

1   Like the names of other student interviewees in this book, "Georgia" is a pseudo-nym. We have also changed some identifying information to protect the confidentiality of our respondents. These matters are discussed in greater detail later in this chapter.

2   UMAS (United Mexican American Students) is a Latinx political club started at CU in 1968. From its inception it has been a far-left force on campus. See Jefferson Dodge and Joel Dyer, "Los Seis De Boulder," *Boulder Weekly*, May 29, 2014, https://www.boulderweekly.com/news/los-seis-de-boulder/. MEXA, also spelled MEChA (Movimiento Estudiantil Chicanx de Aztlán), is a national organization with its own left-wing history. For example, see Gustavo Arellano, "Raza Isn't Racist," *Los Angeles Times*, June 15, 2006, https://www.latimes.com/la-oe-arellano15jun15-story.html. At CU, UMAS and MEXA (while officially distinct groups) are functionally merged as UMAS y MEXA.

3   Georgia is referring to the loose collection of militant left-wing activists commonly known as antifa. Those representing the group frequently wear all black and use masks to conceal their identities. Many on the right consider antifa to be domestic terrorists.

4   The Unite the Right rally was ostensibly an event intended to protest the renaming of Lee Park in Charlottesville and the planned removal of a statue honoring Confederate General Robert E. Lee. The protest was organized by the alt-right figurehead, and UVA alumnus, Jason Kessler. On the night of August 11, 2017, a large number of White supremacists marched through UVA's campus chanting slogans such as "Jews will not replace us" and "White lives matter." The following day, mayhem broke out in the city as alt-right protesters clashed with anti-racist counter-protesters in the streets. Heather Heyer was killed by a car intentionally driven into a crowd of progressive activists. Two police officers also died in a helicopter crash while monitoring the day's events. See Joe Heim, "Recounting a Day of Rage, Hate,

Violence and Death," *Washington Post*, August 14, 2017, https://www.washingtonpost
.com/graphics/2017/local/charlottesville-timeline/.

5 For example, see Andrew Anthony, "Black Power's Coolest Radicals (but Also a Gang
of Ruthless Killers)," *The Guardian*, October 18, 2015, https://www.theguardian.com
/film/2015/oct/18/black-powers-coolest-radicals-black-panthers-vanguard-of-the
-revolution-stanley-nelson-interview.

6 Samuel J. Abrams, "Think Professors Are Liberal? Try School Administrators," *New
York Times*, October 16, 2018, https://www.google.com/search?client=safari&rls=en
&q=Think+Professors+are+Liberal%3F++Try+School+Administrators+NYT&ie
=UTF-8&oe=UTF-8.

7 For example, see David Yamane, *Student Movements for Multiculturalism: Challenging
the Curricular Color Line in Higher Education* (Baltimore, MD: Johns Hopkins University Press, 2001).

8 For a discussion about the relationship between education and wider social change,
see Christopher J. Broadhurst and Angel L. Velez, "Historical and Contemporary
Context of Student Activism in U.S. Higher Education," in *Student Activism, Politics,
and Campus Climate in Higher Education*, ed. Demetri L. Morgan and Charles H. F. Davis III (New York: Routledge, 2019); David K. Cohen and Barbra Neufeld, "The Failure
of High Schools and the Progress of Education," *Daedalus* 110, no. 3 (1981); Becky
Thompson and Sangeeta Tyagi, "Introduction: 'A Wider Landscape . . . without the
Mandate for Conquest,'" in *Beyond a Dream Deferred: Multicultural Education and the
Politics of Excellence*, ed. Becky Thompson and Sangeeta Tyagi (Minneapolis: University of Minnesota Press, 1993).

9 CPAC is an event put on every year by the American Conservative Union, which in
2019 had total expenditures topping $4 million, according to its public tax form,
available through ProPublica's website, accessed November 25, 2020, https://proj
ects.propublica.org/nonprofits/display_990/521294680/12_2019_prefixes_48
–54%2F521294680_201903_990_2019120916936139.

10 For example, see Becky Ropers-Huilman, Laura Carwile, and Kathy Barnett, "Stu-
dent Activists' Characterizations of Administrators in Higher Education: Percep-
tions of Power in 'the System,'" *Review of Higher Education* 28, no. 3 (2005); also see
Jade Agua and Sumun L. Pendakur, "From Resistance to Resilience: Transforming
Institutional Racism from the Inside Out," in *Student Activism, Politics, and Campus
Climate in Higher Education*, ed. Demetri L. Morgan and Charles H. F. Davis III (New
York: Routledge, 2019).

11 Cassie L. Barnhardt, "Philanthropic Foundations' Social Agendas and the Field of
Higher Education," in *Higher Education: Handbook of Theory and Research*, vol. 32, ed.
Michael B. Paulsen (New York: Springer, 2017); Jane Mayer, *Dark Money: The Hidden
History of the Billionaires Behind the Rise of the Radical Right* (New York: Doubleday,
2016).

12 On the professoriate's ideological leanings, see Neil Gross, *Why Are Professors Liberal
and Why Do Conservatives Care?* (Cambridge, MA: Harvard University Press, 2013);
Jon A. Shields and Joshua M. Dunn, *Passing on the Right: Conservative Professors in the
Progressive University* (New York: Oxford University Press, 2016); Matthew Woessner
and April Kelly-Woessner, "Left Pipeline: Why Conservatives Don't Get Doctorates," in *The Politically Correct University: Problems, Scope, and Reforms*, ed. Robert
Maranto et al. (Washington, DC: AEI Press, 2009). On the ideological slant of academic disciplines, see José L. Duarte et al., "Political Diversity Will Improve Social

Psychological Science," *Behavioral and Brain Sciences* 38 (2015); Chris C. Martin, "How Ideology Has Hindered Sociological Insight," *American Sociologist* 47, no. 1 (2016); Nicholas Quinn Rosenkranz, "Intellectual Diversity in the Legal Academy," *Harvard Journal of Law and Public Policy* 37, no. 1 (2014).

13   We analyze historical trends in students' political views and civic participation in chapter 2. Also see Brian O'Leary, "Backgrounds and Beliefs of College Freshmen," *Chronicle of Higher Education*, August 12, 2020, https://www.chronicle.com/interac tives/freshmen-survey; Courtney Kueppers, "Today's Freshman Class Is the Most Likely to Protest in Half a Century," *Chronicle of Higher Education*, February 11, 2016, https://www.chronicle.com/article/Today-s-Freshman-Class-Is/235273/?cid=related -promo. On administrators' ideological leanings, see Abrams, "Think Professors Are Liberal?"

14   For a discussion of conservatives using a civil rights framing, see Mary Becker, "The Legitimacy of Judicial Review in Speech Cases," in *The Price We Pay: The Case against Racist Speech, Hate Propaganda, and Pornography*, ed. Laura J. Lederer and Richard Delgado (New York: Hill and Wang, 1995); Stanley Eugene Fish, *There's No Such Thing as Free Speech, and It's a Good Thing, Too* (New York: Oxford University Press, 1994); Shoon Lio, Scott Melzer, and Ellen Reese, "Constructing Threat and Appropriating 'Civil Rights': Rhetorical Strategies of Gun Rights and English Only Leaders," *Symbolic Interaction* 31, no. 1 (2008). The careers of (and controversies surrounding) Mike Adams and Thomas Cushman, both sociology professors, offer useful illustrations of faculty who feel their campus communities have maligned and censored them for holding heterodox views. See Mike Adams and Adam Kissel, "Censorship in the UNC System: Correcting the Narrative," *Academic Questions* 30, no. 2 (2017); Thomas Cushman, "The Social Structure of Civility and Incivility in the Liberal Academy," *Society* 56, no. 6 (2019).

15   Mayer, *Dark Money*.

16   On civil and provocative forms of conservative student activism, see Amy J. Binder and Kate Wood, *Becoming Right: How Campuses Shape Young Conservatives* (Princeton, NJ: Princeton University Press, 2013). On Republican distrust of higher education, see Pew Research Center, "Sharp Divides in Views of National Institutions," July 10, 2017, http://www.people-press.org/2017/07/10/sharp-partisan-divisions-in-views -of-national-institutions/.

17   See especially Elizabeth A. Armstrong and Laura T. Hamilton, *Paying for the Party: How College Maintains Inequality* (Cambridge, MA: Harvard University Press, 2013); Binder and Wood, *Becoming Right*; Daisy Verduzco Reyes, *Learning to Be Latino: How Colleges Shape Identity Politics* (New Brunswick, NJ: Rutgers University Press 2018).

18   Recent examples of contentious campus protests include: the turmoil over conservative scholar Charles Murray's visit to Middlebury College in 2017 (which we discuss in more detail in chapter 6), the student-led demonstrations and building occupations at Evergreen College that same year, the anti-racist marches and sit-ins two years earlier at the University of Missouri (which led to the resignation of the school's president), and the violent street clashes which canceled a talk at the University of California Berkeley by right-wing provocateur Milo Yiannopoulos in 2017 (which we also address in chapter 6). See (respectively) Taylor Gee, "How the Middlebury Riot Really Went Down," *Politico*, May 28, 2017, https://www.politico .com/magazine/story/2017/05/28/how-donald-trump-caused-the-middlebury -melee-215195; Anemona Hartocollis, "A Campus Argument Goes Viral. Now the

College Is under Siege," *New York Times*, June 16, 2017, https://www.nytimes.com /2017/06/16/us/evergreen-state-protests.html; Elahe Izadi, "The Incidents that Led to the University of Missouri President's Resignation," *Washington Post*, November 9, 2015, https://www.washingtonpost.com/news/grade-point/wp/2015/11/09/the -incidents-that-led-to-the-university-of-missouri-presidents-resignation/; William Wan, "Milo's Appearance at Berkeley Led to Riots. He Vows to Return this Fall for a Week-Long Free-Speech Event," *Washington Post*, April 26. 2017, https://www .washingtonpost.com/news/grade-point/wp/2017/04/26/milos-appearance-at -berkeley-led-to-riots-he-vows-to-return-this-fall-for-a-week-long-free-speech -event/.

19 Ernest T. Pascarella and Patrick T. Terenzini, *How College Affects Students: A Third Decade of Research* (San Francisco: Jossey-Bass Publishers, 2005).

20 Notable examples include: Todd Gitlin, *The Sixties: Years of Hope, Days of Rage*, rev. ed. (New York: Bantam Books, 1993); Doug McAdam, *Freedom Summer* (New York: Oxford University Press, 1988); Demetri L. Morgan and Charles H. F. Davis III, eds., *Student Activism, Politics, and Campus Climate in Higher Education* (New York: Routledge, 2019); Robert A. Rhoads, *Freedom's Web: Student Activism in an Age of Cultural Diversity* (Baltimore, MD: Johns Hopkins University Press, 1998); Fabio Rojas, *From Black Power to Black Studies: How a Radical Social Movement Became an Academic Discipline* (Baltimore, MD: Johns Hopkins University Press, 2007); Yamane, *Student Movements for Multiculturalism*.

21 For examples of conservative student activism, see Binder and Wood, *Becoming Right*; Ziad Munson, "Mobilizing on Campus: Conservative Movements and Today's College Students," *Sociological Forum* 25, no. 4 (2010). For examples of top-down efforts by conservatives to enact institutional change, see Mayer, *Dark Money*; Steven M. Teles, *The Rise of the Conservative Legal Movement: The Battle for Control of the Law* (Princeton, NJ: Princeton University Press, 2008). Rebecca Klatch is one of the few scholars who has attempted to study the interplay of activism from the left and the right. Rebecca E. Klatch, *A Generation Divided: The New Left, the New Right, and the 1960s* (Berkeley: University of California Press, 1999).

22 Beyond our discussion of this matter in chapters 3 and 6, also see Garrett H. Gowen, Kevin M. Hemer, and Robert D. Reason, "Understanding American Conservatism and Its Role in Higher Education," in *Student Activism, Politics, and Campus Climate in Higher Education*, ed. Demetri L. Morgan and Charles H. F. Davis III (New York: Routledge, 2019).

23 Bethany Paige Bryson, *Making Multiculturalism: Boundaries and Meaning in U.S. English Departments* (Stanford, CA: Stanford University Press, 2005); Rojas, *From Black Power to Black Studies*; Yamane, *Student Movements for Multiculturalism*.

24 Greg Lukianoff and Jonathan Haidt, *The Coddling of the American Mind: How Good Intentions and Bad Ideas Are Setting Up a Generation for Failure* (New York: Penguin Press, 2018).

25 See chapter 7.

26 On the share of private and public university students, see Cristobal de Brey, Thomas D. Snyder, Anlan Zhang, and Sally A. Dillow, *Digest of Education Statistics 2019* (Washington, DC: US Department of Education, 2021).

27 Nate Silver, "The Odds of an Electoral College–Popular Vote Split Are Increasing," *FiveThirtyEight*, October 31, 2016, https://fivethirtyeight.com/features/the-odds -of-an-electoral-college-popular-vote-split-are-increasing/.

28   Public universities are more likely to enroll non-traditionally-aged students than private elite universities.

29   We break down national trends in race and political identity among college students in chapter 2. Our past research on conservative activists includes: Binder and Wood, *Becoming Right*; Jeffrey L. Kidder, "College Republicans and Conservative Social Identity," *Sociological Perspectives* 59, no. 1 (2016) and "Civil and Uncivil Places: The Moral Geography of College Republicans," *American Journal of Cultural Sociology* 6, no. 1 (2018). For examples of research on progressive student activists, see Christopher J. Broadhurst and Angel L. Velez, "Historical and Contemporary Context of Student Activism in U.S. Higher Education," in *Student Activism, Politics, and Campus Climate in Higher Education*, ed. Demetri L. Morgan and Charles H. F. Davis III (New York: Routledge, 2019); Veronica Lerma, Laura T. Hamilton, and Kelly Nielsen, "Racialized Equity Labor, University Appropriation and Student Resistance," *Social Problems* 67, no. 2 (2020); Paul Rogat Loeb, *Generation at the Crossroads: Apathy and Action on the American Campus* (New Brunswick, NJ: Rutgers University Press, 1994).

30   UA was recently designated a Hispanic-serving institution and has the lowest percentage of White students: 5 percent Asian, 4 percent Black, 26 percent Latinx, 51 percent White. CU is 8 percent Asian, 3 percent Black, 11 percent Latinx, and 66 percent White. UNC is 13 percent Asian, 8 percent Black, 7 percent Latinx, and 62 percent White. UVA is 13 percent Asian, 6 percent Black, 6 percent Latinx, and 59 percent White.

31   For a discussion about "facts" and subjective perceptions in qualitative interview data, see Shamus Khan and Colin Jerolmack, "Saying Meritocracy and Doing Privilege," *Sociological Quarterly* 54, no. 1 (2013); Iddo Tavory, "Interviews and Inference: Making Sense of Interview Data in Qualitative Research," *Qualitative Sociology* 43, no. 4 (2020). On self-narratives and the social dynamics of the interview setting, see (respectively) Robert Zussman, "Autobiographical Occasions," *Contemporary Sociology* 25, no. 2 (1996); Elliot G. Mishler, *Research Interviewing* (Cambridge, MA: Harvard University Press, 1986).

32   The official name is the Cooperative Institutional Research Program (CIRP) Freshman Survey. Additional analyses of the Freshman Survey data were provided by Edgar Romo.

33   See especially Ezra Klein, *Why We're Polarized* (New York: Avid Reader Press, 2020); Lilliana Mason, *Uncivil Agreement: How Politics Became Our Identity* (Chicago: University of Chicago Press, 2018).

CHAPTER TWO

1   Benefits of utilizing data from the Freshman Survey include its rich history, the consistency with which it has been administered, and the representativeness of the national data. The 2018 survey marked the 53rd consecutive annual administration of the instrument at colleges and universities across the US. While new items are regularly introduced and outdated items are retired, there is a balance between maintaining items with an eye towards historical trends and keeping current with the significant issues in higher education.

2   In the wider political world, not all libertarians feel aligned with conservatives, and we understand that some readers will bristle at our decision to lump the

ideologies together. But we make this move because this is how the libertarians we interviewed—along with the groups they were part of—positioned their activism. And, as our section on libertarians makes clear, we draw out the differences between the two ideologies.

3   However, this item did not appear on the CIRP Freshman Survey in 2016 and 2017.

4   These increases among those in the middle of the road and those to the left of center could be a reflection of students' general sentiments about contemporary campus politics, as well as increased activism resulting from the Black Lives Matter movement since 2014. While this question was not on the survey in 2016 and 2017, it is reasonable to assume the 2016 presidential campaigns and the subsequent election of Trump impacted students' views. It is also interesting to note that while on other measures of activism students who identify as middle-of-the-road are often least engaged, with respect to likelihood of participating in protests, conservatives are at the bottom of the list (16.3%). They are preceded by those on the far right (23.6%). We should add here that historically the term "protest" has negative connotations for right-leaning students, as it is associated with progressivism. Thus, many respondents might want to avoid laying any personal claims to such actions. However, in chapter 3 we propose that many speaking events sponsored by conservative clubs represent a form of protest against the perceived liberal hegemony at their schools.

5   Another metric of civic participation is respondents' voting behavior. But the Freshmen Survey, relying as it does on self-reports, shows numbers incongruent with actual voter turnout among younger adults. That said, even if disconnected from reality, these responses reveal subjective views on the desirability of civic participation. On average, those who identify as middle-of-the-road anticipate voting the least (76.9% say they intend to do so; again relating "middle of the road" with disengagement rather than political moderation). Liberals (88.3%) and those on the far left (86.3%) are slightly more likely to anticipate voting than their right-leaning peers (85.8% for conservatives, 80.7% for those on the far right).

6   Like Georgia, Levi also goes by the gender-neutral pronouns they/them/their.

7   Mark Lilla, *The Once and Future Liberal: After Identity Politics* (New York: HarperCollins, 2017). One can see a strong resonance between Lilla's deprecation of (what he describes as) burned-out-activists-turned-professors glorifying radical protest movements and Iona and Isaac's ideological evolution as college students. That is, their political education—both curricular and extracurricular—seems to have emboldened their nascent critiques of American government as so dysfunctional and inequitable that working within it was felt to be futile.

8   For a critique of liberalism, see Domenico Losurdo, *Liberalism: A Counter-History*, translated by Gregory Elliott (London and New York: Verso Books, 2011 [2005]). On intersecting systems of oppression, see Kimberlé Crenshaw, "Demarginalizing the Intersection of Race and Sex: A Black Feminist Critique of Antidiscrimination Doctrine, Feminist Theory, and Antiracist Politics," *The University of Chicago Legal Forum* 1989, no. 1 (1989). On the capitalist world-system, see Immanuel Wallerstein, *World-System Analysis: An Introduction* (Durham, NC: Duke University Press, 2004).

9   This two-dimensional plotting of ideology is commonly referred to as the political compass. See J. C. Lester, "The Evolution of the Political Compass (and Why Libertarianism Is Not Right-Wing)," *Journal of Social and Evolutionary Systems* 17, no. 3 (1994).

10   David Boaz, *Libertarianism: A Primer* (New York: Free Press, 1997).

11   Adam Gopnik, *A Thousand Small Sanities: The Moral Adventure of Liberalism* (New York: Basic Books, 2019). Also see Lilla, *The Once and Future Liberal*.

12   On this point, see Amy J. Binder and Kate Wood, *Becoming Right: How Campuses Shape Young Conservatives* (Princeton, NJ: Princeton University Press, 2013); Ben Merriman, *Conservative Innovators: How States Are Challenging Federal Power* (Chicago: University of Chicago Press, 2019).

13   Elsewhere, we have elaborated on these divisions, especially as it relates to support-ing (or not) the presidency of Trump. Jeffrey L. Kidder and Amy J. Binder, "Trump-ism on College Campuses," *Qualitative Sociology* 43, no. 2 (2020).

14   Rick Perlstein, *The Invisible Bridge: The Fall of Nixon and the Rise of Reagan* (New York: Simon & Schuster, 2014).

15   Michael Bang Petersen, Mathias Osmundsen, and Kevin Arceneaux, "A 'Need for Chaos' and the Sharing of Hostile Political Rumors in Advanced Democracies," *PsyArXiv*, September 1, 2018, https://doi.org/10.31234/osf.io/6m4ts; Robin Wagner-Pacifici and Iddo Tavory, "Politics as a Vacation," *American Journal of Cultural Sociol-ogy* 5, no. 3 (2017).

16   Alexander Astin, "Diversity and Multiculturalism on the Campus," *Change: The Magazine of Higher Learning* 25, no. 2 (1993); Anne Colby, et al., *Educating for Democ-racy: Preparing Undergraduates for Responsible Political Engagement* (San Francisco: Jossey-Bass, 2003).

17   Peter Kaufman and Kenneth Feldman, "Forming Identities in College: A Sociologi-cal Approach," *Research in Higher Education* 45, no. 5 (2004); Ernest Pascarella and Patrick Terenzini, *How College Affects Students: A Third Decade of Research* (San Fran-cisco: Jossey-Bass, 2005).

18   Kyle Dodson, "The Effect of College on Social and Political Attitudes and Civic Participation," in *Professors and Their Politics*, ed. Neil Gross and Solon Simmons (Baltimore, MD: Johns Hopkins University Press, 2014).

19   For example, see Ezra Klein, *Why We're Polarized* (New York: Avid Reader Press, 2020). Specifically examining the left side of the political spectrum, cultural critics Helen Pluckrose and James Lindsay also make this point in their analysis of post-modernism's transformation from an esoteric intellectual movement (confined to niches within a minority of academic departments) to a set of organizing principles utilized by progressive activists mobilizing for a wide variety of causes. Helen Pluckrose and James Lindsay, *Cynical Theories: How Activist Scholarship Made Every-thing about Race, Gender, and Identity* (Durham, NC: Pitchstone Publishing, 2020).

CHAPTER THREE

1   Clifford Geertz famously argues that the study of culture must move beyond merely charting out group practices and accounting for objects—"thin descriptions" (e.g., an anthropologist reporting on the frequency and popularity of cockfighting in Bali). Instead, analysis should extend into the *meanings* behind people's actions and the symbolic values attributed to them. "Thick description," in other words, offers an appreciation of the larger social context in which people operate (e.g., considering how social status, kindship networks, and cultural ideas about animality intersect in the Balinese cockfight). Clifford Geertz, "Thick Description: Toward an Interpretive Theory of Culture," in *The Interpretation of Cultures* (New York: Basic Books, 1973).

2   Daisy Verduzco Reyes, *Learning to Be Latino: How Colleges Shape Identity Politics* (New Brunswick, NJ: Rutgers University Press 2018).

3   On this approach, also see Demetri L. Morgan and Charles H. F. Davis III, "Preface: Transforming Campus Climates by Reframing Student Political Engagement and Activism," in *Student Activism, Politics, and Campus Climate in Higher Education*, ed. Demetri L. Morgan and Charles H. F. Davis III (New York: Routledge, 2019). On the influence of identity-based clubs in progressive activism on campus see Robert A. Rhoads, *Freedom's Web: Student Activism in the Age of Cultural Diversity* (Baltimore, MD: Johns Hopkins University Press, 1998); Fabio Rojas, *From Black Power to Black Studies: How a Racial Social Movement Became an Academic Discipline* (Baltimore, MD: Johns Hopkins University Press, 2007).

4   Stevens, Armstrong, and Arum argue that universities can be conceptualized using four metaphors to describe their primary social functions. The first is as a system of sieves, which allows only certain students to enter, thrive, and graduate from college. The second is as an incubator, by cultivating new skills and knowledge among its matriculants. Universities also can be viewed as temples, which produce and disseminate legitimate knowledge; and hubs, connecting students to other social sectors, such as the labor force. With minor adjustments, the first two metaphors, sieves and incubators, are especially useful for understanding what happens to students when they join political clubs. Mitchell Stevens, Elizabeth Armstrong, and Richard Arum, "Sieve, Incubator, Temple, Hub: Empirical and Theoretical Advances in the Sociology of Higher Education," *Annual Review of Sociology* 34, no. 1 (2008). For more on how higher education sifts and cultivates students more generally, see Pitirim Sorokin's work on sieves and Ernest Pascarella and Patrick Terenzini's (2005) research on college's influence on life experiences. Pitirim Sorokin, *Social and Cultural Mobility* (New York: Free Press, 1959); Ernest T. Pascarella and Patrick T. Terenzini, *How College Affects Students: A Third Decade of Research* (San Francisco: Jossey-Bass, 2005).

5   On angry town hall meetings, see Trip Gabriel et al., "At Town Halls, Doses of Fury and a Bottle of Tums," *The New York Times*, February 21, 2017, https://www.nytimes.com/2017/02/21/us/politics/town-hall-protests-obamacare.html. On Garrett's meeting with Kessler, see Dartunorro Clark, "GOP Lawmaker Regrets March Meeting with 'Unite the Right' Rally Organizer," *NBC News*, August 14, 2017, https://www.nbcnews.com/politics/congress/gop-lawmaker-regrets-march-meeting-unite-right-rally-organizer-n792496.

6   Mark Lilla, *The Once and Future Liberal: After Identity Politics* (New York: HarperCollins, 2017).

7   George, for example, told us his group went to a rally against gun violence after the mass murders at Marjory Stoneman Douglas High School to hand out "NRA stuff." The response Turning Point got, not surprisingly, was negative: "For the most part they were ticked." But, George reasoned, "We are just counter-protesting."

8   Greg Lukianoff and Jonathan Haidt, *The Coddling of the American Mind: How Good Intentions and Bad Ideas Are Setting Up a Generation for Failure* (New York: Penguin Press, 2018). However, we will explore a positive counter-trend in chapter 7, when we discuss trans-partisan dialogue groups.

9   Objectivism is a branch of philosophy started by Ayn Rand, best known for her books *The Fountainhead* and *Atlas Shrugged*. Objectivism overlaps with libertarianism, and Rand is now an iconic figure in conservative circles.

10   On the conservative social identity in American politics, see Neil Gross, Thomas
      Medvetz, and Rupert Russell, "The Contemporary American Conservative Move-
      ment," *Annual Review of Sociology* 37 (2011). On the conservative social identity
      among collegiate activists, see Jeffrey L. Kidder, "College Republicans and Conserva-
      tive Social Identity," *Sociological Perspectives* 59, no. 1 (2016). On divisions among
      conservatives, see Andrew J. Perrin, J. Micah Roos, and Gordon W. Gauchat, "From
      Coalition to Constraint: Modes of Thought in Contemporary American Conserva-
      tism," *Sociological Forum* 29, no. 2 (2014).

11   Amy J. Binder and Kate Wood, *Becoming Right: How Campuses Shape Young Conserva-
      tives* (Princeton, NJ: Princeton University Press 2013).

12   On the importance of coalition-building, see Suzanne Staggenborg, "Coalition
      Work in the Pro-Choice Movement: Organizational and Environmental Opportuni-
      ties and Obstacles," *Social Problems* 33, no. 5 (1986); Nella Van Dyke, "Crossing Move-
      ment Boundaries: Factors that Facilitate Coalition Protest by American College
      Students, 1930–1990," *Social Problems* 50, no. 2 (2003). For examples of detrimental
      in-fighting among activists, see Kathleen M. Blee, *Democracy in the Making: How
      Activist Groups Form* (New York: Oxford University Press, 2012); Clayborne Carson,
      In Struggle: SNCC and the Black Awakening of the 1960s (Cambridge, MA: Harvard
      University Press, 1981); Lori G. Waite, "Divided Consciousness: The Impact of Black
      Elite Consciousness on the 1966 Chicago Freedom Movement," in *Oppositional
      Consciousness: The Subjective Roots of Social Protest*, ed. Jane Mansbridge and Aldon
      Morris (Chicago: University of Chicago Press, 2001). Conversely, Amin Ghaziani
      makes a compelling case for the potential benefits of some forms of in-fighting
      among activists, arguing that it helps define the parameters of mobilization. Amin
      Ghaziani, *The Dividends of Dissent: How Conflict and Culture Work in Lesbian and Gay
      Marches on Washington* (Chicago: University of Chicago Press, 2008). On divisions
      between conservative student activists specifically, see Jeffrey L. Kidder and Amy J.
      Binder, "Trumpism on College Campuses," *Qualitative Sociology* 43, no. 2 (2020).

13   Nina Eliasoph and Paul Lichterman, "Culture in Interaction," *American Journal of
      Sociology* 108 (2003).

14   Chris Quintana, "Nationalist 'Antics' or the Future of the GOP? College Republicans
      Are at War," *USA Today*, January 17, 2020, accessed August 12, 2020, https://www
      .usatoday.com/story/news/education/2020/01/17/college-republicans-crnc-trump
      -republican-party-gop-turning-point-usa/4476649002/.

15   Nina Eliasoph, *Avoiding Politics: How Americans Produce Apathy in Everyday Life* (New
      York: Cambridge University Press, 1998).

16   For examples, see EJ Dickson, "Swarthmore Frats Disband after 4-Day Student
      Sit-In," *Rolling Stone*, April 30, 2019, https://www.rollingstone.com/culture/culture
      -news/swarthmore-students-protesting-campus-fraternities-829170/; Scott Jaschik,
      "Shifting Narrative at Minnesota," *Inside Higher Ed*, December 19, 2016, https://www
      .insidehighered.com/news/2016/12/19/minnesota-football-players-end-boycott-details
      -emerge-about-why-10-players-were.

17   Although there are notable exceptions. The most prominent of these exceptions
      in recent years has been the Berkeley College Republicans. This conservative (and
      highly provocative) club has been in a long-running set of legal conflicts with the
      University of California. See Jeremy Bauer-Wolf, "Civility at Berkeley," *Inside Higher
      Ed*, November 28, 2018, https://www.insidehighered.com/news/2018/11/28/new
      -policies-student-groups-change-culture-free-speech-berkeley; Joe Khalil, "Judge

Rules College Republicans' Lawsuit against University of California Can Move Forward," *Fox40 Sacramento*, March 19, 2019, https://fox40.com/2019/03/19/judge-rules -college-republicans-lawsuit-against-university-of-california-can-move-forward/; Jonathan Stempel, "UC Berkeley Settles Lawsuit over Treatment of Conservative Speakers," Reuters, December 3, 2018, https://www.reuters.com/article/us-califor nia-lawsuit-ucberkeley/uc-berkeley-settles-lawsuit-over-treatment-of-conservative -speakers-idUSKBN1O22K4. And, from the schools we studied, Young Americans for Freedom (YAF) threatened a lawsuit at UVA when the student council rejected its application to form a chapter on grounds. Kara Peters, "Young Americans for Freedom Claims U.Va. Illegally Denied Conservative Group CIO Status," *Cavalier Daily*, December 20, 2017, https://www.cavalierdaily.com/article/2017/12/young-americans -for-freedom-claims-u-va-illegally-denied-conservative-group-cio-status. The matter was ultimately resolved outside the courts, and YAF started a UVA chapter.

18 This policy agenda includes the conservative analog to progressive activism, such as influencing political leaders to cut funding to programs supporting leftist and liberal causes or crafting legislation to punish protesters. See (respectively) Nick Roll, "UNC Board Bars Litigation by Law School Center," *Inside Higher Ed*, September 11, 2017, https://www.insidehighered.com/news/2017/09/11/north-carolina-board -bars-unc-center-civil-rights-litigating; Michael Hiltzik, "How a Right-Wing Group's Proposed 'Free Speech' Law Aims to Undermine Free Speech on Campus," *Los Angeles Times*, May 30, 2018, https://www.latimes.com/business/hiltzik/la-fi-hiltzik -free-speech-20180530-story.html. These efforts, though, are not the ones to which the right-leaning *student* activists we spoke with were geared.

19 Scholars writing about group styles include Nina Eliasoph and Paul Lichterman, "Culture in Interaction," *American Journal of Sociology* 108, no. 4 (2003); Ann Mische, *Partisan Publics: Communication and Contention across Brazilian Youth Activist Networks* (Princeton, NJ: Princeton University Press, 2008); and Amy Binder and Kate Wood, "'Civil' or 'Provocative'? Varieties of Conservative Student Style and Discourse in American Universities," in *Professors and their Politics*, ed. Neil Gross and Solon Simmons (Baltimore, MD: Johns Hopkins University Press, 2014). Charles Tilly wrote about cultural repertoires for contention in any number of publications, including *Popular Contention in Great Britain, 1758–1834* (Cambridge, MA: Harvard University Press, 1995). See Paul Lichterman and Daniel Cefai, "The Idea of Political Culture," in *The Oxford Handbook of Contextual Political Analysis*, ed. Robert Goodin and Charles Tilly (New York: Oxford University Press, 2006).

CHAPTER FOUR

1 On the conservative network of foundations, think tanks, and advocacy groups, see Thomas Medvetz, *Think Tanks in America* (Chicago: University of Chicago Press, 2012); John Micklethwait and Adrian Wooldridge, *The Right Nation: Conservative Power in America* (New York: Penguin Press, 2004). For a discussion of policy agendas, see Alex Hertel-Fernandez, *State Capture: How Conservative Activists, Big Businesses, and Wealthy Donors Reshaped the American States and the Nation* (New York: Oxford University Press, 2019); Alexander Hertel-Fernandez and Theda Skocpol, "Why US Conservatives Shape Legislation across the Fifty States Much More Effectively than Liberals," *Scholars Strategy Network*, April 6, 2015, http://www.scholars

strategynetwork.org/brief/why-us-conservatives-shape-legislation-across-fifty
-states-much-more-effectively-liberals; Jane Mayer, *Dark Money: The Hidden History
of the Billionaires behind the Rise of the Radical Right* (New York: Doubleday, 2016).

2   Cassie L. Barnhardt, "Philanthropic Foundations' Social Agendas and the Field of
Higher Education," in *Higher Education: Handbook of Theory and Research*, vol. 32, ed.
Michael B. Paulsen (New York: Springer, 2017).

3   See Rebecca E. Klatch, *A Generation Divided: The New Left, the New Right, and the 1960s*
(Berkeley: University of California Press, 1999).

4   Amy J. Binder and Kate Wood, *Becoming Right: How Campuses Shape Young Conservatives* (Princeton, NJ: Princeton University Press, 2013).

5   See Barnhardt, "Philanthropic Foundations' Social Agendas and the Field of Higher
Education"; Amy J. Binder, Daniel B. Davis, and Nick Bloom, "Career Funneling:
How Elite Students Learn to Define and Desire 'Prestigious' Jobs," *Sociology of Educa-
tion* 89, no. 1 (2016).

6   Andrew J. Perrin, J. Micah Roos, and Gordon W. Gauchat, "From Coalition to Constraint: Modes of Thought in Contemporary American Conservatism," *Sociological
Forum* 29, no. 2 (2014).

7   This program is associated with (but not formally attached to) UA's controversial
Center for the Philosophy of Freedom, founded in part by money from the Charles
Koch Foundation. See Tim Steller, "Tim Steller's Opinion: Taxpayers Give UA 'Freedom Center' Prominence, Conflicts after Koch Money Dwindles," *Arizona Daily Star*,
June 21, 2020, https://tucson.com/news/local/tim-stellers-opinion-taxpayers-give
-ua-freedom-center-prominence-conflicts-after-koch-money-dwindles/article
_2698a55a-17e2-5a59-bb00-ca008ea68b3a.html.

8   AEI, "Defending and Promoting Freedom, Opportunity, and Enterprise: 2019 Annual Report," accessed August 21, 2020, http://annualreport.aei.org/.

9   Medvetz, *Think Tanks in America*.

10 Tevi Troy, "The Dilemma of the D.C. Think Tank," *The Atlantic*, December 19, 2017, https://
www.theatlantic.com/politics/archive/2017/12/presidents-and-think-tanks/548765/; also
see AEI, "Defending and Promoting Freedom, Opportunity, and Enterprise."

11 Shortly after our interview with him, Castle moved into another position at AEI.
Christopher Scalia, the son of the late Supreme Court Justice Antonin Scalia, became the Director of Academic Programs. See AEI, "About," accessed December 16,
2020, https://www.aei.org/about/contact/.

12 AEI, "Defending and Promoting Freedom, Opportunity, and Enterprise"; AEI, "Executive Councils," accessed August 31, 2020, https://www.aei.org/academic-programs
/executive-councils/.

13 AEI, "Defending and Promoting Freedom, Opportunity, and Enterprise."

14 For example, see Stephanie Saul, "Dozens of Middlebury Students Are Disciplined
for Charles Murray Protest," *New York Times*, May 24, 2017, https://www.nytimes
.com/2017/05/24/us/middlebury-college-charles-murray-bell-curve.html. The most
frequently cited explanation for the ire directed at Murray concerns positions advocated in a book he co-authored with the Harvard psychologist Richard Herrnstein
in 1994. Richard J. Herrnstein and Charles A. Murray, *The Bell Curve: Intelligence and
Class Structure in American Life* (New York: Free Press, 1994).

15 Eric Siegel, "The Real Problem with Charles Murray and 'The Bell Curve,'" *Scientific
American*, April 12, 2017, https://blogs.scientificamerican.com/voices/the-real-prob
lem-with-charles-murray-and-the-bell-curve/.

16   AEI, "2020 Summer Honors Program," accessed September 9, 2020, https://www
.aei.org/summer-honors-program/. On Yoo's role in the torture memos see Andrew
Cohen, "The Torture Memos, 10 Years Later," *The Atlantic*, February 6, 2012, https://
www.theatlantic.com/national/archive/2012/02/the-torture-memos-10-years
-later/252439/. The short biography on the AEI website emphasizes Yoo's prominence in the George W. Bush administration and his impressive career highlights,
but it omits the controversy concerning his legal legacy. AEI, "The Constitution:
Original Meanings and Modern Times," accessed September 9, 2020, https://www
.aei.org/the-constitution-original-meanings-and-modern-times-2/.

17   AEI, "Internships," accessed August 31, 2020, https://www.aei.org/internships/.

18   This is important because recent studies have documented the many institutional
advantages built up on the right, including financial backers, organizational
complexity, and extensive legislative successes. For example, see Hertel-Fernandez,
State Capture. Yet, we know relatively little about how college students—not those in
graduate school or professional programs, but 18- to 22-year-olds—are groomed to
eventually step into positions of power. AEI intentionally seeks to develop the next
generation of conservative leaders. And they spend a good deal of money, time, and
energy doing so.

19   Walter Mead is Professor of Foreign Affairs and the Humanities at Bard College
and serves on AEI's Council of Academic Advisors. AEI, "Council of Academic Advisors," accessed September 14, 2020, https://www.aei.org/about-old/council-of
-academic-advisers/.

20   Matthew Yglesias offers an illustrative example of the recent critiques written as a
rebuttal to Murray's arguments about class, race, and intelligence in *The Bell Curve*.
Matthew Yglesias, "The Bell Curve Is about Policy. And It's Wrong," *Vox*, April 10,
2018, https://www.vox.com/2018/4/10/17182692/bell-curve-charles-murray-policy
-wrong. Sommers's critiques of contemporary feminism are summed up nicely in
the titles of her books. For example, see Christina Hoff Sommers, *The War against
Boys: How Misguided Feminism Is Harming Our Young Men* (New York: Simon & Schuster, 2000).

21   Turning Point USA, "Our Mission," accessed July 3, 2020, https://www.tpusa.com
/ourmission.

22   In his address to the convention, Kirk referred to Trump as the "bodyguard of Western civilization." Quoted in Julia Manchester, "Charlie Kirk Gets First GOP Convention Address, Calls Trump 'Bodyguard of Western Civilization,'" *The Hill*, August 24,
2020, https://thehill.com/homenews/campaign/513471-charlie-kirk-gives-first
-address-at-gop-convention. Such lofty praise for a president so fundamentally out
of touch with most traditional conservatives' first principles perplexes many of the
Republican Party's former leaders. For example, see David Frum, *Trumpocracy: The
Corruption of the American Republic* (New York: Harper, 2018). On Trump's retweets
of Kirk, see Matthew Rosenberg and Katie Rogers, "For Charlie Kirk, Conservative
Activist, the Virus Is a Cudgel," *New York Times*, April 19, 2020, https://www.nytimes
.com/2020/04/19/us/politics/charlie-kirk-conservatives-coronavirus.html. For an illustration of Trump's relationship with Turning Point see Barbara Sprunt and Alana
Wise, "Trump Addresses Tightly Packed Arizona Crowd amid State's Growing Coronavirus Crisis," *NPR*, June 23, 2020, https://www.npr.org/2020/06/23/881641178/after
-disappointing-tulsa-rally-trump-campaign-moves-to-arizona.

23 Alexandra Yoon-Hendricks, "A Place where Conservative Teenagers Feel Free to Be Themselves," *New York Times*, July 25, 2018, https://www.nytimes.com/2018/07/25/us/politics/turning-point-young-conservatives.html.

24 The membership numbers we cite come from Turning Point. Turning Point USA, "About," accessed July 6, 2020, https://www.tpusa.com/about. However, figuring out the true numbers is impossible. And the Young America's Foundation (an organization fighting for the same niche in the conservative channel) has accused Turning Point of wildly inflating its membership rolls. See Michael Vasquez, "Leaked Memo from Conservative Group Cautions Students to Stay Away from Turning Point USA," *Chronicle of Higher Education*, June 15, 2018, https://www.chronicle.com/article/leaked-memo-from-conservative-group-cautions-students-to-stay-away-from-turning-point-usa/.

25 Turning Point's 2018 form 990 filed with the IRS is available online, accessed August 31, 2020, https://www.documentcloud.org/documents/6983104-Turning-Point-USA-2018-990-With-Redacted-B-2.html. While Turning Point's tax-exempt status means it must be nonpartisan, in 2019 Kirk filed a 501(c)4 application for a separate offshoot called Turning Point Action—the entity under which the revamped Students for Trump now exists. See Brian Schwartz, "Pro-Trump College GOP Activist Charlie Kirk Will Launch a New Group to Target Democrats in 2020," *CNBC*, May 20, 2019, https://www.cnbc.com/2019/05/20/pro-trump-activist-charlie-kirk-to-launch-new-group-to-target-democrats.html. The status of a 501(c)4 permits Turning Point Action to campaign for political candidates. Before being taken over by Kirk, Students for Trump was originally run by two collegians at Campbell University in North Carolina. See Rachel Chason, "National 'Students for Trump' Effort Has NC Roots," *News & Observer*, September 27, 2016, https://www.newsobserver.com/news/politics-government/election/article104522526.html. Started in 2015, the group quickly ballooned, with chapters springing up on campuses across the US, and drew the attention of the Trump campaign. During this time, Turning Point was also a *de facto* club for collegiate support of the president. See Jeffrey L. Kidder and Amy J. Binder, "Trumpism on College Campuses," *Qualitative Sociology* 43, no. 2 (2020). However, local Turning Point chapters could not legally get support from the national organization for campaign events. The creation of Turning Point Action and the revamping of Students for Trump allowed them to do so for the 2020 election.

26 For more on the organizational structure, see Turning Point USA, "Start a Chapter," accessed September 14, 2020, https://www.tpusa.com/startachapter.

27 For more information on the field representative program, see Turning Point USA, "Staff," accessed November 22, 2020, https://www.tpusa.com/staff.

28 Turning Point USA, "Chapter Handbook, College Edition 2018–2019," accessed August 31, 2020, https://drive.google.com/file/d/1j6fEw91X9B8oUIOWWXOyIA9k1ZDBWWn9/view.

29 David R. Dietrich, "Racially Charged Cookies and White Scholarships: Anti-Affirmative Action Protests on American College Campuses," *Sociological Focus* 48, no. 2 (2015). For an example of the sort of uproar affirmative action bake sales can engender, see Jessica Schladebeck, "'Affirmative Action Bake Sale' Charges University of New Mexico Students Based on Race," *Daily News*, September 23, 2017, https://www.nydailynews.com/news/national/affirmative-action-bake-sale-charges-students-based-race-article-1.3515715.

30   We pull this from the promotional materials on the Palm Beach County Convention Center website, accessed September 1, 2020, https://www.pbconventioncenter.com/events/turning-point-usa.

31   At SAS 2020, held in late December at the Palm Beach County Convention Center, few attendees wore masks (in violation of the county's coronavirus protocols and defying common sense amidst a resurgent pandemic). With a rowdy, frat-boy vibe, the event featured "Bang Girls" (named after Bang Energy drinks) in skin-tight outfits firing cash from a money cannon on stage. See Paulina Villegas and David A. Fahrenthold, "Young Conservatives Mingled Maskless at Mar-a-Lago and Partied with a Money Cannon," *Washington Post*, December 21, 2020, https://www.washingtonpost.com/politics/2020/12/21/turning-point-covid-party/. And, despite the conference occurring more than a month after Trump's defeat in the popular election, and after numerous court losses by his campaign, Pence assured the crowd that "As our election contest continues, I'll make you a promise, we're going to keep fighting until every legal vote is counted. We're going to keep fighting until every illegal vote is thrown out." Quoted in Paul Steinhauser, "Pence Urges Conservatives 'to Stay in the Fight' as 'Our Election' Continues," *Fox News*, December 22, 2020, https://www.foxnews.com/politics/pence-election-fight-florida-speech.

32   Turning Point USA, "Profile: Alex Clark," accessed September 4, 2020, https://www.tpusa.com/alexclark; Turning Point USA, "POPlitics," accessed September 4, 2020, https://www.tpusa.com/poplitics.

33   POPlitics, "Ep 180: Fauci's Fail & T. I.'s Ludicrous Reparations," accessed September 8, 2020, https://www.youtube.com/watch?v=oogfOjuAwys&t=197s.

34   On Dr. Fauci's vilification on the right, see Davey Alba and Sheera Frenkel, "Medical Expert Who Corrects Trump Is Now a Target of the Far Right," *New York Times*, March 28, 2020, https://www.nytimes.com/2020/03/28/technology/coronavirus-fauci-trump-conspiracy-target.html. On Trump's claim of an invitation from the Yankees, see Katie Rogers and Noah Weiland, "Trump Announced, then Canceled, a Yankees Pitch. Both Came as a Surprise," *New York Times*, July 25, 2020, accessed September 9, 2020, https://www.nytimes.com/2020/07/27/us/politics/trump-yankees-fauci.html.

35   See (respectively) Professor Watchlist, "About Us," accessed September 1, 2020, https://www.professorwatchlist.org/aboutus; CampusReform.org, "About," accessed September 14, 2020, https://campusreform.org/about/. The Leadership Institute is one of three "partner resources" promoted by Turning Point, along with the Intercollegiate Studies Institute (co-founded by William F. Buckley in 1953) and PragerU (featured in this chapter). See Turning Point USA, "Partner Resources," accessed September 9, 2020, https://www.tpusa.com/partnerresources. For a classic example of conservative critiques of the professoriate, see Roger Kimball, *Tenured Radicals: How Politics Has Corrupted Our Higher Education* (New York: Harper & Row, 1990).

36   Steve Kolowich, "State of Conflict," *Chronicle of Higher of Education*, April 27, 2018, https://www.chronicle.com/interactives/state-of-conflict.

37   Kirk's tweet can be found on Twitter, accessed July 4, 2020, https://twitter.com/charliekirk11/status/1241820673007161345?lang=en.

38   Binder and Wood, *Becoming Right*. On sixties-era leftist political theater, see Todd Gitlin, *The Whole World Is Watching: Mass Media and in the Making and Unmaking of the New Left* (Berkeley: University of California Press, 1980).

39   PragerU, "About," accessed January 20, 2020, https://www.prageru.com/about/.

40 See PragerU's Twitter feed, accessed September 14, 2020, https://twitter.com/prageru
    /status/1259965746186084352?lang=en.

41 See (respectively) PragerU, "Dangerous People Are Teaching Your Kids," accessed
    September 5, 2020, https://www.prageru.com/video/dangerous-people-are-teach
    ing-your-kids/; PragerU, "There Is No Gender Wage Gap!" accessed September 5,
    2020, https://www.prageru.com/video/there-is-no-gender-wage-gap/; PragerU,
    "Why I Left the Left," accessed September 5, 2020, https://www.prageru.com/video
    /why-i-left-the-left/; PragerU, "Democratic Socialism Is Still Socialism," accessed
    September 5, 2020, https://www.prageru.com/video/democratic-socialism-is-still
    -socialism/. We have no way of independently verifying PragerU's claims of viewer-
    ship, but when the reporter Joseph Bernstein consulted independent experts, they
    largely concurred with the organization's self-reports. Joseph Bernstein, "How
    PragerU Is Winning the Right-Wing Culture War without Donald Trump," *BuzzFeed
    News*, March 3, 2018, https://www.buzzfeednews.com/article/josephbernstein/prager
    -university.

42 See (respectively) PragerU, "Black Lives Matter Is a Marxist Movement" (which fea-
    tures PragerU show host Will Witt interviewing Carol Swain, the highly controver-
    sial former political science and law professor from Vanderbilt University), accessed
    September 5, 2020, https://www.prageru.com/video/black-lives-matter-is-a-marxist
    -movement/; PragerU, "Black Lives Matter Is Not Helping Blacks" (which features
    Witt interviewing conservative commentator Derryck Green), accessed Septem-
    ber 5, 2020, https://www.prageru.com/video/black-lives-matter-is-not-helping-blacks/;
    PragerU, "The Media Pushed Lies about Ferguson," accessed September 5, 2020,
    https://www.prageru.com/video/the-media-pushed-lies-about-ferguson/; PragerU,
    "The Mainstream Media Will Not Tell the Truth about Black Lives Matter," accessed
    September 5, 2020, https://www.prageru.com/video/the-mainstream-media-will-not
    -tell-the-truth-about-black-lives-matter/; PragerU, "Larry Elder Eviscerates the Myth
    of 'Systemic Racism,'" accessed September 5, 2020, https://www.prageru.com/video
    /larry-elder-eviscerates-the-myth-of-systemic-racism/.

43 The number of views is listed on many pages, including on https://www.prageru.com/,
    accessed September 15, 2020.

44 PragerU, "2019 Annual Report," accessed September 9, 2020, https://www.prageru
    .com/prageru-2019-annual-report.pdf. PragerU also asserts that 60 percent of its
    audience are under the age of 34 (obliquely revealing that 40 percent of viewers are
    well beyond traditional college age).

45 See PragerU, "2019 Annual Report." On specific donors, see Evan Halper, "How a Los
    Angeles-Based Conservative Became One of the Internet's Biggest Sensations," *Los
    Angeles Times*, August 23, 2019, https://www.latimes.com/politics/story/2019–08–22
    /dennis-prager-university-conservative-internet-sensation; Alex Kotch, "Who Funds
    PragerU's Anti-Muslim Content?" *Sludge*, December 27, 2018, https://readsludge
    .com/2018/12/27/who-funds-pragerus-anti-muslim-content; also see Alex Kotch,
    "Who Funds Conservative Campus Group Turning Point USA? Donors Revealed,"
    International Business Times, November 28, 2017, https://www.ibtimes.com/political
    -capital/who-funds-conservative-campus-group-turning-point-usa-donors-revealed
    -2620325.

46 PragerU, "2019 Annual Report."

47 PragerU, "2019 Annual Report."

48 Restricted content on YouTube is not removed, but it does allow those with control over a computer's settings (like parents or school administrators) to block videos from playing. YouTube has the power to flag content uploaded to the platform as potentially offensive, and thus deserving of the "restricted" designation. PragerU vehemently denies that its videos warrant restrictions, and it also maintains a "Restricted by YouTube" page on its website with a playlist of 99 videos. See PragerU, "Restricted by YouTube," accessed September 1, 2020, https://www.prageru.com /playlist/restricted-by-youtube/. Further, PragerU has (unsuccessfully) pursued a case in federal court asking the government to step in and prevent Google (YouTube's parent company) from restricting its videos (Hamilton 2020), a truly odd strategy for an organization supposedly favoring free markets. See Isobel Asher Hamilton, "YouTube Isn't Bound by the First Amendment and Is Free to Censor PragerU, a Court Ruled," *Business Insider*, February 27, 2020, https://www.businessinsider.com/youtube -google-censor-court-prageru-first-amendment-2020-2; also see Bernstein, "How PragerU Is Winning the Right-Wing Culture War without Donald Trump."

49 See John McCarthy and Mayer Zald, "Resource Mobilization and Social Movements: A Partial Theory," *American Journal of Sociology* 82, no. 6 (1977) for a foundational statement about how elites shape movement activity. Among the hundreds of publications that have taken issue with this formulation is Aldon Morris's classic study *The Origins of the Civil Rights Movement: Black Communities Organizing for Change* (New York: The Free Press, 1984), in which the author argues that the civil rights movement was led by grassroots Black clergy and students, and was activated through local community networks, not elites. As we will see in the next chapter, progressive student activism largely lacks outside entrepreneurial support, but some recent scholarship demonstrates that elites and movement professionals sometimes do direct resources to particular constituencies and successfully influence their mobilization. See, for example, Nella Van Dyke, Marc Dixon, and Helen Carlon, "Manufacturing Dissent: Labor Revitalization, Union Summer and Student Protest," *Social Forces* 86, no.1 (2007) on the AFL-CIO's impact on student labor activism.

CHAPTER FIVE

1 PragerU, "DivestU" (with 2.9 million views), accessed September 29, 2020, https:// www.prageru.com/video/divestu/.

2 For organizational funding in higher education, see Cassie L. Barnhardt, "Philanthropic Foundations' Social Agendas and the Field of Higher Education," in *Higher Education: Handbook of Theory and Research*, vol. 32, ed. Michael B. Paulsen (New York: Springer, 2017). Quoted text comes from Amy J. Binder and Kate Wood, *Becoming Right: How Campuses Shape Young Conservatives* (Princeton, NJ: Princeton University Press, 2013), ix. For partisanship in views on higher education, see Kim Parker, "The Growing Partisan Divide in Views of Higher Education," Pew Research Center, August 19, 2019, https://www.pewsocialtrends.org/essay/the-growing-partisan -divide-in-views-of-higher-education/.

3 As we write this in early 2021, the Republican Party, and conservatism in general, face remarkable internal divisions due to Trumpism. On the electoral challenges facing the Republican Party, see Steven Levitsky and Daniel Ziblatt, "Why Republicans Play Dirty," *New York Times*, September 20, 2019, https://www.nytimes

.com/2019/09/20/opinion/republicans-democracy-play-dirty.html. On the fragmentation of the Democratic Party, see Matt Grossman and David Hopkins, "Ideological Republicans and Group Interest Democrats: The Asymmetry of American Party Politics," *Perspectives on Politics* 13, no. 1 (2015). On organizational advantages, see Alexander Hertel-Fernandez, *State Capture: How Conservative Activists, Big Businesses, and Wealthy Donors Reshaped the American States and the Nation* (New York: Oxford University Press, 2019).

4   Doug McAdam, "Recruitment to High-Risk Activism: The Case of Freedom Summer," *American Journal of Sociology* 92, no. 1 (1986); Nella Van Dyke, "Hotbeds of Activism: Locations of Student Protest," *Social Problems* 45, no. 2 (1998).

5   John McCarthy and Mayer Zald, "Resource Mobilization and Social Movements: A Partial Theory," *American Journal of Sociology* 82, no. 6 (1977).

6   Laura T. Hamilton and Kelly Nielsen, *Broke: The Racial Consequences of Underfunding Public Education* (Chicago: University of Chicago Press, 2021); Lauren D. Olsen, "The Conscripted Curriculum and the Reproduction of Racial Inequalities in Contemporary U.S. Medical Education," *Journal of Health & Social Behavior* 60, no. 1 (2019).

7   US PIRG, "About Us," accessed September 15, 2020, https://uspirg.org/feature/usp/about-us.

8   US PIRG, "Our Staff," accessed November 22, 2020, https://uspirg.org/sites/pirg/files/usp-staff/index.html; for more on Nader's Raiders, see Henriette Mantel and Steve Skrovan, *An Unreasonable Man* (New York: IFC Films, 2006).

9   US PIRG, "About Us."

10   At the University of California San Diego, where one of us is a faculty member, there is a CALPIRG Students group. The fee is voluntary, and students must make the effort to sign up if they want their money to go to the organization. But once they do, the university will collect $10 on CALPIRG Students' behalf every quarter until the students graduate or opt out. In 2018, there was a failed referendum to bar the university from collecting these fees. Opponents of the opt-in fee structure were angered over the types of work CALPIRG engages in (i.e., progressive causes). They also asserted that the funding model lacks transparency. Associated Students, "CALPIRG Voluntary Fee Referendum," AS UC San Diego, accessed May 7, 2020, https://as.ucsd.edu/Home/Referendum/2?name=CALPIRG%20Voluntary%20Fee%20Referendum.

11   Radley Balko, "Nader Scams College Kids," *Fox News*, March 13, 2003, https://www.foxnews.com/story/nader-scams-college-kids.

12   Planned Parenthood Action Fund, "About Us," accessed June 3, 2020, https://www.plannedparenthoodaction.org/about-us. Planned Parenthood's 2018 form 990 filed with the IRS is available online, accessed June 3, 2020, https://pdf.guidestar.org/PDF_Images/2018/133/539/2018-133539048-1062aa15-9O.pdf.

13   The comparatively smaller amount of funding directed toward campus-based political action is implicitly revealed through what students working with the group told us. However, we were unable to verify an exact dollar amount with a Planned Parenthood representative.

14   Planned Parenthood Generation Action, "Planned Parenthood Generation Action . . . ," accessed September 16, 2020, https://www.plannedparenthoodaction.org/communities/planned-parenthood-generation-action.

15   CDA's constitution and bylaws, which includes their mission statement, are available online. CDA, "Constitution of the College Democrats of America," accessed

September 16, 2020, https://democrats.org/wp-content/uploads/sites/2/2019/12/Constitution-and-Bylaws-for-the-College-Democrats-of-America-updated-2.3.19-1.pdf. In addition to CDA, there is also Young Democrats of America (YDA), which is not an official part of the DNC. Many university-level Democratic clubs use the phrase "Young Democrats" in their name, and some may have formal or informal ties with YDA (or perhaps had such ties in the past). However, CDA insists that *all* campus groups seeking to represent the party fall under its umbrella.

16   CDA is not a stand-alone organization. A DNC staffer runs it alongside the president and vice president and sets the annual budget. See CDA, "Constitution of the College Democrats of America." Since the DNC does not file 990s with the IRS, we rely exclusively on this interviewee's information about the dollar amount used to fund CDA.

17   NextGen America, "About Us," accessed June 3, 2020, https://nextgenamerica.org/about-us/.

18   NextGen America, "An Inside Look," accessed August 26, 2020, https://nextgenamerica.org/insider/.

19   NextGen's income tax form 990 is available through ProPublica's website, accessed June 3, 2020, https://projects.propublica.org/nonprofits/display_990/461957345/01_2020_prefixes_45-46%2F461957345_201812_9900_2020011617038677.

20   Wessel's quote here illustrates Mark Lilla's critique of the contemporary progressive movement's general disdain for mainstream politicking. The real action—it is assumed—is in grassroots mobilizing (even within an organization working to elect politicians). Training young people in the necessary (but rather humdrum) aspects of day-to-day governance is pejoratively characterized by Wessel as kids "who like to wear suits," want to "meet Martin O'Malley" (the former governor of Maryland and onetime candidate for the Democratic presidential nomination), and make "references to *The West Wing*." Mark Lilla, *The Once and Future Liberal: After Identity Politics* (New York: HarperCollins, 2017).

21   Samuel J. Abrams, "Think Professors Are Liberal? Try School Administrators," *New York Times*, October 16, 2018, https://www.nytimes.com/2018/10/16/opinion/liberal-college-administrators.html; Neil Gross and Solon Simmons, "The Social and Political Views of American College and University Professors," in *Professors and Their Politics*, ed. Neil Gross and Solon Simmons (Baltimore, MD: Johns Hopkins University Press, 2014).

22   Fabio Rojas, *From Black Power to Black Studies: How a Radical Social Movement Became an Academic Discipline* (Baltimore, MD: Johns Hopkins University Press, 2007).

23   Wallace writes, "There are these two young fish swimming along, and they happen to meet an older fish swimming the other way, who nods at them and says, 'Morning, boys, how's the water?' And the two young fish swim on for a bit, and then eventually one of them looks over at the other and goes, 'What the hell is water?' [. . .] The immediate point of the fish story is that the most obvious, ubiquitous, important realities are often the ones that are the hardest to see and talk about." David Foster Wallace, "Plain Old Untrendy Troubles and Emotions," *The Guardian*, September 19, 2008, https://www.theguardian.com/books/2008/sep/20/fiction.

24   Matthew Woessner and April Kelly-Woessner, "Left Pipeline: Why Conservatives Don't Get Doctorates," in *The Politically Correct University: Problems, Scope, and Reforms*, ed. Robert Maranto et al. (Washington, DC: AEI Press, 2009); also see April Kelly-Woessner and Matthew Woessner, "My Professor Is a Partisan Hack: How

Perceptions of a Professor's Political Views Affect Student Course Evaluations," *PS: Political Science and Politics* 39, no. 3 (2006).

25   Abrams, "Think Professors Are Liberal? Try School Administrators."

26   On the relationship between academia and the military, see Barry Smart, "Military-Industrial Complexities, University Research and Neoliberal Economy," *Journal of Sociology* 52, no. 3 (2016). On the connection between the university and capitalism, see Elizabeth Popp Berman, *Creating the Market University: How Academic Science Became an Economic Engine* (Princeton, NJ: Princeton University Press, 2012). For an overarching critique of contemporary higher education, see Henry A. Giroux, *Neoliberalism's War on Higher Education* (Chicago: Haymarket Books, 2014).

27   MSUA's list of demands is available online, accessed October 2, 2019, https://www.scribd.com/doc/303280642/Marginalized-Students-of-The-University-of-Arizona-MSUA-List-of-Demands.

28   For useful illustrations of these points, see Jade Agua and Sumun L. Pendakur, "From Resistance to Resilience: Transforming Institutional Racism from the Inside Out," in *Student Activism, Politics, and Campus Climate in Higher Education*, ed. Demetri L. Morgan and Charles H. F. Davis III (New York: Routledge, 2019); Sy Stokes and Donté Miller, "Remembering 'the Black Bruins': A Case Study of Supporting Student Activists at UCLA," in *Student Activism, Politics, and Campus Climate in Higher Education*, ed. Demetri L. Morgan and Charles H. F. Davis III (New York: Routledge, 2019).

29   Abrams was pilloried for his op-ed in the *New York Times*. Angry signs were placed on his office door and the campus free speech board was marked with vulgarities about him. The college president personally accused him of attacking the community, and student activists demanded that his tenure be re-evaluated by those more sensitive to multicultural values. See Madeleine Kearns, "Viewpoint Diversity Dies at Sarah Lawrence College," *National Review*, November 6, 2018, https://www.nationalreview.com/2018/11/college-professor-targeted-over-op-ed-viewpoint-diversity/; Colleen Flaherty, "When Students Want to Review a Tenured Professor," *Inside Higher Ed*, March 13, 2019, https://www.insidehighered.com/news/2019/03/13/students-sarah-lawrence-want-review-tenure-conservative-professor-who-criticized.

30   Although we could not verify the salary of the president of College Republicans, tax information for the College Republican National Committee appears on the Open Secrets website, accessed October 3, 2020, https://www.opensecrets.org/527s/527cmtedetail_expends.php?ein=521082055&cycle=2018. In 2018, overall expenditures exceeded $3.5 million, with nearly $364,000 of that amount spent on salaries.

31   We tried to confirm Madeleine's claim, but we could not reach a representative through CDA. On the internet, salaries (or the lack thereof) are difficult to determine, since CDA's finances are linked to the DNC, and we could not find tax information for that organization. A *New York Times* reporter, Maggie Astor, discusses CDA officers having to pay for their own travel, but she does not address the matter of salaries directly. Maggie Astor, "College Democrats, Citing Racism, Force Change in Leadership," *New York Times*, July 1, 2020, https://www.nytimes.com/2020/07/01/us/politics/college-democrats-president-resigns.html.

32   Neil Gross, *Why Are Professors Liberal and Why Do Conservatives Care?* (Cambridge, MA: Harvard University Press, 2013); also see Jon A. Shields and Joshua M. Dunn, *Passing on the Right: Conservative Professors in the Progressive University* (New York: Oxford University Press, 2016); Woessner and Kelly-Woessner, "Left Pipeline."

33   Greg Lukianoff and Jonathan Haidt, *The Coddling of the American Mind: How Good Intentions and Bad Ideas Are Setting up a Generation for Failure* (New York: Penguin Press, 2018).

CHAPTER SIX

1   As mentioned in previous chapters, Milo Yiannopoulos prefers the moniker "Milo."

2   Jake Mauff, "CU Administration Was Aware of Milo Yiannopoulos Incidents; Campus to Host Buffs United and Laverne Cox Events Wednesday," *CU Independent*, January 25, 2017, https://cuindependent.com/2017/01/25/cu-administration-aware-milo-yiannopoulos-incidents-campus-host-buffs-united-laverne-cox-events-wednesday/.

3   For coverage of Seattle, see Katherine Long, Lynn Thompson, and Jessica Lee, "Man Shot during Protests of Breitbart Editor Milo Yiannopoulos' Speech at UW; Suspect Arrested," *Seattle Times*, January 20, 2017, https://www.seattletimes.com/seattle-news/education/violence-punctuates-uw-talk-by-breitbart-editor-milo-yiannopoulos/. For coverage of Berkeley, see Thomas Fuller and Christopher Mele, "Berkeley Cancels Milo Yiannopoulos Speech, and Donald Trump Tweets Outrage," *New York Times*, February 1, 2017, https://www.nytimes.com/2017/02/01/us/uc-berkeley-milo-yiannopoulos-protest.html. For coverage of Boulder, see Sarah Kuta, "Met by Protests, Milo Yiannopoulos Targets Feminists, Liberals at CU Boulder Talk," *Daily Camera*, January 25, 2017, http://www.dailycamera.com/cu-news/ci_30751138/about-100-demonstrators-protesting-milo-yiannopoulos-at-cu.

4   David Uberti, "Milo Yiannopoulos Says He's Broke," *Vice News*, September 9, 2019, https://www.vice.com/en_us/article/59n99q/milo-yiannopoulos-says-hes-broke.

5   See D. D. Guttenplan, "An Interview with the Most Hated Man on the Internet," *The Nation*, October 16, 2016, https://www.thenation.com/article/archive/an-interview-with-the-most-hated-man-on-the-internet/; Maya Oppenheim, "UC Berkeley Protests: Milo Yiannopoulos Planned to 'Publicly Name Undocumented Students' in Cancelled Talk," *Independent*, February 3, 2017, https://www.independent.co.uk/news/world/americas/uc-berkely-protests-milo-yiannopoulos-publicly-name-undocumented-students-cancelled-talk-illegals-a7561321.html; Diana Tourjée, "Trans Student Harassed by Milo Yiannopoulos Speaks Out," *Vice*, January 3, 2017, https://www.vice.com/en_us/article/vb4e44/trans-student-harassed-by-milo-yiannopoulos-speaks-out.

6   Charles R. Lawrence III et al., "Introduction," in *Words that Wound: Critical Race Theory, Assaultive Speech, and the First Amendment*, ed. Mari J. Matsuda et al. (Boulder, CO: Westview Press, 1993).

7   On this point, see especially John G. Palfrey, *Safe Spaces, Brave Spaces: Diversity and Free Expression in Education* (Cambridge, MA: MIT Press, 2017).

8   Scott D. Gerber, "The Politics of Free Speech," *Social Philosophy & Policy* 21, no. 2 (2004). We should also add here that cases which have upheld sexual harassment claims and hostile work environments are an important exception to this otherwise "hands-off" trend in speech regulation. Scholars advocating more restrictive interpretations of the First Amendment to promote diversity often cite these legal precedents.

9   Rodney A. Smolla, "Academic Freedom, Hate Speech, and the Idea of a University," *Law & Contemporary Problems* 53, no. 3 (1990). On the matter of public versus private

schools, see *Harvard Civil Rights–Civil Liberties Law Review*, "First Amendment on Private Campuses," accessed December 7, 2020, https://harvardcrcl.org/first-amend ment-on-private-campuses/.

10   Erwin Chemerinsky and Howard Gillman, *Free Speech on Campus* (New Haven, CT: Yale University Press, 2017), 19.

11   On the assumed virtues of expansive speech rights, see (most famously) John Stuart Mill, *On Liberty* (Mineola, NY: Dover Publications, 2002 [1859]); also see Andrew Jason Cohen, "Psychological Harm and Free Speech on Campus," *Society* 54, no. 4 (2017); Ryan Muldoon, "Free Speech and Learning from Difference," *Society* 54, no. 4 (2017). On Justice Oliver Wendell Holmes's famed Supreme Court dissent that eventually helped to define contemporary laws on free expression, see Thomas Healy, *The Great Dissent: How Oliver Wendell Holmes Changed His Mind—and Changed the History of Free Speech in America* (New York: Henry Holt and Company, 2013).

12   Charles R. Lawrence III, "If He Hollers Let Him Go: Regulating Racist Speech on Campus," in *Words that Wound: Critical Race Theory, Assaultive Speech, and the First Amendment*, ed. Mari J. Matsuda et al. (Boulder, CO: Westview Press, 1993); Richard Delgado, "First Amendment Formalism Is Giving Way to First Amendment Legal Realism," in *The Price We Pay: The Case against Racist Speech, Hate Propaganda, and Por- nography*, ed. Laura J. Lederer and Richard Delgado (New York: Hill and Wang, 1995); also see Catharine A. MacKinnon, *Only Words* (Cambridge, MA: Harvard University Press, 1993).

13   john a. powell, "Worlds Apart: Reconciling Freedom of Speech and Equality," *Kentucky Law Journal* 85, no. 1 (1996); also see Matteo Bonotti, "Religion, Hate Speech, and Non-Domination," *Ethnicities* 17, no. 2 (2017).

14   Jeremy Waldon, *The Harm in Hate Speech* (Cambridge, MA: Harvard University Press, 2012).

15   Jill Gordon and Markus Johnson, "Race, Speech, and a Hostile Educational Environ- ment: What Color Is Free Speech?" *Journal of Social Philosophy* 34, no. 3 (2003). The philosopher Sigal Ben-Porath's emphasis on "dignitary harm" (which she contrasts with "intellectual harm") is instructive here. Dignitary harm prevents members of a campus community from freely participating in the public sphere because they feel unwelcome and threatened. Intellectual harm, on the other hand, challenges in- dividuals to question their pre-existing beliefs. The latter is a beneficial experience for collegians; the former is injurious. Sigal R. Ben-Porath, *Free Speech on Campus* (Philadelphia: University of Pennsylvania Press, 2017).

16   Laura Beth Nielsen, *License to Harass: Law, Hierarchy, and Offensive Public Speech* (Princeton, NJ: Princeton University Press, 2004).

17   See especially Dan M. Kahan, "The Politically Motivated Reasoning Paradigm, Part 1: What Politically Motivated Reasoning Is and How to Measure It," in *Emerging Trends in the Social and Behavioral Sciences*, ed. Robert A. Scott et al. (Hoboken, NJ: John Wiley & Sons, 2016); also see Geoffrey L. Cohen, "Party over Policy: The Dominating Impact of Group Influence on Political Beliefs," *Journal of Personality & Social Psychol- ogy* 85, no. 5 (2002); Ziva Kunda, "The Case for Motivated Reasoning," *Psychological Bulletin* 108, no. 3 (1990). In one especially notable study, the legal scholar Dan Kahan and his co-authors find that ideological orientations influence assessments of speech rights by altering how people actually perceive reality. Subjects were shown video footage of the *exact same* demonstration; some were told they were watching an anti-abortion protest and others were told it was a protest against the military's

"don't ask, don't tell" policy. Afterwards, what people reported viewing—ostensibly an objective statement of fact—fell in line with their political outlooks. Asked to consider the footage as if they were jurors in a First Amendment case, subjects disinclined to support the demonstrators' purported cause asserted that the video proved protesters had harassed and threatened bystanders (making the protest illegal conduct). Subjects supportive of the stated purpose of the rally, on the other hand, did not see any untoward behavior (i.e., instead of illegality these subjects saw constitutionally protected speech). See Dan M. Kahan et al., " 'They Saw a Protest': Cognitive Illiberalism and the Speech-Conduct Distinction," *Stanford Law Review* 64, no. 4 (2012).

18   On the Free Speech Movement, see Robert Cohen, "The Many Meanings of the FSM: In Lieu of an Introduction," in *The Free Speech Movement: Reflections on Berkeley in the 1960s*, ed. Robert Cohen and Reginald E. Zelnik (Berkeley: University of California Press, 2002). On critiques of free speech, see (respectively) P. E. Moskowitz, *The Case against Free Speech: The First Amendment, Fascism, and the Future of Dissent* (New York: Bold Type Books, 2019), 18; Stanley Eugene Fish, *There's No Such Thing as Free Speech, and It's a Good Thing, Too* (New York: Oxford University Press, 1994). On partisan application of speech protections, see Jason Giersch, "Punishing Campus Protesters Based on Ideology," *Research & Politics* 6, no. 4 (2019).

19   On critiques of Murray's work, see Eric Siegel, "The Real Problem with Charles Murray and 'the Bell Curve,' " *Scientific American*, April 12, 2017, https://blogs.scientificam erican.com/voices/the-real-problem-with-charles-murray-and-the-bell-curve/; also see Matthew Yglesias, "The Bell Curve Is about Policy. And It's Wrong," *Vox*, April 10, 2018, https://www.vox.com/2018/4/10/17182692/bell-curve-charles-murray-policy -wrong; Ezra Klein, "Sam Harris, Charles Murray, and the Allure of Race Science," *Vox*, March 27, 2018, https://www.vox.com/policy-and-politics/2018/3/27/15695060 /sam-harris-charles-murray-race-iq-forbidden-knowledge-podcast-bell-curve. On the Middlebury protest, see Taylor Gee, "How the Middlebury Riot Really Went Down," *Politico*, May 28, 2017, https://www.politico.com/magazine/story/2017/05/28 /how-donald-trump-caused-the-middlebury-melee-215195.

20   William Wan, "Milo's Appearance at Berkeley Led to Riots. He Vows to Return this Fall for a Week-Long Free-Speech Event," *Washington Post*, April 26, 2017, https:// www.washingtonpost.com/news/grade-point/wp/2017/04/26/milos-appearance -at-berkeley-led-to-riots-he-vows-to-return-this-fall-for-a-week-long-free-speech -event/.

21   Such comments echo the famed (although misattributed) Voltairean dictum, "I disapprove of what you say, but I will defend to the death your right to say it."

22   Moskowitz, *The Case against Free Speech*.

23   On the impact of professor watchlists to academic freedom, see Nell Gluckman, "The Outrage Peddlers Are Here to Stay," *Chronicle of Higher Education*, November 17, 2020, https://www.chronicle.com/article/the-outrage-peddlers-are-here-to-stay. For a few examples of threats to progressive professors' jobs over their political speech, see Katie Robertson, "Nikole Hannah-Jones Denied Tenure at University of North Carolina," *New York Times*, May 19, 2021, https://www.nytimes.com/2021/05/19/business /media/nikole-hannah-jones-unc.html. Devna Bose, " 'Tweets Are My Own': How James Thomas's Twitter Sparked a Conversation about Academic Freedom," *Daily Mississippian*, March 4, 2019, https://thedmonline.com/james-thomas-jt/; Colleen Flaherty, "Professor Loses Job over Iran Joke," *Inside Higher Ed*, January 10, 2020, https://www.insidehighered.com/quicktakes/2020/01/10/professor-loses-job-over

-iran-joke; Dan Frosch, "Fired Colorado Professor Defends 9/11 Remarks," *New York Times*, March 23, 2009, https://www.nytimes.com/2009/03/24/us/24churchill.html; Emma Pettit, "'Ousted' from Academe, Steven Salaita Says He's Driving a School Bus to Make Ends Meet," *Chronicle of Higher Education*, February 19, 2019, https://www.chronicle.com/article/Ousted-From-Academe/245732. On the relative success of disinvitation initiatives, see Sean Stevens, "Campus Speaker Disinvitation Trends (Part 2 of 2)," *Heterodox Academy*, February 7, 2017, https://heterodoxacademy.org/campus-speaker-disinvitations-recent-trends-part-2-of-2/. It is worth noting that Stevens's research shows that while the right is more successful in getting speakers disinvited, the left initiates far more attempts to prevent talks from happening. And, given the relative imbalance of conservative speakers on college campuses, this latter point is notable.

24   Mike McPhate, "California Today: Price Tag to Protect Speech at Berkeley: $600,000," *New York Times*, September 15, 2017, https://www.nytimes.com/2017/09/15/us/california-today-price-tag-to-protect-speech-at-berkeley-600000.html; Sabrina Schnur, "Hundreds March, Dozens Protest Outside Ben Shapiro's Speech," *Boston University News Service*, November 13, 2019, https://bunewsservice.com/hundreds-march-dozens-protest-outside-ben-shapiros-speech/.

25   Allegra Kirkland, "How Did Sebastian Gorka Go from the Anti-Muslim Fringe to White House Aide?" *TPM*, February 9, 2017, https://talkingpointsmemo.com/dc/sebastian-gorka-washington-experts-dc-anti-islam-ties; Tina Nguyen, "Far-Right Trump Advisor Tied to Anti-Semitic Paramilitary Group," *Vanity Fair*, April 4, 2017, https://www.vanityfair.com/news/2017/04/sebastian-gorka-anti-semitism-hungarian-guard.

26   Charity Lackey, the organizer of a walkout for Shapiro's talk at UNC, was quoted in the school paper. "These are not conservative lecturers. This is hate speech. [. . .] We can walk out of a space and show that we will not engage; we will not give you that satisfaction. I will not waste my energy because it took a lot of energy to sit in there for five minutes to be quite honest." Quoted in Acy Jackson and Natalie Conti, "Conservative Writer Ben Shapiro Speaks, Students Walk Out," *Daily Tar Heel*, March 31, 2016, https://www.dailytarheel.com/article/2016/03/ben-shapiro-speaks-students-walk-out.

27   Jeffrey Herbst, "Addressing the Real Crisis of Free Expression on Campus," *Newseum*, April 25, 2017, https://www.freedomforuminstitute.org/wp-content/uploads/2017/04/WhitePaper_Herbst_FreeExpressionOnCampus.pdf.

28   In January 2015, the University of Chicago released a statement related to speech, which reads in part: "Because the University is committed to free and open inquiry in all matters, it guarantees all members of the University community the broadest possible latitude to speak, write, listen, challenge, and learn [. . . . I]t is not the proper role of the University to attempt to shield individuals from ideas and opinions they find unwelcome, disagreeable, or even deeply offensive." This is an example of a school producing a transportable cultural script, although it is not clear whether the majority of progressive students, even at the University of Chicago, embrace it. The full Chicago Statement is available from FIRE, "Adopting the Chicago Statement," accessed December 7, 2020, https://www.thefire.org/get-involved/student-network/take-action/adopting-the-chicago-statement/.

29   As Warren indicated above, Gorka strongly refutes such a characterization. Also see Jacey Fortin, "Who Is Sebastian Gorka? A Trump Adviser Comes Out of the

Shadows," *New York Times*, February 17, 2017, https://www.nytimes.com/2017/02/17
/us/politics/dr-sebastian-gorka.html. Most importantly for the point being made in
this chapter, none of the clubs that brought Gorka to UNC—Christians United for
Israel, College Republicans, and Turning Point—labeled themselves as alt-right,
and they certainly did not consider themselves neo-Nazis.

30   For example, see Katherine Gelber and Luke McNamara, "Evidencing the Harms of
Hate Speech," *Social Identities* 22, no. 3 (2016). Further, it is instructive to contrast the
argument made by Gelber and McNamara with the comparatively glib treatment of
psychological harm advanced by Andrew Cohen. See Cohen, "Psychological Harm
and Free Speech on Campus."

31   Emily Ekins, "The State of Free Speech and Tolerance in America," Cato Institute,
October 31, 2017, https://www.cato.org/survey-reports/state-free-speech-tolerance
-america; Knight Foundation, "Free Expression on College Campuses," May 13, 2019,
https://knightfoundation.org/reports/free-expression-college-campuses/.

32   Palfrey, for example, writes, "Our system of governance must also allow a point
at which the tolerant may become intolerant of the intolerance. The intolerant
should not be able to dominate merely by calling on the tolerant to tolerate their
intolerance. The hard problem of hate speech is where that line—between political
speech we tolerate, no matter how obnoxious, and the hate speech we should not
tolerate—is drawn." This is to say, Palfrey punts on the actual answer to the "hard
problem." Palfrey, *Safe Spaces, Brave Spaces*, 105–6. Ben-Porath stresses the need to
protect students from dignitary harm, but again, how such harms are to be assessed
(especially in relation to counterclaims from other parties) remains murky. "Deciding when, if ever, the harm done or risked is significant enough to justify putting a
limitation on the free exchange of ideas can be difficult [. . .]. Again, some issues in
this area are easier than others." See Ben-Porath, *Free Speech on Campus*, 76. This advice, useful as it is, still leaves the "hard problem" of drawing the line unanswered.

33   For example, see Matthew d'Ancona, "There Must Be Free Speech, Even for Milo
Yiannopoulos," *The Guardian*, February 6, 2017, https://www.theguardian.com/com
mentisfree/2017/feb/06/free-speech-milo-yiannopoulos-alt-right-far-right; Emma
Grey Ellis, "Milo, Ann Coulter, and 'Free Speech Week' Add Up to the Right's Best
Troll Yet," *Wired*, September 28, 2017, https://www.wired.com/story/free-speech
-week-milo-best-troll-yet/; Andrew Marantz, "How Social-Media Trolls Turned U.C.
Berkeley into a Free-Speech Circus," *The New Yorker*, June 25, 2018, https://www
.newyorker.com/magazine/2018/07/02/how-social-media-trolls-turned-uc-berkeley
-into-a-free-speech-circus.

34   Moskowitz, *The Case against Free Speech*.

35   On Milo's banning from Twitter, see Abby Ohlheiser, "Just How Offensive Did Milo
Yiannopoulos Have to Be to Get Banned from Twitter?" *Washington Post*, July 21,
2016, https://www.washingtonpost.com/news/the-intersect/wp/2016/07/21/what-it
-takes-to-get-banned-from-twitter/. At a West Virginia University speaking event,
Milo projected a photograph of Daniel Brewster, a sociology instructor, with the label "Fat Faggot." Brewster is an advocate for LGBTQ+ issues at the school. Milo went
on to call Brewster "Professor Fat Ass" and "Professor Stuff Your Face with Froot
Loops," and denigrated sociology as one of many "burger-flipping majors." See
Scott Jaschik, "Free Speech, Both Ways," *Inside Higher Ed*, December 5, 2016, https://
www.insidehighered.com/news/2016/12/05/west-virginia-university-lets-contro
versial-speaker-appear-and-answers-his-attack. At the University of

Wisconsin-Milwaukee, Milo used a photograph of a former student, Adelaide Kramer (who was also in the audience), to denounce the trans community by cracking jokes about her appearance. Kramer later recalled, "I didn't know if I was going to get attacked or not. I was just like, 'Dear god, I hope nobody recognizes me.'" Quoted in Tourjée, "Trans Student Harassed by Milo Yiannopoulos Speaks Out." It was these incidents that led to a widespread fear at UC Berkeley that Milo was planning to publicly identify undocumented students. See Oppenheim, "UC Berkeley Protests." On the types of intolerant speech not worthy of toleration, see Palfrey, *Safe Spaces, Brave Spaces.*

36 Gelber and McNamara, "Evidencing the Harms of Hate Speech."

37 Greg Lukianoff and Jonathan Haidt, *The Coddling of the American Mind: How Good Intentions and Bad Ideas Are Setting up a Generation for Failure* (New York: Penguin Press, 2018). Scholars such as Musa Al-Gharbi and Sean Stevens (both affiliated with Heterodox Academy, which we discuss in the next chapter) have offered additional evidence of a speech crisis on campus. See Musa Al-Gharbi, "Vox's Consistent Errors on Campus Speech, Explained," *Heterodox Academy*, August 16, 2018, https://heterodoxacademy.org/vox-consistent-errors-explained/; Sean Stevens, "The Skeptics Are Wrong, Part 1: Attitudes about Free Speech on Campus Are Changing," *Heterodox Academy*, March 4, 2018, https://heterodoxacademy.org/blog/skeptics-are-wrong-about-campus-speech/. Conversely, others, such as Jeffrey Sachs (a politics professor) and Lee Bollinger (the president of Columbia University), have forcefully pushed back on the idea of a campus speech crisis. For example, see Lee C. Bollinger, "Free Speech on Campus Is Doing Just Fine, Thank You," *The Atlantic*, June 12, 2019, https://www.theatlantic.com/ideas/archive/2019/06/free-speech-crisis-campus-isnt-real/591394/; Jeffrey Adam Sachs, "There Is No Campus Free Speech Crisis: The Right's New Moral Panic Is Largely Imaginary," *Salon*, May 1, 2018, https://www.salon.com/2018/05/01/there-is-no-campus-free-speech-crisis-the-rights-new-moral-panic-is-largely-imaginary/; also see Ben-Porath, *Free Speech on Campus.*

38 The vast majority of the speakers affiliated with these national organizations are not firebrands. However, the marquee figures tend to be provocateurs.

39 On the influence of national organization in campus speech controversies, see Amy J. Binder, "There's a Well-Funded Campus Industry behind the Ann Coulter Incident," *Washington Post*, May 1, 2017, https://www.washingtonpost.com/news/monkey-cage/wp/2017/05/01/theres-a-well-funded-campus-outrage-industry-behind-the-ann-coulter-incident/?utm_term=.1d91f11e5a2a. On the role of Robert Mercer in Milo's college tour, see Joseph Bernstein, "Leaked Documents Suggest Secretive Billionaire Trump Donors Are Milo's Patrons," *BuzzFeed News*, July 13, 2017, https://www.buzzfeednews.com/article/josephbernstein/leaked-documents-suggest-secretive-billionaire-trump-donors.

40 Amy J. Binder and Kate Wood, *Becoming Right: How Campuses Shape Young Conservatives* (Princeton, NJ: Princeton University Press, 2013); Garrett H. Gowen, Kevin M. Hemer, and Robert D. Reason, "Understanding American Conservatism and Its Role in Higher Education," in *Student Activism, Politics, and Campus Climate in Higher Education*, ed. Demetri L. Morgan and Charles H. F. Davis III (New York: Routledge, 2019).

41 For example, see John Hardin, "You Can't Legislate Free Inquiry on Campus," *New York Times*, May 21, 2018, https://www.nytimes.com/2018/05/21/opinion/free-inquiry-campus.html. Hardin is the director of university relations at the Charles Koch

Foundation. Also see PEN America, "Chasm in the Classroom: Campus Free Speech in a Divided America," April 2, 2019, https://pen.org/chasm-in-the-classroom-campus-free-speech-in-a-divided-america/.

42 On the political grindstone of FIRE's founders, see Alan Charles Kors and Harvey A. Silverglate, *The Shadow University: The Betrayal of Liberty on America's Campuses* (New York: Free Press, 1998). On perceptions of FIRE as partisan, see Jim Sleeper, "The Conservatives behind the Campus 'Free Speech' Crusade," *The American Prospect*, October 19, 2016, https://prospect.org/education/conservatives-behind-campus-free-speech-crusade/; also see FIRE, "Mission," accessed December 7, 2020, https://www.thefire.org/about-us/mission/.

43 Binder and Wood, *Becoming Right*.

44 Paul Fain, "Deep Partisan Divide on Higher Education," *Inside Higher Ed*, July 11, 2017, https://www.insidehighered.com/news/2017/07/11/dramatic-shift-most-republicans-now-say-colleges-have-negative-impact.

45 On this point, also see Ben-Porath, *Free Speech on Campus*. Ben-Porath discusses the need to promote "inclusive freedom"—that is, strong support of speech rights within a campus environment that protects the dignity of all members of the community.

46 To be clear, PEN America is nonpartisan. However, it is associated in the public eye with progressive causes.

47 See (respectively) American Sociological Association, "Protecting Our Speech," accessed December 27, 2020, https://www.asanet.org/protecting-our-speech; National Center for Free Speech and Civic Engagement's website, accessed December 27, 2020, https://freespeechcenter.universityofcalifornia.edu.

48 It is also worth noting (as one of our reviewers did) that it is possible that K–12 education fails to adequately teach young people about the overarching values behind free expression. During their early school years, such a critique goes, students are primarily taught about the harm that words can cause and how bullying is unacceptable. They then—perhaps—arrive on college campuses unprepared for and shocked by the prevalence of what they consider to be hate speech.

49 Murray has been a polarizing figure for decades, but there is evidence that (at least at this stage in his career) much of the vitriol directed towards him by progressives has less to do with the content of his recent work and more to do with his reputation as a conservative. See Wendy M. Williams and Stephen J. Ceci, "Charles Murray's 'Provocative' Talk," *New York Times*, April 15, 2017, https://www.nytimes.com/2017/04/15/opinion/sunday/charles-murrays-provocative-talk.html.

50 See Elliot Kaufman, "Campus Conservatives Gave the Alt-Right a Platform," *National Review*, August 15, 2017, https://www.nationalreview.com/2017/08/campus-conservative-organizations-alt-right-platform-free-speech-milo-yiannopoulos-charlottesville-terrorist-attack/; Gowen et al., "Understanding American Conservatism and Its Role in Higher Education."

51 powell, "Worlds Apart."

52 On philosophical grey areas see Waldon, *The Harm in Hate Speech*. On normative restraints, see Fish, *There's No Such Thing as Free Speech*.

53 On divisions among progressives over speech rights, see Cohen, "The Meaning of FSM." On the possibilities of synergy between free expression and inclusion, see Nadine Strossen, *Hate: Why We Should Resist It with Free Speech, not Censorship* (New York: Oxford University Press, 2018); also see Ben-Porath, *Free Speech on Campus*.

54   Nancy Thomas and Margaret Brower, with Tufts University's Institute for Democracy and Higher Education, identify five attributes promoting positive political climates on campus: social cohesion, compositional diversity, social mobility and equal opportunity, facilitations of political discussion, and support for student activism. Nancy Thomas and Margaret Brower, "Politics 365: Fostering Campus Climates for Student Political Learning & Engagement," Institute for Democracy and Higher Education, April 2017, https://tischcollege.tufts.edu/sites/default/files/Politics%20365.pdf. Thomas and Brower's ideas fit nicely with Ben-Porath's concept of inclusive freedom. See Ben-Porath, *Free Speech on Campus.*

55   Binder and Wood, *Becoming Right;* Daisy Verduzco Reyes, *Learning to Be Latino: How Colleges Shape Identity Politics* (New Brunswick, NJ: Rutgers University Press, 2018).

CHAPTER SEVEN

1   Ezra Klein, *Why We're Polarized* (New York: Avid Reader Press, 2020); Lilliana Mason, *Uncivil Agreement: How Politics Became Our Identity* (Chicago: University of Chicago Press, 2018).

2   Daniel Yankelovich, *The Magic of Dialogue: Transforming Conflict into Cooperation* (New York: Simon & Schuster, 1999), 14, 15; also see Martin Buber, *I and Thou,* translated by Ronald Gregor Smith (New York: Scribner, 1958 [1923]).

3   For example, see José L. Duarte et al., "Political Diversity Will Improve Social Psychological Science," *Behavioral and Brain Sciences* 38 (2015); Chris C. Martin, "How Ideology Has Hindered Sociological Insight," *American Sociologist* 47, no. 1 (2016); Nicholas Quinn Rosenkranz, "Intellectual Diversity in the Legal Academy," *Harvard Journal of Law and Public Policy* 37, no. 1 (2014).

4   For information about the Sustained Dialogue Institute, see Sustained Dialogue, "About Us," accessed October 20, 2020, https://sustaineddialogue.org/about-us/. For information about the Sustained Dialogue Campus Network, see Sustained Dialogue, "Our Work," accessed October 20, 2020, https://sustaineddialogue.org/our-work/campus/. For information about Sustained Dialogue's impact, see Sustained Dialogue, "Our Impact," accessed October 20, 2020, https://sustaineddialogue.org/our-impact/.

5   Anne Bromley, "UVA Group Learns about Transformative Power of Dialogue," *UVA Today,* August 18, 2014, https://www.news.virginia.edu/content/uva-group-learns-about-transformative-power-dialogue.

6   See BridgeUSA's website, accessed October 19, 2020, https://www.bridgeusa.org/. Information about the coalition members within the larger Bridge Alliance can be found at "Our Members," accessed October 19, 2020, https://www.bridgealliance.us/our_members_bridging_ideological_divides. There are currently 100 organizations listed as participating groups, including BridgeUSA, Sustained Dialogue, Living Room Conversations, allsides.com, and The Village Square.

7   See especially Jonathan Haidt, *The Righteous Mind: Why Good People Are Divided by Politics and Religion* (New York: Pantheon Books, 2012). For information on Bill Shireman, see *In This Together,* "Bill Shireman," accessed November 6, 2020, https://inthistogetheramerica.org/bill-shireman/. Two of Bridge's leaders, Manu Meel and Jonathan Ampallor, told us that Van Jones consulted with the group. For Haidt's centrist leanings, see Peter Wehner, "Jonathan Haidt Is Trying to Heal America's

Divisions," *The Atlantic*, May 24, 2020, https://www.theatlantic.com/ideas/archive/2020/05/jonathan-haidt-pandemic-and-americas-polarization/612025/.

8 BridgeUSA, "Our Mission," accessed November 5, 2020, https://www.bridgeusa.org/about-us/.

9 Arlie Russell Hochschild, *Strangers in Their Own Land: Anger and Mourning on the American Right* (New York: New Press, 2016).

10 Abraham H. Maslow, *Religions, Values, and Peak-Experiences* (Columbus: Ohio State University Press, 1964).

11 Jeremy Bauer-Wolf, "Civility at Berkeley," *Inside Higher Ed*, November 28, 2018, https://www.insidehighered.com/news/2018/11/28/new-policies-student-groups-change-culture-free-speech-berkeley; Jenna Massengale, "Appalachian Welcomes Sustained Dialogue as Catalyst for Change on Campus," *Appalachian Magazine*, May 2, 2016, http://appalachianmagazine.org/stories/id/581.

12 Veronica Lerma, Laura T. Hamilton, and Kelly Nielsen, "Racialized Equity Labor, University Appropriation and Student Resistance," *Social Problems* 67, no. 2 (2020).

13 Quoted in Jack Stripling, "Trump Picked a Fight with Higher Ed. It's Still Learning to Punch Back," *Chronicle of Higher Education*, November 2, 2020, https://www.chronicle.com/article/trump-picked-a-fight-with-higher-ed-its-still-learning-to-punch-back.

14 Jürgen Habermas, *Between Facts and Norms: Contributions to a Discourse Theory of Law and Democracy*, translated by William Rehg (Cambridge, MA: MIT Press 1996 [1992]).

15 Evan Mandery, "What Teaching Ethics in Appalachia Taught Me about Bridging America's Partisan Divide," *Politico*, October 13, 2019, https://www.politico.com/magazine/story/2019/10/13/america-cultural-divide-red-state-blue-state-228111.

16 See Michael Bérubé, *What's Liberal about the Liberal Arts? Classroom Politics and "Bias" in Higher Education* (New York: W. W. Norton, 2006); Neil Gross, *Why Are Professors Liberal and Why Do Conservatives Care?* (Cambridge, MA: Harvard University Press, 2013).

17 Christopher Rim, "How Student Activism Shaped the Black Lives Matter Movement," *Forbes*, June 4, 2020, https://www.forbes.com/sites/christopherrim/2020/06/04/how-student-activism-shaped-the-black-lives-matter-movement/?sh=4e4225194414.

18 On this point, one need look no further back in history than the origins of the Tea Party movement, which arose when Barack Obama was elected president in 2008. The Tea Party was funded by the Americans for Prosperity advocacy group, which was backed by conservative mega-donors Charles and David Koch. See Christopher S. Parker and Matt A. Barreto, *Change They Can't Believe In: The Tea Party and Reactionary Politics in America* (Princeton, NJ: Princeton University Press, 2013). For illustrations of conservatives' critiques directed at higher education, see David Horowitz, *Indoctrination U: The Left's War against Academic Freedom* (New York: Encounter Books, 2007); Roger Kimball, *Tenured Radicals: How Politics Has Corrupted Our Higher Education* (New York: Harper & Row, 1990); Alan Charles Kors and Harvey A. Silverglate, *The Shadow University: The Betrayal of Liberty on America's Campuses* (New York: Free Press, 1998); Heather Mac Donald, *The Diversity Delusion: How Race and Gender Pandering Corrupt the University and Undermine Our Culture* (New York: St. Martin's Press, 2018).

19 Frank Donoghue, *The Last Professors: The Corporate University and the Fate of the Humanities* (New York: Fordham University Press, 2008); Henry A. Giroux,

Neoliberalism's War on Higher Education (Chicago: Haymarket Books, 2014); Christopher Newfield, *The Great Mistake: How We Wrecked Public Universities and How We Can Fix Them* (Baltimore, MD: Johns Hopkins University Press, 2016); Bill Readings, *The University in Ruins* (Cambridge, MA: Harvard University Press, 1996).

20   Elizabeth A. Armstrong and Laura T. Hamilton, *Paying for the Party: How College Maintains Inequality* (Cambridge, MA: Harvard University Press, 2013); Amy J. Binder and Kate Wood, *Becoming Right: How Campuses Shape Young Conservatives* (Princeton, NJ: Princeton University Press, 2013); Mitchell L. Stevens, Elizabeth A. Armstrong, and Richard Arum, "Sieve, Incubator, Temple, Hub: Empirical and Theoretical Advances in the Sociology of Higher Education," *Annual Review of Sociology* 34, no.1 (2008).

21   See Gross, *Why Are Professors Liberal and Why Do Conservatives Care?*; April Kelly-Woessner and Matthew Woessner, "My Professor Is a Partisan Hack: How Perceptions of a Professor's Political Views Affect Student Course Evaluations," *PS: Political Science and Politics* 39, no. 3 (2006); Jon A. Shields and Joshua M. Dunn, *Passing on the Right: Conservative Professors in the Progressive University* (New York: Oxford University Press, 2016); Matthew Woessner and April Kelly-Woessner, "Left Pipeline: Why Conservatives Don't Get Doctorates," in *The Politically Correct University: Problems, Scope, and Reforms*, ed. Robert Maranto et al. (Washington, DC: AEI Press, 2009).

22   For example, see Sarah Kuta, "What's It Like to Be a Conservative Student at CU Boulder?" *Daily Camera*, October 29, 2016, http://www.dailycamera.com/news/boulder/ci_30519985/whats-it-like-be-conservative-student-at-cu.

23   On this point, see Shields and Dunn, *Passing on the Right*.

References

Abrams, Samuel J. 2018. "Think Professors Are Liberal? Try School Administrators." *New York Times*, October 16. https://www.nytimes.com/2018/10/16
/opinion/liberal-college-administrators.html.

Adams, Mike, and Adam Kissel. 2017. "Censorship in the UNC System: Correcting the Narrative." *Academic Questions* 30 (2): 210–23.

Agua, Jade, and Sumun L. Pendakur. 2019. "From Resistance to Resilience:
Transforming Institutional Racism from the Inside Out." In *Student Activ-
ism, Politics, and Campus Climate in Higher Education*, edited by Demetri L.
Morgan and Charles H. F. Davis III, 164–82. New York: Routledge.

Alba, Davey, and Sheera Frenkel. 2020. "Medical Expert Who Corrects Trump
Is Now a Target of the Far Right." *New York Times*, March 28. https://www
.nytimes.com/2020/03/28/technology/coronavirus-fauci-trump-conspiracy
-target.html.

Al-Gharbi, Musa. 2018. "Vox's Consistent Errors on Campus Speech, Explained." *Heterodox Academy*, August 16. https://heterodoxacademy.org
/vox-consistent-errors-explained/.

American Enterprise Institute. "Defending and Promoting Freedom, Opportunity, and Enterprise: 2019 Annual Report." Accessed August 21, 2020.
http://annualreport.aei.org/.

Anthony, Andrew. 2015. "Black Power's Coolest Radicals (but Also a Gang of
Ruthless Killers)." *The Guardian*, October 18. https://www.theguardian.com
/film/2015/oct/18/black-powers-coolest-radicals-black-panthers-vanguard
-of-the-revolution-stanley-nelson-interview.

Arellano, Gustavo. 2006. "Raza Isn't Racist." *Los Angeles Times*, June 15. https://www.latimes.com/la-oe-arellano15jun15-story.html.

Armstrong, Elizabeth A., and Laura T. Hamilton. 2013. *Paying for the Party: How College Maintains Inequality*. Cambridge, MA: Harvard University Press.

Astin, Alexander. 1993. "Diversity and Multiculturalism on the Campus." *Change: The Magazine of Higher Learning* 25 (2): 44–49.

Astor, Maggie. 2020. "College Democrats, Citing Racism, Force Change in Leadership." *New York Times*, July 1. https://www.nytimes.com/2020/07/01/us/politics/college-democrats-president-resigns.html.

Balko, Radley. 2003. "Nader Scams College Kids." *Fox News*, March 13. https://www.foxnews.com/story/nader-scams-college-kids.

Barnhardt, Cassie L. 2017. "Philanthropic Foundations' Social Agendas and the Field of Higher Education." In *Higher Education: Handbook of Theory and Research*, vol. 32, edited by Michael B. Paulsen, 181–257. New York: Springer.

Bauer-Wolf, Jeremy. 2018. "Civility at Berkeley." *Inside Higher Ed*, November 28. https://www.insidehighered.com/news/2018/11/28/new-policies-student-groups-change-culture-free-speech-berkeley.

Becker, Mary. 1995. "The Legitimacy of Judicial Review in Speech Cases." In *The Price We Pay: The Case against Racist Speech, Hate Propaganda, and Pornography*, edited by Laura J. Lederer and Richard Delgado, 208–15. New York: Hill and Wang.

Ben-Porath, Sigal R. 2017. *Free Speech on Campus*. Philadelphia: University of Pennsylvania Press.

Berman, Elizabeth Popp. 2012. *Creating the Market University: How Academic Science Became an Economic Engine*. Princeton, NJ: Princeton University Press.

Bernstein, Joseph. 2017. "Leaked Documents Suggest Secretive Billionaire Trump Donors Are Milo's Patrons." *BuzzFeed News*, July 13. https://www.buzzfeednews.com/article/josephbernstein/leaked-documents-suggest-secretive-billionaire-trump-donors.

Bernstein, Joseph. 2018. "How PragerU Is Winning the Right-Wing Culture War without Donald Trump." *BuzzFeed News*, March 3. https://www.buzzfeednews.com/article/josephbernstein/prager-university.

Bérubé, Michael. 2006. *What's Liberal about the Liberal Arts? Classroom Politics and "Bias" in Higher Education*. New York: W. W. Norton.

Binder, Amy J. 2017. "There's a Well-Funded Campus Industry behind the Ann Coulter Incident." *Washington Post*, May 1. https://www.washingtonpost.com

/news/monkey-cage/wp/2017/05/01/theres-a-well-funded-campus-outrage
-industry-behind-the-ann-coulter-incident/?utm_term=.1d91f11e5a2a.

Binder, Amy J., Daniel B. Davis, and Nick Bloom. 2016. "Career Funneling: How
Elite Students Learn to Define and Desire 'Prestigious' Jobs." *Sociology of
Education* 89 (1): 20–39.

Binder, Amy J., and Kate Wood. 2013. *Becoming Right: How Campuses Shape
Young Conservatives.* Princeton, NJ: Princeton University Press.

Binder, Amy J., and Kate Wood. 2014. "'Civil' or 'Provocative'? Varieties of
Conservative Student Style and Discourse in American Universities." In
Professors and Their Politics, edited by Neil Gross and Solon Simmons,
158–87. Baltimore, MD: Johns Hopkins University Press.

Blee, Kathleen M. 2012. *Democracy in the Making: How Activist Groups Form.*
New York: Oxford University Press.

Boaz, David. 1997. *Libertarianism: A Primer.* New York: Free Press.

Bollinger, Lee C. 2019. "Free Speech on Campus Is Doing Just Fine, Thank
You." *The Atlantic*, June 12. https://www.theatlantic.com/ideas/archive
/2019/06/free-speech-crisis-campus-isnt-real/591394/.

Bonotti, Matteo. 2017. "Religion, Hate Speech, and Non-Domination." *Ethnicities*
17 (2): 259–74.

Bose, Devna. 2019. "'Tweets Are My Own': How James Thomas's Twitter
Sparked a Conversation about Academic Freedom." *Daily Mississippian*,
March 4. https://thedmonline.com/james-thomas-jt/.

Brey, Cristobal de, Thomas D. Snyder, Anlan Zhang, and Sally A. Dillow. 2021.
Digest of Educational Statistics 2019. National Center for Education Statistics,
Institute of Education Sciences. Washington, DC: US Department of Edu-
cation. https://nces.ed.gov/programs/coe/pdf/2021/cha_508c.pdf.

Broadhurst, Christopher J., and Angel L. Velez. 2019. "Historical and Contem-
porary Context of Student Activism in U.S. Higher Education." In *Student
Activism, Politics, and Campus Climate in Higher Education*, edited by Demetri L.
Morgan and Charles H. F. Davis III, 3–20. New York: Routledge.

Bromley, Anne. 2014. "UVA Group Learns about Transformative Power of
Dialogue." *UVA Today*, August 18. https://www.news.virginia.edu/content
/uva-group-learns-about-transformative-power-dialogue.

Bryson, Bethany Paige. 2005. *Making Multiculturalism: Boundaries and Meaning
in U.S. English Departments.* Stanford, CA: Stanford University Press.

Buber, Martin. 1958 [1923]. *I and Thou.* Translated by Ronald Gregor Smith. New
York: Scribner.

Carson, Clayborne. 1981. *In Struggle: SNCC and the Black Awakening of the 1960s.* Cambridge, MA: Harvard University Press.

Chason, Rachel. 2016. "National 'Students for Trump' Effort Has NC Roots." *News & Observer*, September 27. https://www.newsobserver.com/news /politics-government/election/article104522526.html.

Chemerinsky, Erwin, and Howard Gillman. 2017. *Free Speech on Campus.* New Haven, CT: Yale University Press.

Clark, Dartunorro. 2017. "GOP Lawmaker Regrets March Meeting with 'Unite the Right' Rally Organizer." *NBC News*, August 14. https://www.nbcnews .com/politics/congress/gop-lawmaker-regrets-march-meeting-unite -right-rally-organizer-n792496.

Cohen, Andrew. 2012. "The Torture Memos, 10 Years Later." *The Atlantic*, February 6. https://www.theatlantic.com/national/archive/2012/02/the-torture -memos-10-years-later/252439/.

Cohen, Andrew Jason. 2017. "Psychological Harm and Free Speech on Campus." *Society* 54 (4): 320–25.

Cohen, David K., and Barbara Neufeld. 1981. "The Failure of High Schools and the Progress of Education." *Daedalus* 110 (3): 69–89.

Cohen, Geoffrey L. 2003. "Party over Policy: The Dominating Impact of Group Influence on Political Beliefs." *Journal of Personality & Social Psychology* 85 (5): 808–22.

Cohen, Robert. 2002. "The Meaning of the FSM: In Lieu of an Introduction." In *The Free Speech Movement: Reflections on Berkeley in the 1960s*, edited by Robert Cohen and Reginald E. Zelnik, 1–53. Berkeley: University of California Press.

Colby, Anne, Elizabeth Beaumont, Thomas Ehrlich, and Josh Corngold. 2003. *Educating for Democracy: Preparing Undergraduates for Responsible Political Engagement.* San Francisco: Jossey-Bass.

Crenshaw, Kimberlé. 1989. "Demarginalizing the Intersection of Race and Sex: A Black Feminist Critique of Antidiscrimination Doctrine, Feminist Theory, and Antiracist Politics." *The University of Chicago Legal Forum* 1989 (1): 139–67.

Cushman, Thomas. 2019. "The Social Structure of Civility and Incivility in the Liberal Academy." *Society* 56 (6): 590–600.

d'Ancona, Matthew. 2017. "There Must Be Free Speech, Even for Milo Yiannopoulos." *The Guardian*, February 6. https://www.theguardian.com /commentisfree/2017/feb/06/free-speech-milo-yiannopoulos-alt-right -far-right.

Delgado, Richard. 1995. "First Amendment Formalism Is Giving Way to First Amendment Legal Realism." In *The Price We Pay: The Case against Racist Speech, Hate Propaganda, and Pornography*, edited by Laura J. Lederer and Richard Delgado, 327–31. New York: Hill and Wang.

Dickson, EJ. 2019. "Swarthmore Frats Disband after 4-Day Student Sit-In." *Rolling Stone*, April 30. https://www.rollingstone.com/culture/culture-news /swarthmore-students-protesting-campus-fraternities-829170/.

Dietrich, David R. 2015. "Racially Charged Cookies and White Scholarships: Anti-Affirmative Action Protests on American College Campuses." *Sociological Focus* 48 (2): 105–25.

Dodge, Jefferson, and Joel Dyer. 2014. "Los Seis de Boulder." *Boulder Weekly*, May 29. https://www.boulderweekly.com/news/los-seis-de-boulder/.

Dodson, Kyle. 2014. "The Effect of College on Social and Political Attitudes and Civic Participation." In *Professors and Their Politics*, edited by Neil Gross and Solon Simmons, 135–57. Baltimore, MD: Johns Hopkins University Press.

Donoghue, Frank. 2008. *The Last Professors: The Corporate University and the Fate of the Humanities*. New York: Fordham University Press.

Duarte, José L., Jarret T. Crawford, Charlotta Stern, Jonathan Haidt, Lee Jussim, and Philip E. Tetlock. 2015. "Political Diversity Will Improve Social Psychological Science." *Behavioral and Brain Sciences* 38: 1–58.

Ekins, Emily. 2017. "The State of Free Speech and Tolerance in America." Cato Institute, October 31. https://www.cato.org/survey-reports/state-free -speech-tolerance-america.

Eliasoph, Nina. 1998. *Avoiding Politics: How Americans Produce Apathy in Everyday Life*. New York: Cambridge University Press.

Eliasoph, Nina, and Paul Lichterman. 2003. "Culture in Interaction." *American Journal of Sociology* 108 (4): 735–94.

Ellis, Emma Grey. 2017. "Milo, Ann Coulter, and 'Free Speech Week' Add up to the Right's Best Troll Yet." *Wired*, September 28. https://www.wired.com /story/free-speech-week-milo-best-troll-yet/.

Fain, Paul. 2017. "Deep Partisan Divide on Higher Education." *Inside Higher Ed*, July 11. https://www.insidehighered.com/news/2017/07/11/dramatic-shift -most-republicans-now-say-colleges-have-negative-impact.

Fish, Stanley Eugene. 1994. *There's No Such Thing as Free Speech, and It's a Good Thing, Too*. New York: Oxford University Press.

Flaherty, Colleen. 2019. "When Students Want to Review a Tenured Professor." *Inside Higher Ed*, March 13. https://www.insidehighered.com/news/2019

/03/13/students-sarah-lawrence-want-review-tenure-conservative
-professor-who-criticized.

Flaherty, Colleen. 2020. "Professor Loses Job over Iran Joke." *Inside Higher Ed*,
January 10. https://www.insidehighered.com/quicktakes/2020/01/10
/professor-loses-job-over-iran-joke.

Fortin, Jacey. 2017. "Who Is Sebastian Gorka? A Trump Adviser Comes out of
the Shadows." *New York Times*, February 17. https://www.nytimes.com/2017
/02/17/us/politics/dr-sebastian-gorka.html.

Frosch, Dan. 2009. "Fired Colorado Professor Defends 9/11 Remarks." *New York
Times*, March 23. https://www.nytimes.com/2009/03/24/us/24churchill
.html.

Frum, David. 2018. *Trumpocracy: The Corruption of the American Republic.*
New York: Harper.

Fuller, Thomas, and Christopher Mele. 2017. "Berkeley Cancels Milo Yiannopoulos Speech, and Donald Trump Tweets Outrage." *New York Times*,
February 1. https://www.nytimes.com/2017/02/01/us/uc-berkeley-milo
-yiannopoulos-protest.html.

Gabriel, Trip, Thomas Kaplan, Lizette Alvarez, and Emmarie Huetteman.
2017. "At Town Halls, Doses of Fury and a Bottle of Tums." *New York Times*,
February 21. https://www.nytimes.com/2017/02/21/us/politics/town-hall
-protests-obamacare.html.

Gee, Taylor. 2017. "How the Middlebury Riot Really Went Down." *Politico*,
May 28. https://www.politico.com/magazine/story/2017/05/28/how-donald
-trump-caused-the-middlebury-melee-215195.

Geertz, Clifford. 1973. "Thick Description: Toward an Interpretive Theory of
Culture." In *The Interpretation of Cultures*, 3–30. New York: Basic Books.

Gelber, Katherine, and Luke McNamara. 2016. "Evidencing the Harms of Hate
Speech." *Social Identities* 22 (3): 324–41.

Gerber, Scott D. 2004. "The Politics of Free Speech." *Social Philosophy & Policy*
21 (2): 23–47.

Ghaziani, Amin. 2008. *The Dividends of Dissent: How Conflict and Culture Work
in Lesbian and Gay Marches on Washington.* Chicago: University of Chicago
Press.

Giersch, Jason. 2019. "Punishing Campus Protesters Based on Ideology."
Research & Politics 6 (4): 1–6.

Giroux, Henry A. 2014. *Neoliberalism's War on Higher Education.* Chicago:
Haymarket Books.

Gitlin, Todd. 1980. *The Whole World Is Watching: Mass Media in the Making and Unmaking of the New Left*. Berkeley: University of California Press.

Gitlin, Todd. 1993. *The Sixties: Years of Hope, Days of Rage*. Revised edition. New York: Bantam Books.

Gluckman, Nell. 2020. "The Outrage Peddlers Are Here to Stay." *Chronicle of Higher Education*, November 17. https://www.chronicle.com/article/the -outrage-peddlers-are-here-to-stay.

Gopnik, Adam. 2019. *A Thousand Small Sanities: The Moral Adventure of Liberalism*. New York: Basic Books.

Gordon, Jill, and Markus Johnson. 2003. "Race, Speech, and a Hostile Educational Environment: What Color Is Free Speech?" *Journal of Social Philosophy* 34 (3): 414–36.

Gowen, Garrett H., Kevin M. Hemer, and Robert D. Reason. 2019. "Understanding American Conservatism and Its Role in Higher Education." In *Student Activism, Politics, and Campus Climate in Higher Education*, edited by Demetri L. Morgan and Charles H. F. Davis III, 43–59. New York: Routledge.

Gross, Neil. 2013. *Why Are Professors Liberal and Why Do Conservatives Care?* Cambridge, MA: Harvard University Press.

Gross, Neil, Thomas Medvetz, and Rupert Russell. 2011. "The Contemporary American Conservative Movement." *Annual Review of Sociology* 37: 325–54.

Gross, Neil, and Solon Simmons. 2014. "The Social and Political Views of American College and University Professors." In *Professors and Their Politics*, edited by Neil Gross and Solon Simmons, 19–51. Baltimore, MD: Johns Hopkins University Press.

Grossman, Matt, and David Hopkins. 2015. "Ideological Republicans and Group Interest Democrats: The Asymmetry of American Party Politics." *Perspectives on Politics* 13 (1): 119–39.

Guttenplan, D. D. 2016. "An Interview with the Most Hated Man on the Internet." *The Nation*, October 16. https://www.thenation.com/article/archive /an-interview-with-the-most-hated-man-on-the-internet/.

Habermas, Jürgen. 1996 [1992]. *Between Facts and Norms: Contributions to a Discourse Theory of Law and Democracy*. Translated by William Rehg. Cambridge, MA: MIT Press.

Haidt, Jonathan. 2012. *The Righteous Mind: Why Good People Are Divided by Politics and Religion*. New York: Pantheon Books.

Halper, Evan. 2019. "How a Los Angeles–Based Conservative Became One of the Internet's Biggest Sensations." *Los Angeles Times*, August 23. https://

www.latimes.com/politics/story/2019–08–22/dennis-prager-university
-conservative-internet-sensation.

Hamilton, Isobel Asher. "YouTube Isn't Bound by the First Amendment and Is
Free to Censor PragerU, a Court Ruled." *Business Insider*, February 27, 2020.
https://www.businessinsider.com/youtube-google-censor-court-prageru
-first-amendment-2020-2.

Hamilton, Laura T., and Kelly Nielsen. 2021. *Broke: The Racial Consequences of
Underfunding Public Education*. Chicago: University of Chicago Press.

Hardin, John. 2018. "You Can't Legislate Free Inquiry on Campus." *New York
Times*, May 21. https://www.nytimes.com/2018/05/21/opinion/free-inquiry
-campus.html.

Hartocollis, Anemona. 2017. "A Campus Argument Goes Viral. Now the College Is under Siege." *New York Times*, June 16. https://www.nytimes.com
/2017/06/16/us/evergreen-state-protests.html.

Healy, Thomas. 2013. *The Great Dissent: How Oliver Wendell Holmes Changed His
Mind—and Changed the History of Free Speech in America*. New York: Henry
Holt and Company.

Heim, Joe. 2017. "Recounting a Day of Rage, Hate, Violence and Death." *Washington Post*, August 14. https://www.washingtonpost.com/graphics/2017
/local/charlottesville-timeline/?utm_term=.b42ecdbe55ab.

Herbst, Jeffrey. 2017. "Addressing the Real Crisis of Free Expression on Campus."
Newseum, April 25. https://www.freedomforuminstitute.org/wp-content
/uploads/2017/04/WhitePaper_Herbst_FreeExpressionOnCampus.pdf.

Herrnstein, Richard J., and Charles A. Murray. 1994. *The Bell Curve: Intelligence
and Class Structure in American Life*. New York: Free Press.

Hertel-Fernandez, Alexander. 2019. *State Capture: How Conservative Activists,
Big Businesses, and Wealthy Donors Reshaped the American States and the Nation*. New York: Oxford University Press.

Hertel-Fernandez, Alexander, and Theda Skocpol. 2015. "Why US Conservatives Shape Legislation across the Fifty States Much More Effectively than
Liberals." *Scholars Strategy Network*, April 6. http://www.scholarsstrategy
network.org/brief/why-us-conservatives-shape-legislation-across-fifty
-states-much-more-effectively-liberals.

Hiltzik, Michael. 2018. "How a Right-Wing Group's Proposed 'Free Speech'
Law Aims to Undermine Free Speech on Campus." *Los Angeles Times*,
May 30. https://www.latimes.com/business/hiltzik/la-fi-hiltzik-free-speech
-20180530-story.html.

Hochschild, Arlie Russell. 2016. *Strangers in Their Own Land: Anger and Mourning on the American Right*. New York: New Press.

Horowitz, David. 2007. *Indoctrination U: The Left's War against Academic Freedom*. New York: Encounter Books.

Izadi, Elahe. 2015. "The Incidents that Led to the University of Missouri President's Resignation." *Washington Post*, November 9. https://www.wash ingtonpost.com/news/grade-point/wp/2015/11/09/the-incidents-that-led -to-the-university-of-missouri-presidents-resignation/.

Jackson, Acy, and Natalie Conti. 2016. "Conservative Writer Ben Shapiro Speaks, Students Walk Out." *Daily Tar Heel*, March 31. https://www.dailytar heel.com/article/2016/03/ben-shapiro-speaks-students-walk-out.

Jaschik, Scott. 2016a. "Shifting Narrative at Minnesota." *Inside Higher Ed*, December 19. https://www.insidehighered.com/news/2016/12/19/minne sota-football-players-end-boycott-details-emerge-about-why-10-players -were.

Jaschik, Scott. 2016b. "Free Speech, Both Ways." *Inside Higher Ed*, December 5. https://www.insidehighered.com/news/2016/12/05/west-virginia -university-lets-controversial-speaker-appear-and-answers-his-attack.

Kahan, Dan M. 2016. "The Politically Motivated Reasoning Paradigm, Part 1: What Politically Motivated Reasoning Is and How to Measure It." In *Emerging Trends in the Social and Behavioral Sciences*, edited by Robert A. Scott et al., 1–16 Hoboken, NJ: John Wiley & Sons.

Kahan, Dan M., David A. Hoffman, Donald Braman, Danieli Evans, and Jeffrey J. Rachlinski. 2012. "'They Saw a Protest': Cognitive Illiberalism and the Speech-Conduct Distinction." *Stanford Law Review* 64 (4): 851–906.

Kaufman, Elliot. 2017. "Campus Conservatives Gave the Alt-Right a Platform." *National Review*, August 15. https://www.nationalreview.com/2017/08 /campus-conservative-organizations-alt-right-platform-free-speech -milo-yiannopoulos-charlottesville-terrorist-attack/.

Kaufman, Peter, and Kenneth A. Feldman. 2004. "Forming Identities in College: A Sociological Approach." *Research in Higher Education* 45 (5): 463–96.

Kearns, Madeleine. 2018. "Viewpoint Diversity Dies at Sarah Lawrence College." *National Review*, November 6. https://www.nationalreview.com /2018/11/college-professor-targeted-over-op-ed-viewpoint-diversity/.

Kelly-Woessner, April, and Matthew Woessner. 2006. "My Professor Is a Partisan Hack: How Perceptions of a Professor's Political Views Affect

Student Course Evaluations." *PS: Political Science and Politics* 39 (3): 495–501.

Khalil, Joe. 2019. "Judge Rules College Republicans' Lawsuit against University of California Can Move Forward." *Fox40 Sacramento*, March 19. https://fox40.com/2019/03/19/judge-rules-college-republicans-lawsuit-against-university-of-california-can-move-forward/.

Khan, Shamus, and Colin Jerolmack. 2013. "Saying Meritocracy and Doing Privilege." *Sociological Quarterly* 54 (1): 9–19.

Kidder, Jeffrey L. 2016. "College Republicans and Conservative Social Identity." *Sociological Perspectives* 59 (1): 177–200.

Kidder, Jeffrey L. 2018. "Civil and Uncivil Places: The Moral Geography of College Republicans." *American Journal of Cultural Sociology* 6 (1): 161–88.

Kidder, Jeffrey L., and Amy J. Binder. 2020. "Trumpism on College Campuses." *Qualitative Sociology* 43 (2): 145–63.

Kimball, Roger. 1990. *Tenured Radicals: How Politics Has Corrupted Our Higher Education*. New York: Harper & Row.

Kirkland, Allegra. 2017. "How Did Sebastian Gorka Go from the Anti-Muslim Fringe to White House Aide?" *TPM*, February 9. https://talkingpointsmemo.com/dc/sebastian-gorka-washington-experts-dc-anti-islam-ties.

Klatch, Rebecca E. 1999. *A Generation Divided: The New Left, the New Right, and the 1960s*. Berkeley: University of California Press.

Klein, Ezra. 2018. "Sam Harris, Charles Murray, and the Allure of Race Science." *Vox*, March 27. https://www.vox.com/policy-and-politics/2018/3/27/15695060/sam-harris-charles-murray-race-iq-forbidden-knowledge-podcast-bell-curve.

Klein, Ezra. 2020. *Why We're Polarized*. New York: Avid Reader Press.

Knight Foundation. 2019. "Free Expression on College Campuses." May 13. https://knightfoundation.org/reports/free-expression-college-campuses/.

Kolowich, Steve. 2018. "State of Conflict." *Chronicle of Higher of Education*, April 27. https://www.chronicle.com/interactives/state-of-conflict.

Kors, Alan Charles, and Harvey A. Silverglate. 1998. *The Shadow University: The Betrayal of Liberty on America's Campuses*. New York: Free Press.

Kotch, Alex. 2017. "Who Funds Conservative Campus Group Turning Point USA? Donors Revealed." *International Business Times*, November 28. https://www.ibtimes.com/political-capital/who-funds-conservative-campus-group-turning-point-usa-donors-revealed-2620325.

Kotch, Alex. 2018. "Who Funds PragerU's Anti-Muslim Content?" *Sludge*, December 27. https://readsludge.com/2018/12/27/who-funds-pragerus -anti-muslim-content/.

Kueppers, Courtney. 2016. "Today's Freshman Class Is the Most Likely to Protest in Half a Century." *Chronicle of Higher Education*, February 11. https://www.chronicle.com/article/Today-s-Freshman-Class-Is/235273 /?cid=related-promo.

Kunda, Ziva. 1990. "The Case for Motivated Reasoning." *Psychological Bulletin* 108 (3): 480–98.

Kuta, Sarah. 2016. "What's It Like to Be a Conservative Student at CU Boulder?" *Daily Camera*, October 29. https://www.dailycamera.com/2016/10 /29/whats-it-like-to-be-a-conservative-student-at-cu-boulder/.

Kuta, Sarah. 2017. "Met by Protests, Milo Yiannopoulos Targets Feminists, Liberals at CU Boulder Talk." *Daily Camera*, January 25. http://www.daily camera.com/cu-news/ci_30751138/about-100-demonstrators-protesting -milo-yiannopoulos-at-cu.

Lawrence, Charles R., III. 1993. "If He Hollers Let Him Go: Regulating Racist Speech on Campus." In *Words that Wound: Critical Race Theory, Assaultive Speech, and the First Amendment*, edited by Mari J. Matsuda et al., 53–88. Boulder, CO: Westview Press.

Lawrence, Charles R., III, Mari J. Matsuda, Richard Delgado, and Kimberlé Williams Crenshaw. 1993. "Introduction." In *Words that Wound: Critical Race Theory, Assaultive Speech, and the First Amendment*, edited by Mari J. Matsuda et al., 1–15. Boulder, CO: Westview Press.

Lerma, Veronica, Laura T. Hamilton, and Kelly Nielsen. 2020. "Racialized Equity Labor, University Appropriation and Student Resistance." *Social Problems* 67 (2): 286–303.

Lester, J. C. 1994. "The Evolution of the Political Compass (and Why Libertarianism Is Not Right-Wing)." *Journal of Social and Evolutionary Systems* 17 (3): 231–41.

Levitsky, Steven, and Daniel Ziblatt. 2019. "Why Republicans Play Dirty." *New York Times*, September 20. https://www.nytimes.com/2019/09/20/opinion /republicans-democracy-play-dirty.html.

Lichterman, Paul, and Daniel Cefai. 2006. "The Idea of Political Culture." In *The Oxford Handbook of Contextual Political Analysis*, edited by Robert E. Goodin and Charles Tilly, 392–415. New York: Oxford University Press.

Lilla, Mark. 2017. *The Once and Future Liberal: After Identity Politics*. New York: HarperCollins.

Lio, Shoon, Scott Melzer, and Ellen Reese. 2008. "Constructing Threat and Appropriating 'Civil Rights': Rhetorical Strategies of Gun Rights and English Only Leaders." *Symbolic Interaction* 31 (1): 5–31.

Loeb, Paul Rogat. 1994. *Generation at the Crossroads: Apathy and Action on the American Campus*. New Brunswick, NJ: Rutgers University Press.

Long, Katherine, Lynn Thompson, and Jessica Lee. 2017. "Man Shot during Protests of Breitbart Editor Milo Yiannopoulos' Speech at UW; Suspect Arrested." *Seattle Times*, January 20. https://www.seattletimes.com/seattle -news/education/violence-punctuates-uw-talk-by-breitbart-editor -milo-yiannopoulos/.

Losurdo, Domenico. 2011 [2005]. *Liberalism: A Counter-History*. Translated by Gregory Elliott. London and New York: Verso Books.

Lukianoff, Greg, and Jonathan Haidt. 2018. *The Coddling of the American Mind: How Good Intentions and Bad Ideas Are Setting Up a Generation for Failure*. New York: Penguin Press.

Mac Donald, Heather. 2018. *The Diversity Delusion: How Race and Gender Pandering Corrupt the University and Undermine Our Culture*. New York: St. Martin's Press.

MacKinnon, Catharine A. 1993. *Only Words*. Cambridge, MA: Harvard University Press.

Manchester, Julia. 2020. "Charlie Kirk Gets First GOP Convention Address, Calls Trump 'Bodyguard of Western Civilization.'" *The Hill*, August 24. https://thehill.com/homenews/campaign/513471-charlie-kirk-gives-first -address-at-gop-convention.

Mandery, Evan. 2019. "What Teaching Ethics in Appalachia Taught Me about Bridging America's Partisan Divide." *Politico*, October 13. https://www .politico.com/magazine/story/2019/10/13/america-cultural-divide-red -state-blue-state-228111.

Mantel, Henriette, and Steve Skrovan. 2006. *An Unreasonable Man*. New York: IFC Films.

Marantz, Andrew. 2018. "How Social-Media Trolls Turned U.C. Berkeley into a Free-Speech Circus." *The New Yorker*, June 25. https://www.newyorker.com /magazine/2018/07/02/how-social-media-trolls-turned-uc-berkeley -into-a-free-speech-circus.

Martin, Chris C. 2016. "How Ideology Has Hindered Sociological Insight." *American Sociologist* 47 (1): 115–30.

Maslow, Abraham H. 1964. *Religions, Values, and Peak-Experiences*. Columbus: Ohio State University Press.

Mason, Lilliana. 2018a. *Uncivil Agreement: How Politics Became Our Identity*. Chicago: University of Chicago Press.

Mason, Lilliana. 2018b. "Ideologues without Issues: The Polarizing Consequences of Ideological Identities." *Public Opinion Quarterly* 82 (S1): 280–301.

Massengale, Jenna. 2016. "Appalachian Welcomes Sustained Dialogue as Catalyst for Change on Campus." *Appalachian Magazine*, May 2. http:// appalachianmagazine.org/stories/id/581.

Mauff, Jake. 2017. "CU Administration Was Aware of Milo Yiannopoulos Incidents; Campus to Host Buffs United and Laverne Cox Events Wednesday." *CU Independent*, January 25. https://cuindependent.com/2017/01/25 /cu-administration-aware-milo-yiannopoulos-incidents-campus-host -buffs-united-laverne-cox-events-wednesday/.

Mayer, Jane. 2016. *Dark Money: The Hidden History of the Billionaires behind the Rise of the Radical Right*. New York: Doubleday.

McAdam, Doug. 1986. "Recruitment to High-Risk Activism: The Case of Freedom Summer." *American Journal of Sociology* 92 (1): 64–90.

McAdam, Doug. 1988. *Freedom Summer*. New York: Oxford University Press.

McCarthy, John, and Mayer Zald. 1977. "Resource Mobilization and Social Movements: A Partial Theory." *American Journal of Sociology* 82 (6): 1212–41.

McPhate, Mike. 2017. "California Today: Price Tag to Protect Speech at Berkeley: $600,000." *New York Times*, September 15. https://www.nytimes.com /2017/09/15/us/california-today-price-tag-to-protect-speech-at-berkeley -600000.html.

Medvetz, Thomas. 2012. *Think Tanks in America*. Chicago: University of Chicago Press.

Merriman, Ben. 2019. *Conservative Innovators: How States Are Challenging Federal Power*. Chicago: University of Chicago Press.

Micklethwait, John, and Adrian Wooldridge. 2004. *The Right Nation: Conservative Power in America*. New York: Penguin Press.

Mill, John Stuart. 2002 [1859]. *On Liberty*. Mineola, NY: Dover Publications.

Mische, Ann. 2008. *Partisan Publics: Communication and Contention across Brazilian Youth Activist Networks*. Princeton, NJ: Princeton University Press.

Mishler, Elliot G. 1986. *Research Interviewing*. Cambridge, MA: Harvard University Press.

Morgan, Demetri L., and Charles H. F. Davis III, eds. 2019a. *Student Activism, Politics, and Campus Climate in Higher Education*. New York: Routledge.

Morgan, Demetri L., and Charles H. F. Davis III. 2019b. "Preface: Transforming Campus Climates by Reframing Student Political Engagement and Activism." In *Student Activism, Politics, and Campus Climate in Higher Education*, edited by Demetri L. Morgan and Charles H. F. Davis III, xv–xxiv. New York: Routledge.

Morris, Aldon D. 1984. *The Origins of the Civil Rights Movement: Black Communities Organizing for Change*. New York: Free Press.

Moskowitz, P. E. 2019. *The Case against Free Speech: The First Amendment, Fascism, and the Future of Dissent*. New York: Bold Type Books.

Muldoon, Ryan. 2017. "Free Speech and Learning from Difference." *Society* 54 (4): 331–36.

Munson, Ziad. 2010. "Mobilizing on Campus: Conservative Movements and Today's College Students." *Sociological Forum* 25 (4): 769–86.

Newfield, Christopher. 2016. *The Great Mistake: How We Wrecked Public Universities and How We Can Fix Them*. Baltimore, MD: Johns Hopkins University Press.

Nguyen, Tina. 2017. "Far-Right Trump Advisor Tied to Anti-Semitic Paramilitary Group." *Vanity Fair*, April 4. https://www.vanityfair.com/news/2017/04/sebastian-gorka-anti-semitism-hungarian-guard.

Nielsen, Laura Beth. 2004. *License to Harass: Law, Hierarchy, and Offensive Public Speech*. Princeton, NJ: Princeton University Press.

Ohlheiser, Abby. 2016. "Just How Offensive Did Milo Yiannopoulos Have to Be to Get Banned from Twitter?" *Washington Post*, July 21. https://www.washingtonpost.com/news/the-intersect/wp/2016/07/21/what-it-takes-to-get-banned-from-twitter/.

O'Leary, Brian. 2020. "Backgrounds and Beliefs of College Freshmen." *Chronicle of Higher Education*, August 12. https://www.chronicle.com/interactives/freshmen-survey.

Olsen, Lauren D. 2019. "The Conscripted Curriculum and the Reproduction of Racial Inequalities in Contemporary U.S. Medical Education." *Journal of Health & Social Behavior* 60 (1): 55–68.

Oppenheim, Maya. 2017. "UC Berkeley Protests: Milo Yiannopoulos Planned to 'Publicly Name Undocumented Students' in Cancelled Talk." *Independent*, February 3. https://www.independent.co.uk/news/world/americas

/uc-berkely-protests-milo-yiannopoulos-publicly-name-undocumented
-students-cancelled-talk-illegals-a7561321.html.

Palfrey, John G. 2017. *Safe Spaces, Brave Spaces: Diversity and Free Expression in Education.* Cambridge, MA: MIT Press.

Parker, Christopher S., and Matt A. Barreto. 2013. *Change They Can't Believe In: The Tea Party and Reactionary Politics in America.* Princeton, NJ: Princeton University Press.

Parker, Kim. 2019. "The Growing Partisan Divide in Views of Higher Education." Pew Research Center, August 19. https://www.pewsocialtrends.org /essay/the-growing-partisan-divide-in-views-of-higher-education/.

Pascarella, Ernest T., and Patrick T. Terenzini. 2005. *How College Affects Students: A Third Decade of Research.* San Francisco: Jossey-Bass Publishers.

PEN America. 2019. "Chasm in the Classroom: Campus Free Speech in a Divided America." April 2. https://pen.org/chasm-in-the-classroom-campus -free-speech-in-a-divided-america/.

Perlstein, Rick. 2014. *The Invisible Bridge: The Fall of Nixon and the Rise of Reagan.* New York: Simon & Schuster.

Perrin, Andrew J., J. Micah Roos, and Gordon W. Gauchat. 2014. "From Coalition to Constraint: Modes of Thought in Contemporary American Conservatism." *Sociological Forum* 29 (2): 285–300.

Peters, Kara. 2017. "Young Americans for Freedom Claims U.Va. Illegally Denied Conservative Group CIO Status." *Cavalier Daily*, December 20. https://www.cavalierdaily.com/article/2017/12/young-americans-for -freedom-claims-u-va-illegally-denied-conservative-group-cio-status.

Petersen, Michael Bang, Mathias Osmundsen, and Kevin Arceneaux. 2018. "A 'Need for Chaos' and the Sharing of Hostile Political Rumors in Advanced Democracies." *PsyArXiv*, September 1. https://doi.org/10.31234 /osf.io/6m4ts.

Pettit, Emma. 2019. "'Ousted' from Academe, Steven Salaita Says He's Driving a School Bus to Make Ends Meet." *Chronicle of Higher Education*, February 19. https://www.chronicle.com/article/Ousted-From-Academe/245732.

Pew Research Center. 2017. "Sharp Divides in Views of National Institutions." Pew Research Center, July 10. http://www.people-press.org/2017/07/10 /sharp-partisan-divisions-in-views-of-national-institutions/.

Pluckrose, Helen, and James Lindsay. 2020. *Cynical Theories: How Activist Scholarship Made Everything about Race, Gender, and Identity—and Why This Harms Everybody.* Durham, NC: Pitchstone Publishing.

powell, john a. 1996. "Worlds Apart: Reconciling Freedom of Speech and Equality." *Kentucky Law Journal* 85 (1): 9–95.

Quintana, Chris. 2020. "Nationalist 'Antics' or the Future of the GOP? College Republicans Are at War." *USA Today*, January 17. https://www.usatoday.com /story/news/education/2020/01/17/college-republicans-crnc-trump-repub lican-party-gop-turning-point-usa/4476649002/.

Readings, Bill. 1996. *The University in Ruins.* Cambridge, MA: Harvard University Press.

Reyes, Daisy Verduzco. 2018. *Learning to Be Latino: How Colleges Shape Identity Politics.* New Brunswick, NJ: Rutgers University Press.

Rhoads, Robert A. 1998. *Freedom's Web: Student Activism in an Age of Cultural Diversity.* Baltimore, MD: Johns Hopkins University Press.

Rim, Christopher. 2020. "How Student Activism Shaped the Black Lives Matter Movement." *Forbes*, June 4. https://www.forbes.com/sites/christopher rim/2020/06/04/how-student-activism-shaped-the-black-lives-matter -movement/?sh=4e4225194414.

Robertson, Katie. 2021. "Nikole Hannah-Jones Denied Tenure at University of North Carolina." *New York Times*, May 19. https://www.nytimes.com/2021 /05/19/business/media/nikole-hannah-jones-unc.html.

Rogers, Katie, and Noah Weiland. 2020. "Trump Announced, then Canceled, a Yankees Pitch. Both Came as a Surprise." *New York Times*, July 25. https:// www.nytimes.com/2020/07/27/us/politics/trump-yankees-fauci.html.

Rojas, Fabio. 2007. *From Black Power to Black Studies: How a Radical Social Movement Became an Academic Discipline.* Baltimore, MD: Johns Hopkins University Press.

Roll, Nick. 2017. "UNC Board Bars Litigation by Law School Center." *Inside Higher Ed*, September 11. https://www.insidehighered.com/news/2017/09/11 /north-carolina-board-bars-unc-center-civil-rights-litigating.

Ropers-Huilman, Becky, Laura Carwile, and Kathy Barnett. 2005. "Student Activists' Characterizations of Administrators in Higher Education: Perceptions of Power in 'the System.'" *Review of Higher Education* 28 (3): 295–312.

Rosenberg, Matthew, and Katie Rogers. 2020. "For Charlie Kirk, Conservative Activist, the Virus Is a Cudgel." *New York Times*, April 19. https://www .nytimes.com/2020/04/19/us/politics/charlie-kirk-conservatives-corona virus.html.

Rosenkranz, Nicholas Quinn. 2014. "Intellectual Diversity in the Legal Academy." *Harvard Journal of Law and Public Policy* 37 (1): 137–43.

Sachs, Jeffrey Adam. 2018. "There Is No Campus Free Speech Crisis: The Right's New Moral Panic Is Largely Imaginary." *Salon*, May 1. https://www.salon .com/2018/05/01/there-is-no-campus-free-speech-crisis-the-rights-new -moral-panic-is-largely-imaginary/.

Saul, Stephanie. 2017. "Dozens of Middlebury College Students Are Disciplined for Charles Murray Protest." *New York Times*, May 24. https://www .nytimes.com/2017/05/24/us/middlebury-college-charles-murray-bell -curve.html?mcubz=3.

Schladebeck, Jessica. 2017. "'Affirmative Action Bake Sale' Charges University of New Mexico Students Based on Race." *Daily News*, September 23. https:// www.nydailynews.com/news/national/affirmative-action-bake-sale -charges-students-based-race-article-1.3515715.

Schnur, Sabrina. 2019. "Hundreds March, Dozens Protest Outside Ben Shapiro's Speech." *Boston University News Service*, November 13. https://bunewsservice .com/hundreds-march-dozens-protest-outside-ben-shapiros-speech/.

Schwartz, Brian. 2019. "Pro-Trump College GOP Activist Charlie Kirk Will Launch a New Group to Target Democrats in 2020." *CNBC*, May 20. https:// www.cnbc.com/2019/05/20/pro-trump-activist-charlie-kirk-to-launch -new-group-to-target-democrats.html.

Shields, Jon A., and Joshua M. Dunn. 2016. *Passing on the Right: Conservative Professors in the Progressive University*. New York: Oxford University Press.

Siegel, Eric. 2017. "The Real Problem with Charles Murray and 'the Bell Curve.'" *Scientific American*, April 12. https://blogs.scientificamerican.com /voices/the-real-problem-with-charles-murray-and-the-bell-curve/.

Silver, Nate. 2016. "The Odds of an Electoral College–Popular Vote Split Are Increasing." *FiveThirtyEight*, October 31. https://fivethirtyeight.com /features/the-odds-of-an-electoral-college-popular-vote-split-are -increasing/.

Sleeper, Jim. 2016. "The Conservatives behind the Campus 'Free Speech' Crusade." *The American Prospect*, October 19. https://prospect.org/education /conservatives-behind-campus-free-speech-crusade/.

Smart, Barry. 2016. "Military-Industrial Complexities, University Research and Neoliberal Economy." *Journal of Sociology* 52 (3): 455–81.

Smolla, Rodney A. 1990. "Academic Freedom, Hate Speech, and the Idea of a University." *Law & Contemporary Problems* 53 (3): 195–225.

Sommers, Christina Hoff. 2000. *The War against Boys: How Misguided Feminism Is Harming Our Young Men*. New York: Simon & Schuster.

Sorokin, Pitirim. 1959. *Social and Cultural Mobility*. New York: Free Press.

Sprunt, Barbara, and Alana Wise. 2020. "Trump Addresses Tightly Packed Arizona Crowd amid State's Growing Coronavirus Crisis." *NPR*, June 23. https://www.npr.org/2020/06/23/881641178/after-disappointing-tulsa-rally-trump-campaign-moves-to-arizona.

Staggenborg, Suzanne. 1986. "Coalition Work in the Pro-Choice Movement: Organizational and Environmental Opportunities and Obstacles." *Social Problems* 33 (5): 374–90.

Steinhauser, Paul. 2020. "Pence Urges Conservatives 'to Stay in the Fight' as 'Our Election' Continues." *Fox News*, December 22. https://www.foxnews.com/politics/pence-election-fight-florida-speech.

Steller, Tim. 2020. "Tim Steller's Opinion: Taxpayers Give UA 'Freedom Center' Prominence, Conflicts after Koch Money Dwindles." *Arizona Daily Star*, June 21. https://tucson.com/news/local/tim-stellers-opinion-taxpayers-give-ua-freedom-center-prominence-conflicts-after-koch-money-dwindles/article_2698a55a-17e2-5a59-bb00-ca008ea68b3a.html.

Stempel, Jonathan. 2018. "UC Berkeley Settles Lawsuit over Treatment of Conservative Speakers." Reuters, December 3. https://www.reuters.com/article/us-california-lawsuit-ucberkeley/uc-berkeley-settles-lawsuit-over-treatment-of-conservative-speakers-idUSKBN1O22K4.

Stevens, Mitchell L., Elizabeth A. Armstrong, and Richard Arum. 2008. "Sieve, Incubator, Temple, Hub: Empirical and Theoretical Advances in the Sociology of Higher Education." *Annual Review of Sociology* 34 (1): 127–51.

Stevens, Sean. 2017. "Campus Speaker Disinvitation Trends (Part 2 of 2)." *Heterodox Academy*, February 7. https://heterodoxacademy.org/campus-speaker-disinvitations-recent-trends-part-2-of-2/.

Stevens, Sean. 2018. "The Skeptics Are Wrong, Part 1: Attitudes about Free Speech on Campus Are Changing." *Heterodox Academy*, March 4. https://heterodoxacademy.org/blog/skeptics-are-wrong-about-campus-speech/.

Stokes, Sy, and Donté Miller. 2019. "Remembering 'the Black Bruins': A Case Study of Supporting Student Activists at UCLA." In *Student Activism, Politics, and Campus Climate in Higher Education*, edited by Demetri L. Morgan and Charles H. F. Davis III, 143–63. New York: Routledge.

Stripling, Jack. 2020. "Trump Picked a Fight with Higher Ed. It's Still Learning to Punch Back." *Chronicle of Higher Education*, November 2. https://www.chronicle.com/article/trump-picked-a-fight-with-higher-ed-its-still-learning-to-punch-back.

Strossen, Nadine. 2018. *Hate: Why We Should Resist It with Free Speech, Not Censorship*. New York: Oxford University Press.

Tavory, Iddo. 2020. "Interviews and Inference: Making Sense of Interview Data in Qualitative Research." *Qualitative Sociology* 43 (4): 449–65.

Teles, Steven M. 2008. *The Rise of the Conservative Legal Movement: The Battle for Control of the Law*. Princeton, NJ: Princeton University Press.

Thomas, Nancy, and Margaret Brower. 2017. "Politics 365: Fostering Campus Climates for Student Political Learning & Engagement." *Institute for Democracy and Higher Education*, April. https://tischcollege.tufts.edu/sites/default/files/Politics%20365.pdf.

Thompson, Becky, and Sangeeta Tyagi. 1993. "Introduction: 'A Wider Landscape . . . without the Mandate for Conquest.'" In *Beyond a Dream Deferred: Multicultural Education and the Politics of Excellence*, edited by Becky Thompson and Sangeeta Tyagi. Minneapolis: University of Minnesota Press.

Tilly, Charles. 1995. *Popular Contention in Great Britain, 1758–1834*. Cambridge, MA: Harvard University Press.

Tourjée, Diana. 2017. "Trans Student Harassed by Milo Yiannopoulos Speaks Out." *Vice*, January 3. https://www.vice.com/en_us/article/vb4e44/trans-student-harassed-by-milo-yiannopoulos-speaks-out.

Troy, Tevi. 2017. "The Dilemma of the D.C. Think Tank." *The Atlantic*, December 19. https://www.theatlantic.com/politics/archive/2017/12/presidents-and-think-tanks/548765/.

Uberti, David. 2019. "Milo Yiannopoulos Says He's Broke." *Vice News*, September 9. https://www.vice.com/en_us/article/59n99q/milo-yiannopoulos-says-hes-broke.

Van Dyke, Nella. 1998. "Hotbeds of Activism: Locations of Student Protest." *Social Problems* 45 (2): 205–20.

Van Dyke, Nella. 2003. "Crossing Movement Boundaries: Factors that Facilitate Coalition Protest by American College Students, 1930–1990." *Social Problems* 50 (2): 226–50.

Van Dyke, Nella, Marc Dixon, and Helen Carlon. 2007. "Manufacturing Dissent: Labor Revitalization, Union Summer and Student Protest." *Social Forces* 86 (1): 193–214.

Vasquez, Michael. 2018. "Leaked Memo from Conservative Group Cautions Students to Stay Away from Turning Point USA." *Chronicle of Higher Education*, June 15. https://www.chronicle.com/article/leaked-memo-from-conservative-group-cautions-students-to-stay-away-from-turning-point-usa/.

Villegas, Paulina, and David A. Fahrenthold. 2020. "Young Conservatives Mingled Maskless at Mar-a-Lago and Partied with a Money Cannon." *Washington Post*, December 21. https://www.washingtonpost.com/politics /2020/12/21/turning-point-covid-party/.

Wagner-Pacifici, Robin, and Iddo Tavory. 2017. "Politics as a Vacation." *American Journal of Cultural Sociology* 5 (3): 307–21.

Waite, Lori G. 2001. "Divided Consciousness: The Impact of Black Elite Consciousness on the 1966 Chicago Freedom Movement." In *Oppositional Consciousness: The Subjective Roots of Social Protest*, edited by Jane Mansbridge and Aldon Morris, 170–203. Chicago: University of Chicago Press.

Waldron, Jeremy. 2012. *The Harm in Hate Speech.* Cambridge, MA: Harvard University Press.

Wallace, David Foster. 2008. "Plain Old Untrendy Troubles and Emotions." *The Guardian*, September 19. https://www.theguardian.com/books/2008 /sep/20/fiction.

Wallerstein, Immanuel. 2004. *World-System Analysis: An Introduction.* Durham, NC: Duke University Press.

Wan, William. 2017. "Milo's Appearance at Berkeley Led to Riots. He Vows to Return this Fall for a Week-Long Free-Speech Event." *Washington Post*, April 26. https://www.washingtonpost.com/news/grade-point/wp/2017 /04/26/milos-appearance-at-berkeley-led-to-riots-he-vows-to-return-this -fall-for-a-week-long-free-speech-event/.

Wehner, Peter. 2020. "Jonathan Haidt Is Trying to Heal America's Divisions." *The Atlantic*, May 24. https://www.theatlantic.com/ideas/archive/2020/05 /jonathan-haidt-pandemic-and-americas-polarization/612025/.

Williams, Wendy M., and Stephen J. Ceci. 2017. "Charles Murray's 'Provocative' Talk." *New York Times*, April 15. https://www.nytimes.com/2017/04/15 /opinion/sunday/charles-murrays-provocative-talk.html.

Woessner, Matthew, and April Kelly-Woessner. 2009. "Left Pipeline: Why Conservatives Don't Get Doctorates." In *The Politically Correct University: Problems, Scope, and Reforms*, edited by Robert Maranto et al., 38–59. Washington, DC: AEI Press.

Yamane, David. 2001. *Student Movements for Multiculturalism: Challenging the Curricular Color Line in Higher Education.* Baltimore: Johns Hopkins University Press.

Yankelovich, Daniel. 1999. *The Magic of Dialogue: Transforming Conflict into Cooperation.* New York: Simon & Schuster.

Yglesias, Matthew. 2018. "The Bell Curve Is about Policy. And It's Wrong." *Vox*, April 10. https://www.vox.com/2018/4/10/17182692/bell-curve-charles -murray-policy-wrong.

Yoon-Hendricks, Alexandra. 2018. "A Place where Conservative Teenagers Feel Free to Be Themselves." *New York Times*, July 25. https://www.nytimes .com/2018/07/25/us/politics/turning-point-young-conservatives.html.

Zussman, Robert. 1996. "Autobiographical Occasions." *Contemporary Sociology* 25 (2): 143–48.

Index

Made in the USA
Las Vegas, NV
04 March 2024

86685472R00128